FIVE EUPHEMIAS

Also by Elizabeth Sutherland

FICTION

Lent Term
The Seer of Kintail
Hannah Hereafter
The Eye of God
The Weeping Tree

NON-FICTION

The Black Isle: a Portrait of the Past
The Prophecies of the Brahan Seer (Editor)
The Rosemarkie Symbol Stones
Ravens and Black Rain: the Story of Highland Second Sight
The Gold Key and the Green Life (Editor)
In Search of the Picts

FIVE EUPHEMIAS

Women in Medieval Scotland

1200–1420

ELIZABETH SUTHERLAND

CONSTABLE · LONDON

First published in Great Britain 1999
by Constable and Company Limited
3 The Lanchesters, 162 Fulham Palace Road
London W6 9ER
Copyright © Elizabeth Sutherland 1999
ISBN 0 09 478250 4

The right of Elizabeth Sutherland to be identified as author
of this work has been asserted by her in accordance
with the Copyright, Designs and Patents Act 1988

Typeset in Linotron Sabon 11pt by
Rowland Phototypesetting Limited
Printed in Great Britain by
St Edmundsbury Press Limited
both of Bury St Edmunds, Suffolk

A CIP catalogue record for this book
is available from the British Library

For my dear grand-daughters Shakti and Mayva
in California to remind them of their roots

CONTENTS

LIST OF ILLUSTRATIONS

between pages 96 and 97

THE FIRST EUPHEMIA

1. Applecross Stone (*Copyright T.E. Gray*)
2. Matthew Paris Map showing Dingwall (*British Library*)
3. Dingwall today (*Copyright T.E. Gray*)
4. Reconstruction of Duffus by Historic Scotland (*Copyright T.E. Gray*)
5. Duffus Castle (*Copyright T.E. Gray*)
6. Frearn Abbey (*Copyright T.E. Gray*)
7. Farquhar's Tomb in Fearn Abbey (*Copyright T.E. Gray*)

THE SECOND EUPHEMIA

8. Balliol offers homage to Edward I (*British Library*)
9. Urquhart Castle (*Copyright T.E. Gray*)
10. Robert the Bruce (*Courtesy the National Trust for Scotland. Copyright T.E. Gray*)
11. St Duthac's Church (*Copyright T.E. Gray*)
12. Celtic Warriors (*Copyright T.E. Gray*)

between pages 192 and 193

THE THIRD EUPHEMIA

13. Dunbar Castle (*Copyright T.E. Gray*)

[9]

Five Euphemias

14. Reconstruction of Dundonald Castle (*Crown copyright. Historic Scotland*)
15. Dundonald Castle today (*Copyright T.E. Gray*)
16. Edinburgh Castle (*Copyright T.E. Gray*)

THE FOURTH EUPHEMIA

17. Dingwall Castle today (*Copyright T.E. Gray*)
18. Ruthven Barracks (*Copyright T.E. Gray*)
19. Wolf of Badenoch's tomb (*Copyright T.E. Gray*)
20. Fortrose Castle (*Copyright T.E. Gray*)

THE FIFTH EUPHEMIA

21. Doune Castle (*Copyright T.E. Gray*)
22. Dirleton Castle(*Copyright T.E. Gray*)
23. Cistercian Nunnery, North Berwick (*Copyright T.E. Gray*)
24. North Berwick Harbour (*Copyright T.E. Gray*)
25. Nuns singing in chapel. Poor Clares at Service from Richard II's psalter. (*British Library/Bridgeman Art Library, London/New York*)

ACKNOWLEDGEMENTS

Twenty years ago after the publication of my novel *The Eye of God*, which was set in Ross-shire, I had a letter from Dr A. C. Gordon Ross, a medical practitioner and amateur historian living in St Andrews. He suggested that I write a novel about the five Euphemias of Ross who had lived in Scotland between c.1200 and c.1420 AD and who had captured his own imagination. He had already done much of the research but believed he was too old to write the book himself. He sent me his manuscript as a gift in the hopes that one day I would complete the work for him. A short time later he died and the typescript entitled *The Chronicles of Ross* languished among my files and at the bottom of my mind awaiting a decision. After re-reading it carefully a couple of years ago, I realised that the story would be much better told as fact than fiction. Here was a chance for me to explore what it was like to be a woman in medieval Scotland.

The task was perhaps the most difficult I have ever undertaken because women feature hardly at all in the charts and records of that period. Much of Dr Ross's cherished embellishments to the characters and behaviour of the five women had to be discarded as fiction, while the recorded facts were minimal. However, using them as symbols of their age, I have tried to show how aristocratic women coped with the culture clash between Anglo-Norman and Celt, what it was like to be a lone wife in the Wars of Independence, or a nun in a busy Cistercian convent. I have tried to demonstrate how a woman was on the one hand a possession first of her father then of her husband and finally of her eldest son, yet, at the same time, a figure of power and influence within the politics of her castle. This has been an absorbing journey of discovery for me and I am more grateful to Dr Ross for his suggestion than, sadly, he can ever know.

I would also like to thank the following for their personal support and advice: Monica Clough, Bridget Mackenzie, Dr Jean Munro and Dr I. L. Gordon; the librarians in Dingwall and Inverness, especially Norman Newton and Alastair Macleod; Sheila Mackenzie and Dr Iain G. Brown from the Department of Manuscripts at the National Library of Scotland.

Out of all the many historians whose works have guided and inspired me, I am particularly indebted to Professor Geoffrey Barrow, Dr Ranald Nicholson and Dr Alexander Grant for their lucid presentations of the Middle Ages in Scotland; above all to Dr Stephen Boardman and Tuckwell Press whose *Early Stewart Kings* was my constant companion for at least a year. A very special thank-you to Mary Beith and her publisher Polygon for allowing me to quote from *Healing Threads*, that marvellous portrait of medicine in the Highlands. Thanks also to Ronald Williams and the House of Lochar for allowing me to quote from *The Lordship of the Isles*; to Alan Macquarrie and John Donald Publishers for quotations from *Scotland and the Crusades*; to A. A. M. Duncan and Canongate Books Ltd for extracts from *The Bruce*. I have quoted freely from Alexander Carmichael's *Carmina Gadelica*, as these songs, prayers and incantations give the flavour of Gaeldom as it used to be. I am grateful to Floris Publishers for their edition of this marvellous work and making it so widely accessible.

I particularly want to thank Dr Henrietta Leyser and Phoenix Publishers for showing me what it was like to be a woman in the Middle Ages and granting permission to reproduce extracts from *Medieval Women, a Social History of Women in England, 450–1500*; also Nicholas Orme and Methuen & Co, for permission to reproduce extracts from *From Childhood to Chivalry*; Sylvia Lansberg and the British Museum Press for permission to quote from *The Medieval Garden* and George Duby and Polity Press for his splendid account of *Love and Marriage in the Middle Ages*.

I am particularly grateful to Mrs Mary-Flora Murchison of Balmacara and Mrs Anne Jack of Fortrose, both Latin scholars, for translating certain medieval Latin letters and documents pertaining to my Euphemias. Thank you, too, to Pauline Jacobs of Fortrose who arranged my family trees, no easy task as she quickly found out.

Acknowledgements

Thank you, also, to Carol O'Brien and Maggie Body for working so hard on my text. I am truly grateful.

Above all I am indebted to Robert A. J. Macdonald FSA Scot of St Andrews who did so much of my research for me, worked out complicated genealogical tables, trawled through obscure documents and references, read my manuscript and generally advised and encouraged me. Thank you, Rob. I couldn't have done it without you.

ILLUSTRATIONS

Once again I am entirely grateful to my friend and colleague, Tom E. Gray, for the gift of his beautiful evocative photographs which greatly enhance the text in every way. Thank you, Tom, for your support, your skill and your generosity.

I am also grateful to Historic Scotland for permission to reproduce reconstructions of Duffus and Dundonald castles; the Trustees of the National Library of Scotland and Sir Francis Ogilvie, Bart., for permission to reproduce the illustration of Robert II and Queen Euphemia from the Seton Armorial; the British Library for permission to reproduce MS ROYAL 20 c.VII.f28 'John Balliol Offering Homage to Edward I' and MS COTTON CLAUDIUS D VI f12v, 'Matthew Paris Map of Great Britain'; the British Library/Bridgeman Art Library for permission to reproduce COTT DOM A XVII f.74v 'Poor Clares at Service' from Richard II's Psalter.

ELIZABETH SUTHERLAND

FOREWORD

A HALLOWED HOMELAND

Applecross, birth home of Farquhar Mactaggart and his daughter, our first Euphemia, has nothing to do with apples, and only incidentally with a cross. It translates from the Gaelic *Apurcrosan* somewhat prosaically as 'the mouth of the River Crosan'. This hallowed homeland however is anything but dull. According to the *Statistical Account of Scotland* for Ross-shire 1791–9, 'The modern name Applecross was given to the parish by the proprietor of the estate' in the eighteenth century 'in commemoration of which event five apples trees had been planted crossways in the proprietor's garden'. Farquhar, however, like Gaelic-speakers of today, would have called his homeland *A'Chomraich*, the Sanctuary (in Latin, *Refugium*). This name describes the ancient right of protection which extended for six miles in all directions marked by long-gone stone crosses around the Picto-Celtic monastery founded by St Maelrubha (Mulru-a) in 673 AD.

Dr William Reeves suggests that *Comrich*, the word for sanctuary, may actually have been *Comchris* which translates as 'belly-belt'. Local tradition records that when Maelrubha and his companions approached the bay in their coracle, one of his monks pulled off his belt, flung it before him on the shore crying out, '*Mo chromchris ort*' (My belly-belt upon you). In 1854, when Dr Reeves visited Applecross, this spot where the monks first landed was still marked with four trees.

Even after thirteen hundred years, Applecross retains its aura of holiness. Perhaps this is because the journey over the famous Bealach na Bo (Pass of the Cattle) which rises in a series of hairpin bends to a dizzy height of 774m (2054ft) still retains something of the old effort of pilgrimage. Today the bealach is metalled and there are crash barriers which give a semblance of safety as the single-track road snakes upwards between the great rocky bulk of Sgurr a-Chaorachain (Shepherd's Peak) and Meall Gorm (Blue Mound). The plateau at the top is a lunar wilderness strewn with stones, but the views of the island of Raasay to the west with its dead crater of Dun Ca'an (possibly Fortress of Battles), and beyond, the blue-hazed mountains of Skye with the smaller islets of the Inner Sound in the foreground are rare and precious.

Looking south, the wild moorland is patterned with sixty little lochs that glint like silver shillings in the sunlight. Such glimpses are to be treasured for the bealach is more likely to be swathed in mist than bathed in sunshine. The road descends as steeply as it has risen. There are no sheep here, no ruined crofts, no fields, only innumerable springs and black peaty corries, silver cataracts, and grey lichened boulders, a waste-land of water and stone where even the heather finds it hard to grow.

In the *Old Statistical Account* for 1790 the Revd John M'Queen, minister of the parish, wrote: 'The extent of the parish is considerable and cannot, with precision, be ascertained, as there is neither public road nor bridge from one extremity of it to the other. The foot traveller is guided, according to the season of the year which course to take, over rugged hill, rapid waters and deep marshy moors.'

Apart from the road and the telegraph poles which march bravely over the bealach, the mountains have not changed since John M'Queen climbed them in the eighteenth century nor since the thirteenth century when our first Euphemia was a child, nor indeed since the seventh century in the days when St Maelrubha, the missionary monk from Ireland, established his monastery at their feet.

Suddenly as the road descends, a flash of vivid green appears in a fold of the hills. Slowly the scenery changes. Forest and woodland, grassland and field begin to clothe the glen of the great river that tumbles down to the sheltered bay that gave Applecross its name. Here at the mouth of the river is the clachan, now no more than a manse, an eighteenth-century church and a graveyard. This is all that remains of the great enclosed site of the original monastery. The tiny roofless chapel overgrown with laurel and ivy within the graveyard is pre-Reformation but not thought to be part of the original monastery. At the gate, however, there is a great cross-slab. Eaten with lichen, leaning a little, worn a lot, this stone cross still stands nine foot tall. It was raised by the monks of Applecross to the glory of God and perhaps in memory of their founder or one of his successors. Like John M'Queen, like thousands of long-forgotten pilgrims, priests and passers-by, like myself, Euphemia too may have touched it with love and wonder.

Standing in the lea of the cross, feeling the warmth of late summer sunshine, listening to the stir of wind in the hazel and hawthorn trees, to the murmur of sea and river, it is not hard to see why Maelrubha settled here. It is easy to understand how this remote glen became one of the great centres of Dark Age Christianity. The sense of peace and sanctuary still pervades the place.

A HOLY ANCESTOR

A lot of history has passed since 671 when Maelrubha – which translates as 'patient servant' – left the great monastery of Bangor in Ulster at the age of thirty with his *familia* of fellow monks and beached his coracle in Applecross bay. He may have come at the invitation of the Pictish king of Skye who, during exile in Ireland, is thought to have been converted. When freed, he invited Maelrubha to rebuild the mission established by St Donnan, a contemporary of Columba, who with his fellow monks had been murdered on Eigg in 617. In those days Applecross, like Iona, was not on the edge of civilization as it must seem to the tourists of today but in the centre of a growing and busy world of Irish expansion into Alba, the land of the Picts.

We know very little about Maelrubha and Donnan, the two great saints of Wester Ross who worked independently of Columba and Iona. They were not supported by the Dal Riadan dynasty in Argyll which produced the early kings of Scotland. Nor was there anyone of the stature of St Adamnan – St Columba's hagiographer – to record their missions to the Picts. Nor, when the Vikings are thought to have raided the monastery, looted its treasures and destroyed its archives in the ninth century, was there any evacuation of the monks to Ireland, as in the case of Iona. No one remained to keep its annals, though the last abbot is said to have escaped and fled to Bangor.

We do know however that Maelrubha was nobly born, descended

through his father from the great Niall of the Nine Hostages of the Cinel Owen race. According to Irish authorities he died a natural death on Tuesday 21st April 722 at the age of eighty. There are numerous dedications to him in the west, north and east of Scotland. Most famous of these is Loch Maree. One of its many islands became his hermitage. There the dead tree above his healing well is still studded with copper nails and coins, thank offerings from countless pilgrims of another age, and there alone among all the other islands, the holly tree symbolising Christianity re-seeds itself beside the pagan oak.

Maelrubha is said to have been buried in the north-east corner of his monastery under a green mound – *Claodh Maree* – in an unmarked grave identified by two big stones lying nearby. Allegedly a princess of Norway ordered a more imposing stone of red granite to mark the grave but it was broken up when the modern manse was built centuries later. Travellers and pilgrims still take a pinch of earth from the site for blessing and protection and local tradition maintains that no one is able to commit suicide or injure himself within view of the monastery.

Maelrubha was succeeded by Failbhe, son of Guaire, who according to the annalist Tighernach was drowned with twenty-two of his community in 737. Towards the end of the same century a monk called Mac Oigi from Applecross became abbot of Bangor. His obituary is recorded in the *Annals of Ulster* for 801 and Dr Reeves was 'strongly of the opinion that he is the individual familiarly known at Applecross as *Ruadhri mor Mac Caoigan*' to whom the great cross-slab was raised.

This is the last reference to Applecross in the Irish annals but in the early thirteenth century a member of Maelrubha's family 'commonly known by the epithet *Mac-an-t'sagairt*, son of the priest' distinguished himself by his military exploits, as is recorded in the *Chronicle of Melrose* in the year 1215.

The office of *herenach*, or hereditary lord, of monastic lands was originally both in Ireland and Scotland of a semi-clerical nature. In the days of the monastery the heir to the abbacy and church lands was a monk elected from the founder's kin, but with the passage of time the inheritance became a matter of direct succession. Applecross therefore became an heirloom eventually inherited by Farquhar Mactaggart of the clan O'Beolan.

THE MONASTERY

We know what the monastic site looks like today, a lumpy green sward scattered with gravestones and a ruined chapel all set within a circle of pines. We also know what it probably looked like in Maelrubha's time. Enclosed within a roughly circular path, or dry-stone dyke, the monks – perhaps twelve in the first instance, though the number soon increased – lived in wattle and wooden cells with a communal refectory for their meals, perhaps a scriptorium and a guest house. There would be a barn, stable, byre, a water mill and a bakery, a kiln for drying corn and a little stone church thatched with heather, with a sacristy opening on one side to house the monastic bell and the sacred vessels and relics.

The abbot lived apart, but as simply as his monks. He organised his community into those who laboured to support the others, those who studied, taught, copied the gospels in a scriptorium, those who looked after the sacred relics and those who went 'a wandering for Christ'. Celtic monks as part of their discipline spent several lonely and dangerous years evangelising the Picts or in solitary communion with God in such isolated places as Isle Maree, or Priest Island in the Summer Isles and the Holy Cave at Torridon Bay.

A well-organised foundation such as *A Chromraich*, built in a lush and sheltered valley that had the support of the kings of Skye, that was on the busy sea-route between Ireland, Dal Riada in Argyll and the Western Isles, could only thrive. The abbot was a leader of importance, usually of aristocratic birth, as Maelrubha had been, and the abbacy hereditary. It was retained within the family of the founder. After the sacking – if indeed that is what happened to it – the monastery became secularised and by 1200 AD its territories reached into Torridon, Gairloch, Lochalsh, Lochcarron and part of Lochbroom.

Farquhar's father, from whom presumably he inherited the lay abbacy of Applecross, seems also to have been a priest. It is tempting to associate him with the building of the tiny chapel in the monastic grounds. But M'Queen tells us that there were several surnames surviving in the parish in the eighteenth century that clearly derive from the clergy: 'Macvriar, the prior's son; Macficher, the vicar's son; Macpherson, the parson's son and Macantagaird, the priest's son.' These presumably all dated from a pre-celibate clergy.

So we know a little about the origins of the monastery. We also know a little about the place at the time of the Reformation (1560) when most of the carved stones and crosses were destroyed as relics of 'idolatry'. An ancient font was discovered in 1874, used by the ministers as a drinking trough for their poultry. Several beautiful fragments carved with interlace may now be seen in the modern church vestibule, but these are all that remain of what must once have been a treasure house of early Christian art.

We know that for some two hundred years the Mackenzies of Applecross owned 144,000 acres, including the Applecross peninsula, and that they derived their rents mainly from the three thousand black cattle that grazed the mountain valleys. We also know that in the middle of the last century the Mackenzies sold out to the duke of Leeds for £135,000. Eventually, in the 1860s, Applecross itself was bought by another wealthy Yorkshire landowner, the eighth Lord Middleton who turned the estate into a deer forest and took away the grazing rights from local people, forcing them to eke a living and build themselves crofts further along the shore at Lonbain, Kalnakill and Cuaig. Only within the last twenty years have they become linked to Applecross and Torridon by road.

We know that the estate was bought by the Wills family in 1929 who turned the one-time shooting lodge of Hartfield on the west side of the river into an adventure school for boys from dockland settlements. Today the Hartland Venture Trust operates a scheme for conservation.

We can see with our own eyes what it looks like today, with the beautiful eighteenth-century mansion house, still owned by the Wills family, set in finely wooded grounds and paddocks, surrounded by forestry plantations with rhododendrons now growing wild on either side of the river. We can visit the great walled garden, slowly being brought back to life after years of neglect. We can drive down the coast for seven miles to visit Milltown, or worship in any one of three churches, but we know nothing at all about Applecross during Euphemia's childhood.

We can only guess.

Foreword

SOURCES

Dr William Reeves' description of Applecross and St Maelrubha is taken from his paper published in the *Proceedings of the Society of Antiquaries of Scotland*, Volume III, 1857–60. Previous to his research nothing had been done towards the identification of St Maelrubha or his church of *Apercrosan*.

The Statistical Account of Scotland, compiled by the parish ministers in the 1790s, edited by Sir John Sinclair and printed in twenty-one volumes, is an unrivalled source of information as to the moral, economic and political state of the country. The Revd John M'Queen gives a fascinating account of Applecross. Alfred Smyth, in his readable and scholarly *Warlords and Holy Men* (1984), describes and emphasises the importance of St Maelrubha and his monastery and puts him into the context of his times.

PART ONE

◆

THE FIRST EUPHEMIA

Daughter of Applecross, Lady of Duffus

Euphemia . . . the name chimes like a silver bell down the centuries, musical, classical and aristocratic. Derived from the Greek, it means 'pleasant speech' or 'euphemism', but it can also mean 'silence'. When the pagan priests offered a sacrifice they ordered those attending to 'speak pleasantly' in order not to annoy the gods. Thus for safety's sake, nobody spoke at all.

How then did a thirteenth-century Gaelic-speaking warrior and hereditary lay abbot called Farquhar Mactaggart and his wife (whose name is not known), living in remote Applecross, come to choose such a fancy unfamiliar name for their eldest daughter? Perhaps she was called after St Euphemia of Bithynia, a virgin martyr who was tortured and thrown to the lions during Diocletian's persecution of the Christians in 307 AD. Her courage was legendary and the name spread throughout Europe reaching England about 1100 AD. Perhaps – even more unlikely – her father had heard of Euphemia, prioress of Ickleton in Cambridgeshire, who seems to have taken the name of the convent's foundress, Euphemia de Vere, countess of Oxford in the mid-twelfth century.

The probability is that he had never even heard of the name Euphemia. He and his wife may have chosen his mother's or mother-in-law's name, as was the custom, and she was baptised *Eighrig* (Eyrik) which was changed by genealogists of a later date into the nearest English, or more probably French, equivalent.

Similarly her father's name was *Fearchar* (Fe-ru-hur) anglicised to Farquhar, a common Celtic name meaning 'dearest one'. Descended, as we have seen, from Niall of the Nine Hostages, St Maelrubha's clan and the Irish King Beolan, his distinguishing title – in those days there were no surnames – was *Mac an t-saigairt* which translates as 'son of the priest'. All that is known of his background is that by inheritance he became lay abbot and lord of Applecross, and that he grew up to be a courageous and successful warrior with strong Christian convictions.

Euphemia – for the time being we will call her Eighrig – must have been born in the first decade of the thirteenth century. We don't know where she came in the family of four surviving children but we know she had a younger sister *Cairistiona* or Christina and two brothers, *Uilleam* or William, the elder, who was to be heir to the earldom, and *MaolCholuim* or Malcolm who inherited the lay abbacy of Applecross.

Farquhar's choice of names is revealing. William was still king of Scots, a man of fifty-seven in 1200, styled today as 'the Lion' from his adoption of the lion rampant on his coat of arms, and as 'the Brawny' to contemporary Gaels. It was his aim to consolidate those parts of Alba (Scotland) which were still rebellious, including Caithness, Moray and Ross. In 1187 he had taken his army north and while staying at Inverness, his young warriors had defeated the rebel claimant to the throne and in true Celtic tradition presented his head in triumph to their king. William had thereafter planted great defensive castles in Moray, the Black Isle and in Easter Ross. He had then gone on to subdue the powerful earl of Caithness and Orkney, putting in place of the rebel chieftains Anglo-French or Flemish knights of his own choosing, some of whose descendants were later to play an important part in Eighrig's life.

The younger Farquhar probably fought for and certainly admired his brawny king who was as famed for his courage as for his personal piety. Perhaps he called his eldest son William in his honour. Applecross, unlike the Western Isles which were Norse, was part of the Scottish kingdom. Farquhar's admiration, loyalty and support of the Scottish crown were later to be extended to William the Brawny's young heir, Alexander II, and would eventually lead Farquhar to fortune and the founding of a dynasty.

Malcolm, too, was a king's name. William the Brawny's older brother Malcolm IV, known as 'the Maiden', was only eleven years old when he was crowned in 1153. He died unmarried at the age of twenty-three. Although so young, he seems to have been an effective ruler and also a great patron of the church. But perhaps Farquhar chose the name in honour of St Columba for it means 'tonsured follower of Colum Cille'. The name Christina was brought to Scotland in the eleventh century by Queen Margaret, English wife of King Malcolm III (*Ceann Mor* or 'Big Head'), and speaks for itself. All these names reflect the age that combined the feudal and Celtic values of chivalry, warriorship and an extraordinary piety.

It is hard today to imagine a world where belief in Christ and all that is entailed by biblical Christianity was unquestioned. But the old pagan customs and beliefs were slow to die out – indeed they have not yet entirely disappeared from *a'Ghaidhealtachd* (the Gaelic-speaking Highlands and Islands). Thus while the devout Celtic warrior could also see in Christ, a shadow of Cuchullin the great god-hero of his ancestors, his wife could see in St Bridget not only the foundress of a religious community at Kildare in the fifth to sixth centuries but also Bride, the legendary foster-mother of Christ, whose *alter ego* was *Bridhde*, the ancient Celtic goddess of the hearth.

The name therefore whom Eighrig's mother would have invoked at childbirth was an amalgam of pagan, saint and midwife the one as bound to the others as the three persons of the Trinity.

'AID ME, O BRIDE'

Let us imagine then that as soon as Eighrig's birth was imminent, the midwife would have gone to the door of Farquhar's house and called out to Bride to come in.

> Tha do bheatha deanta,
> Tabhair cobhair dha na bhean,
> S' tabh an gein dh'an Triana.
>
> You are truly welcome,
> Give relief to the woman
> And give the conception to the Trinity.

Childbirth was cloaked in a great mantle of ritual and incantation and Eighrig's mother for all her Christian beliefs would have mingled pagan with Christian practice and seen no sin in it. A piece of iron in the bed would keep away the *sithean* (fairies), a relic from the

[27]

days when Goibnui the Celtic smith-god was associated with healing and protection. A burning peat carried sunwise seven times round the house was double insurance against abduction of the newborn babe by the *sithean*. Otters were thought to have a magical skin which acted as a charm against a difficult birth.

When Eighrig was born she would have been handed to and fro across the central hearth-fire three times in the name of the Trinity, then carried sunwise three times round the hearth in honour of the sun. A piece of silver or gold would be put into the water she was washed in and while the nurse splashed her with nine little waves all those present might have chanted an incantation which sums up the best that could be wished for any child.

> A wavelet for thy form
> A wavelet for thy voice
> A wavelet for sweet speech;
>
> A wavelet for thy luck
> A wavelet for thy good
> A wavelet for thy health;
>
> A wavelet for thy throat
> A wavelet for thy pluck
> A wavelet for thy graciousness;
> Nine waves for thy graciousness.

Immediately after the birth the child was baptised by the midwife, or in Gaelic terminology, the knee-woman. In *baisteadh ban-ghluin* (knee-woman's baptism) three drops of water were spilled on the baby's head in the name of the Trinity with all present as witnesses, the reason being that if the child were to die unbaptised he or she could not be buried in consecrated ground. Near St Moluag's burial ground on the Island of Lismore there was a place known as *Cladh na Cloinne gun Bailsteadh*, the 'Burial Place of the Unbaptised Children'. More often, however, these infants were buried in the dark between sunset and dawn in rocky inaccessible places. It was thought that such a child had no soul, only a spirit which could enter into a rock and become *Mac Talla*, Son of the Rock. This is also the Gaelic term for 'echo'.

As soon as possible thereafter Eighrig would have been baptised by a priest. Her soul was now safe and her body protected from the power of the fairies to exchange her for one of their own. Baptism was a great social occasion. The infant was handed from person to person around the hearth in a sunwise direction. In true Sleeping Beauty fashion, every guest was expected to make a wish for the child, preferably in original verse. Some would have travelled a distance to greet a new relative, while godparents, or those anxious to please her father, would have presented her with a gift of a calf or perhaps a lamb.

An old tale, undoubtedly fictitious, but reflecting the superstitions of the age, relates how an old woman cried out when it was her turn to hold the infant Eighrig, '*Iseam deiridh linne cinnidh e no theid dholaidh!*' (The last chicken of a brood comes to either grief or good). When Farquhar told her to pray for the child, she promised to make a charm that would protect her, but not others bearing the same name.

'BLESS THIS HOUSE FROM FOUND TO SUMMIT'

Eighrig's early years were spent in a farming community. Sadly, according to Peter Yeoman in *Medieval Scotland*, 'the archaeology of medieval farming communities is one of the greatest mysteries of our past.' The nearest perhaps we can get to it is by looking at Finlaggan in Argyll, which was the headquarters of the Macdonald lords of the Isles and excavated in the 1990s. Although Farquhar was lord of Applecross, he was not in the same league as the powerful Somerled, progenitor of the Macdonalds, but probably his homestead was constructed in much the same manner.

Just as today in the Western Isles you can still find a white-washed modern bungalow built next door to a rectangular stone cottage with corrugated iron roof and beside it a low stone hut, still with its shred of blackened thatch, so there would have been a variety of styles in the thirteenth century. Farquhar's house was probably of cruck construction, that is a pair of curved timbers supporting a thatched roof, with wooden, turf or clay walls. Because Applecross was so near the Norse-owned islands, the building may even have had a stone sub-basement overlaid with a wooden floor. It would probably have measured about 6m (20ft) by 12m (40ft), and been divided into rooms with a fire in the central chamber.

Farquhar might even had had his own hall, not as grand as the one at Finlaggan which was 20m (66ft) long with a great high roof supported on stone corbels carved with human heads, but a sizeable place for feasting and celebration with a kitchen at the far end. As a place of sanctuary and pilgrimage, Applecross had many visitors – warriors, priests, and traders – and Gaels have always been renowned for their hospitality.

His homestead would have been set within some sort of enclosure, palisaded or stone-walled, which contained guest houses and smaller dwellings for his servants and relatives, including stables, a byre, a large barn and store houses. His position as lay abbot would have granted him teinds – ten per cent of income usually paid in produce to the church – and as landowner, an income from his scattered properties which would include venison, salmon, goats, pigs and calves, oats or barley, butter and cheese and skins which he in turn could trade for the luxuries of the day.

The farm would have been near the old monastery, perhaps built on the lush and level pasture where Applecross House stands today. The old monastic site was a ruin even in his day, but he would have seen to it that the tiny chapel – perhaps the ruin in existence today – was well-appointed with embroidered hangings and reliquaries, tended by a priest, and surrounded by the graves of his ancestors, including the saintly Maelrubha.

His servants in exchange for a rig or two of a field and a share of the grazing ground would have ploughed his acres with a team of oxen, fertilising the land with seaweed from the shore. But his true wealth – like that of his neighbours – lay in sheep and particularly cattle. A Highland chief was above all a cattle baron. The mountainous peninsula of Applecross was no bar to trade and raiding. The waters of the Minch and the Inner Sound were highways in continual use and cattle were regularly rowed or swum between the islands and the mainland. How large the community at Applecross was in those days it is impossible to know, but it is certain that it would have been self-sufficient, producing not only enough food to survive – just – during the long winter storms, but also young men to accompany Farquhar on his warrior expeditions.

Among the leaders of the community, the priest, probably a relative, would have had an all-important influence. The seanachie, an inherited position and almost certainly a relative, acted as genealogist and family historian, while the bard chanted poetry, satire and songs to the accompaniment of the harper. All these men were in direct descent from the druids, who had been the priests and law-givers, historians and poets of their race. The seanachie provided the family with a strong sense of its own value and standing in the world. The bard provided poetic inspiration, while the priest gave spiritual sustenance. These men would have kept a critical and guiding eye on the young Eighrig and her siblings.

There was certainly a blacksmith, one of the most important of all craftsmen to the farmer-warrior Gaels who needed weapons as well as axes and cooking pots. According to the *Statistical Account of Scotland*, in the eighteenth century Applecross supported three smiths who were 'anciently' entitled to the heads of all slaughtered cows, 'a privilege they still claim but it is rarely complied with'. Iron ore was obtained from peat bogs and smelted in the summer on the spot when the bogs were comparatively dry. There would have been carpenters to make the staved cogs and pails, tubs and churns and turned bowls, possibly a potter, certainly a baker and surely a tanner.

Boatwrights would have played an enormously important part in the community. Coracles made of hides stretched over wooden frameworks dating back into prehistoric times were still in use until comparatively recent years. By Farquhar's time the Gaels had started to use the clinker-built wooden ships with single masts and square sails evolved from Viking vessels. The West Highland galleys, carved on so many medieval tombstones, could take as many as twenty-four oars, while a *birlinn* took up to sixteen and in time of war carried three men to an oar. In the twelfth century Somerled, king of the Hebrides, had command of some hundred and sixty galleys. How many Farquhar had is unknown, but certainly he would have had several craft, both coracles and *birlinns*.

Although dangerous, travel by sea was generally preferable to over land with no roads and no bridges through the high mountain passes. Eighrig would have spent her scant free time on the shore waving farewell to her father and his warrior companions or watching anxiously for their return. In a country of about half a million people, Applecross may have supported a population of several hundred, led by Farquhar who was more often absent than at home. Eighrig's mother would have been responsible for the smooth running of the extended family, with perhaps Eighrig's grandmother, together with an elderly male relative, to help and advise. Eighrig would have learned at an early age how to take responsibility for the lives and welfare of a tight-knit community.

'O BEING OF LIFE, SHEPHERD ME THIS DAY'

The young Eighrig must have woken in her cradle to the country sounds of barking dogs, lowing cattle, the neighing of her father's horses, if he were at home, the chime of the chapel bell, and above all the noisy cocks. She would have been able to recognise the difference between the crow of the big cock – remarkably accurate – and that of the little cock who at under a year old was unreliable. When the big cock crowed it was safe to get up. The dangers of the night, supernatural and real, were gone for another day.

She would hear her mother or possibly a house servant rekindling the smoored peat fire and murmuring the first prayer of the morning.

> I will raise the hearth-fire
> As Mary would.
> The encirclement of Bride and of Mary
> On the fire, and on the floor,
> And on the household all.

From then on her day would be punctuated with little croons of prayer or murmured charms for protection. Her childhood, indeed her whole life was imbued with respect for Christ's family and the saints, her human family and for the beautiful, unpredictable, all-encompassing family of the natural world. Before rising she would dedicate herself, her thoughts and words, her deeds and desires to God. As soon as she stepped outside she would reverence the sun. 'Glory to thee, thou glorious sun. Glory to thee, thou face of the God of Life.' Until recently old men removed their caps at first sight of the sun. Perhaps some still do. Today, as in the remote past, the sun is a blessing unsurpassed by the most modern of conveniences to those who live between towering mountains and an implacable sea. It gentles, colours and warms a harsh world.

And it was a harsh world. Eighrig in the comparative luxury of her later life might well have remembered the drenching rain and driving winds that shook the rafters, blew acrid peat smoke into her eyes and chilled her to the bone; the stench of animal and human ordure from the midden, the mud and muck around her home; the daily grind of necessary chores. As soon as she was old enough she and her sister and the other young girls in the settlement would take their share of the numerous tasks that kept the women busy from dawn till dark. The first of these might have been to collect the eggs. The following chant sounds like a child's game.

> I will close my two eyes quickly,
> As in blind-man's buff moving, slowly;
> I will stretch my left hand over thither
> To the nest of my hen on yonder side.

Soon she would be old enough to help with the milking, crooning to the cattle as she had been taught or in words of her own invention.

> Lovely black cow, pride of the shieling,
> First cow of the byre, choice mother of calves . . .
> Ho my heifer, ho my gentle heifer
> My heifer dear, generous and kind . . .
> She moves not against me feet nor head,
> She moves not against me hoof nor side;
> She fills the pitcher for the children
> After giving the calf his fill . . .

The beasts grew so accustomed to these songs sung with a lilt that often they refused to yield their milk without them. Herd-owners like Farquhar would prize milkmaids with sweet voices. One of the first things Eighrig would have learned was how to sing.

Then there was butter to churn. A long and wearisome task to judge by the length of the churn charms which urged the butter to come. As she grew stronger she would have taken her turn at fetching water from the Applecross river known to her as *amhain Maree* (Maelrubha's river) or from the well beside the monastery. Water from pagan times had a magical significance for Celts and certain wells or springs could harm or heal, grant wishes, or ward off the evil eye in return for a gift to the guardian spirit of the water. No doubt when Eighrig took her turn at the well in Applecross she crossed herself, turned three times sunwise, spilled three palmfuls back into the water and offered a prayer for protection, thus appeasing every deity.

At an early age she would have been taught to spin wool from her father's flocks. The spindle whorl dating back to the Iron Age was an old implement, even in the thirteenth century, and the process comparatively simple, if lengthy. Yarn was twisted and lengthened by the dangling spindle and weighted by the whorl, a stone with a hole in it. The spinner would wind the wool round a longer piece of wood called the distaff which she could carry in the crook of her arm while she herded cattle. The last woman known to spin with a distaff in Applecross was still alive at the beginning of the present century.

Linen was also fabricated in those long ago days, for warriors all wore the saffron-dyed tightly pleated linen shirt (*leine chroich*) in battle. Whether flax was grown in Applecross or imported there is no means of knowing but I. F. Grant in *Highland Folk Ways* writes that it grew well in the Highlands. 'It was a troublesome crop, exhausting the ground and requiring hand-weeding (a woman's job).' It then had to be soaked to rot, a process known as retting and extremely smelly. The earliest looms for weaving were upright. They were in use all over the Highlands from prehistoric times. There would most certainly have been looms in Farquhar's community. Perhaps Eighrig helped to wind the bobbins for the weavers. This was seen as children's work.

She would have helped to collect the herbs used for dyeing the wool. Crotal, a coarse rock lichen, produced that reddish brown so typical of Harris tweed, while the roots of the yellow flag, still profuse at the edge of the lochs, gave a greyish blue. Lady's bedstraw produced red, a difficult recipe to get right. While I. F. Grant tells us that 'the real expert can get a brilliant clear yellow from heather in flower'. Probably this rather than the rare saffron crocus was used to dye the warriors' shirts. It took hours to produce the dyes and as they could only be made in small quantities – there were no vats in the Highlands – it was almost impossible to match the different batches of wool. I. F. Grant suggests ingeniously that this may have been why Gaels wore checkered clothing.

Eighrig would have learned at an early age a prudent economy where food was concerned. As was the custom, her father would have kept an open table for his visitors, tenants and servants, but it was his wife's responsibility to see that there was sufficient food for all without wastage. The staple diet was milk and cheese, porridge and barley broth, eggs and fish and bannocks, but on feast days and festivals or entertainment of important guests there would have been roast beef, mutton or venison.

Ale brewed from a good part of the barley crop was regularly drunk. Whisky too – *uisge beatha* the water of life – was probably distilled locally from malted barley. Although traditionally it was thought to have been brought over from Ireland in the fifth or sixth centuries, archaeological excavation on the island of Rum in 1986 found spores and pollen suggesting that some sort of alcoholic drink was distilled there six thousand years ago. But Farquhar and his children may also have enjoyed imported wine. This was to become such a popular drink in the Hebrides that by the seventeenth century the Privy Council passed an act limiting its consumption by some of the chiefs to an amount between one and four tuns (500–2,000 gallons).

Eighrig's tasks would have been governed by the weather, the seasons and the festivals. The herds had to be taken to the hills in spring, returned to the harvested fields in autumn and to the homesteads in winter. Summer saw the collection of herbs for medicines and dyes, peat-cutting for the fires and autumn the ingathering of the harvest, the wild fruits and nuts. And so the days would pass, with no thought of book study. There were too many other lessons to be learned, too many tasks to perform. The local priest would have taught the children the Lord's Prayer and the Ten Commandments but it is unlikely that she or indeed her parents would have learned to read or write. The seanachie would have taught her and her siblings their family history, making them chant their genealogy from the Irish King Niall of the Nine Hostages down to Farquhar himself. Gaels were above all proud of their ancestry.

Her mother or grandmother would have taught her how to knit, perhaps even how to embroider the rare and costly silks and damasks brought back by her father from his travels or imported in exchange for hides and produce. These might be used to adorn the chapel or make priestly vestments, but rarely for clothes. They were too precious.

The wise woman or man in the community with a knowledge of medicine would have taught her the use of herbs and charms for healing. The traditional medicines of the Highlands, combined with the correct incantations, were often extraordinarily effective, combining psychology with time-tested remedies. For example, St John's wort, known in Gaelic as *Achlasan Choluim Cille* (the Oxterful of Columba) was one of the most effective of all medicines. Traditionally Columba was said to have put the plant in the armpit of a herdsboy whose nerves had become upset by long and lonely nights on the hills. Thereafter he recovered. The armpit, like the groin, is well-endowed with nerve-endings, glands and blood vessels. Thus it readily absorbs treatment through the skin. St John's wort contains rutin which affects the flow of adrenaline and so alters the whole nervous system. St John's wort is known today as 'nature's Prozac' and may still be used in the treatment of depression. Eighrig would have learned to murmur a prayer as she gathered the herb.

> . . . I will pluck my Columba plant,
> As a prayer to my King,
> That mine be the power of Columba's plant
> Over everyone I see . . .

If Eighrig and her sister were talented musically they might have learned to play the harp to perform and accompany themselves singing not just to their father's guests in the hall but also around the hearth fire in the evening when the outdoor chores were done.

This was the best time of the day. Though the women's fingers would still be busy knitting and mending, while the men twisted twigs of heather into ropes or plaited bent grass into baskets and the boys perched precariously in the rafters and the girls hugged the grown-ups' knees and nursed the babies, this was the time for music, poetry and stories. Such stories!

If Farquhar and his companion warriors were at home, they would recount their adventures, perhaps a little exaggerated, but all the better for that. There would be much laughter, riddles and comic stories. Above all the Gaels enjoyed a joke and a tale of trickery. There would be serious discussions, too, on whether the king was introducing too many French and Flemish foreigners into Alba. Were Gaels not good enough for him? And Farquhar might try to explain why he continued to support the king rather than the rebels, although they were Gaels like himself.

The seanachie would recite favourite tales of feuds and challenges to single combat in the past, great sea battles lost and won by Farquhar's ancestors, and afterwards there would be discussion and argument and songs. Eighrig, her fingers twisted in the ruff of her father's sleeping deerhound, would listen enthralled. And she would learn and remember.

When the men were away – more often than at home – the stories would change. Others would take their turn to tell tales of faery and romance, of magic and the second sight, of talking birds and kelpies and ghosts, of the Blue Men of the Minch, the giant *bodach* (old man) that slept under the mountain and the *Cailleach Bheur* (sharp old woman) with her blue-black face, her matted hair 'white as aspen covered with hoar frost' and her rust-red teeth.

The Cailleach seems to have been a universal figure of fear in the thirteenth century. At one moment she could be a beautiful virgin, at another Thomas the Rhymer's Queen of the Fairies 'her body as blow [blue] as ony bede' and thirdly that 'loathly hag' described in Chaucer's *Wife of Bath's Tale* who when kissed by the hero-knight becomes as fair 'as any lady, empress or queen'.

She was winter, 'a wild hag with a venomous temper, hurrying about with a magic wand in her withered hand, switching the grass and keeping down vegetation to the detriment of man and beast'. When spring came she threw her wand into a whin bush and disappeared under a holly tree which is why no grass grows there. Eighrig had only to look out over the water to Skye to see her in the guise of a great menacing mountain rising beyond the island of Raasay. Here she kept prisoner a beautiful maiden whom her son loved. Only at the end of winter could the young couple escape together in spite of the great storms she raised to keep them apart. And then in her *alter ego* she became spring, the beautiful virgin who in turn became summer the nurturer, the queen mother of all fruitfulness.

Not only the seasons had their personalities and stories but also the trees and rocks and rivers. The landscape was full of haunts and giants and fairies. There would most certainly have been rowans in or about Farquhar's homestead to ward away ghosts. The hazel was sacred because of the 'milk' contained in its green nut and because its wood was used to make fire by friction. Holly berries protected animals and humans from the evil eye. Birds and beasts, seals and sea creatures had their special place and personality in the family of nature and their stories were legion.

All this and so much more that has long ago been forgotten constituted Eighrig's schooling. A rich education indeed, passed on from one generation to another through the oral tradition of her race. And so the busy day drew to a close.

Perhaps Eighrig left the crowded smoky gathering to breathe the fresh night air and look up at the moon and the stars. If so she would sing to herself with wonder one of the many incantations which survive.

> Hail unto thee,
> Jewel of the night!
> Beauty of the heavens
> Mother of the stars,
> Fosterling of the sun,
> Majesty of the stars,
> Jewel of the night!

Just as the sun was lord of the day, the eye of God, so the moon was queen of the night, mistress of the tides and the mysteries of women. Perhaps the young Eighrig ran with her companions to the nearest knoll to be first to see the rising of a new moon. Together they would look to the west, turning slowly sunwise on the right heel till the new moon appeared. '*Fhaic! Fhaic!*' (See! See!) they would cry, making the sign of the cross on their palms with spit. Those herding cattle on the hill would whisper to their beasts, 'There is the new moon, beloved one among cows.' Or she might have cut a cross on the ground for the absent Farquhar whispering, 'I have wounded you or bled you dear earth. Let not my father be wounded.' The new moon – *gob soillse* (beak of the light) – was propitious for clipping hair, cutting peats, reaping corn, shearing sheep. No journey would be undertaken without consulting the phase of the moon.

A waning moon was 'in her black boundaries'. Withies for creels and baskets were cut at this time. Eggs laid in the wane were preserved for hatching because they produced hens rather than cocks. The second moon in autumn, the 'ripening moon', was thought to ripen the crops as effectively as the sun. The last moon in harvest was 'the hunter's moon' and the first moon of winter, 'the reddening moon', when vegetation grew as much by night as by day.

'I think myself that it is a matter for thankfulness, the golden-bright sun of virtues giving us warmth and light by day, and the white moon of the seasons giving us guidance and leading by night.' So, according to Carmichael, said an old cottar from Barra a hundred and fifty years ago. Farquhar and his family probably thought the same.

The last act of the day was to smoor the fire, another ceremony surrounded with ritual. Eighrig would have watched and learned as the embers were spread evenly on the central hearth in the shape of a circle divided into three sections with a boss in the centre. Peats were then laid over them in the name of the God of Life, the God of Peace and the God of Grace. The whole was carefully covered over with ashes – not too many and not too few – in the name of the Three of Light. The woman of the house – perhaps Eighrig's mother, perhaps her grandmother – closed her eyes and stretched out her hands and intoned one of the many incantations to keep the fire alight.

And then bed, all in the same room around the fire, perhaps lying on heather arranged with the brush uppermost or sea-grass carefully washed and dried and covered with blankets. Farquhar, if he were at home, or his wife led the family in the final prayers of the day.

> I lie down tonight
> With fair Mary and with her Son,
> And pure-white Michael,
> And with Bride beneath her mantle...

As she grew older so her tasks increased, some heavy and hard, some enjoyable like preparing for the great and lesser festivals, lay and religious, that punctuated the long and busy year.

'GOD, BLESS TO ME THE NEW YEAR'

Eighrig would not have known the months by name. The passing of time was computed by the moon and punctuated with festivals that mingled Christian with the secular and pagan. There were so many that only a few can be remembered here.

Samhain the first day of winter provided more fun and excitement mingled with terror than any other season of the year. With the harvest ingathered the families collected round the fire for what we call Hallowe'en. Ceremonies included divination. Perhaps Eighrig threw two nuts on the fire to represent herself and some young lad she admired. As they burned together or alone, or leapt away from each other, so the future of the couple was foreseen. Perhaps she drew a straw from a stack and counted the grains to find out how many children she would have.

Samhain was also the season when the dead were remembered with dread. Their ghosts could return to their own homes to haunt the living. Rowans placed over the door of every house helped to keep them away. This, too, was a night for bonfires when all the rubbish of summer was burned, one for each house and there was great rivalry as to who should have the biggest blaze.

Then came Christmas Eve. Oidhche nam Bannagan may have meant the Night of Cakes or the Feast of Women. Eighrig might have helped her mother to give everyone on her father's land a *bannag,* or large round cake, the most luxurious kind covered after cooking with a batter of eggs, milk and butter and baked before the fire. The seven days between Christmas and new year (*Nollaig*) were for games, good food and friendly festivities.

Our Hogmanay was known as Calluinn, the Night of the Blows, when the young lads visited all the houses, marched round them sunwise and struck the walls shouting to be let in. After all had entered they entertained with rhymes and riddles and were duly fed. Perhaps Eighrig's brothers were whipped with holly and assured that they would live a year for every drop of blood spilled.

January and part of February was known as the Dead Month. St Bride's Day, 1st February, calculated as one month and three days after Nollaig was not to be confused with Candlemas on 2nd February. 'The women make up a bed of birch twigs and then they

cry at the door, *"Bride, Bride, thig astigh, tha do leaba dean-te!"'*
(Bride, Bride enter, your bed is ready.)

The season of spring was heralded by the Wolf-Month a time of
'cold hail-stones', after which came Gearran which means 'complaint'. Gearran was however the best time for sowing. The high
winds dried the ground and it was said that the seeds preferred a
dry bed.

Inid was Shrovetide, the beginning of Lent, a moveable feast
reckoned from 'the first Tuesday of the Spring Light' – the new moon
in spring. This was a time for the saining of cattle when juniper was
burned before them to keep away evil. March 25th was celebrated
as *Feill Mhoire*, Lady Day, when Christ was conceived but it was
also *Latha na Caillich*, the Cailleach's Day, when the Cailleach was
finally overthrown by spring. In Eighrig's time and up till December
1599, 25th March was also recognised as New Year's Day.

Maundy Thursday was known as *La Brochain Mhora*, the Day
of the Big Porridge. If winter had failed to produce the seaweed
needed to fertilize the land, a pot of porridge prepared with butter
and cream was taken to the headland above the shore and poured
into the sea.

> Come and come is seaweed,
> Come and come is red sea-ware,
> Come is yellow weed, come is tangle,
> Come is food which the wave enwraps.
> Come is warrior Michael of fruitage,
> Come is fair Bride of gentleness,
> Come is mild Mother Mary,
> And come is glorious Connan of guidance.

And when the seaweed was thrown on shore by the strong prevailing
west wind, the community would always give thanks.

On Crucifixion Friday, mindful of the nails, no iron was put into
the ground, which meant no ploughing and no grave-digging. So
strong did this tradition become that in some places it was extended
to every Friday. On Caisg, Easter, it was said that the sun used to
dance after dawn. Exactly when it became the tradition for boys to
steal and hide as many eggs as they could find and thereafter make
themselves pancakes is not known.

The days before the great May festival of Beltain were auspicious for going on pilgrimage. No doubt there were many from far and wide who visited the grave of St Maelrubha on his feast day, 21st April, to make their special requests. As his sacred well on Isle Maree was associated with healing of madness, this may have been one of the reasons for pilgrimage to Applecross.

The *Crois Sliachdaidh*, or Cross of Prostration, marked the first sighting of the sanctuary. The pilgrim would have prostrated himself, said his prayers and made his requests there before going on to the shrine to make his offering. One wonders how many thousands of pilgrims must have knelt below that lichened cross that still stands today by the gateway to the monastery. And Farquhar's family would have fed and housed them to the best of their ability.

But the greatest secular festival of the year, apart from Samhain, was Beltain, May Day, the feast of 'the big sun' whose origins go back into distant pagan times. The rituals were mainly concerned with protecting the cattle from the power of evil, and getting them out to the hills. Great bonfires were lit and the beasts driven between them for purification. A torch kindled from the Beltain fires was used to relight the house fires which for one only night in the year had been allowed to go out.

Caingis or Whitsun was followed by Feill Choim Cille, St Columba's Festival, celebrated on a Thursday, the day between two fasts, technically 9th June. This was the luckiest day in the year.

> Day to send sheep on prosperity
> Day to send cow on calf
> Day to put the web in the warp
> Day to put coracle on the brine . . .
> Day to hunt the heights,
> Day to put horses in harness,
> Day to send herds to pasture,
> Day to make prayer efficacious . . .

On Feill-Sheathain, St John's Day or Midsummer Eve, the cuckoo was said to 'enter its winter house' and was no longer heard to sing. Like other migrating birds it was called one of the seven sleepers believed to spend winter underground.

The Dog-Days preceded Lammas, 1st–12th August, so called

because of the shortage of supplies before the new harvest was in-gathered. It was a sad time for putting down old and hungry dogs. In Lammastide the cattle were 'sained' by putting tar on their tails and ears, charms on their udders, and coloured threads on their tails, all for protection against evil.

Roodmas in September celebrated the rutting season in the hills. If the deer 'took their head wet into the rutting season', the weather would be dry for harvest. The night before the festival was called the Night of the Holy Nut but no one knows why. The end of September heralded the Feast of St Michael, subduer of the dragon, patron of horses, one of the best-loved characters in the Christian pantheon.

> Thou chief of chiefs,
> Thou chief of the needy . . .
> Thou chief of angels
> Spread thy wings
> Over sea and land
> For thine is their fullness . . .

The celebrations included dancing, games and horse-racing.

Thus the busy years of Eighrig's childhood in Applecross were stitched with the ancient customs of her race. Soon, however, were to come great changes for her and for her family.

FARQUHAR'S PROMOTION

On Thursday 4th December 1214 William the Lion died in Stirling. 'The next day, very early in the morning,' seven earls with Malvoison, the French bishop of St Andrews and the queen-mother, Ermengarde, in charge, 'took the king's son, Alexander, a lad of sixteen years and a half; and bringing him as far as Scone, they raised him to the throne, in honour and peace, with the approval of God and man, and with more grandeur and glory than any one until then'. On the following Monday 'the Little Red Fox', as Alexander was styled, followed by 'all the nobility of the whole kingdom, save a few nobles who guarded the uttermost parts' met William's body at Perth bridge on its way to burial in front of the high altar at the church he had built at Arbroath. It is more than likely that Farquhar would have been there too.

But Alexander's coronation was the trigger to spark off a rebellion in Moray, led by the son of that claimant to the throne, Donald MacWilliam, who had been decapitated by King William's warriors in 1187. He was supported by Kenneth, son of Malcolm MacHeth who may have been *mormaor* (a Pictish office corresponding to an earl) of Ross who had also been deposed by King William. This was Farquhar's chance to prove himself a loyal subject and he seized it.

'The foes were attacked by Macentagart and mightily overthrown; and the latter having cut off their heads, presented them as new gifts to the new king, Alexander, and was therefore graced, by the king, with the honour of knighthood.'

To be a knight in the feudal system involved a mutual acceptance of lordship and homage between two free persons. The lord, in this case the king, granted an estate and fortified residence (fief) to the knight (vassal) and his heirs in exchange for loyalty and military service. It is almost certain that Sir Farquhar was rewarded with the land in Ross lost by the MacHeths and the castle of Delny in Easter Ross for his residence. It is not known when he was created earl, but it must have been fairly soon after he received his knighthood. Perhaps he had to prove his ability to control great tracts of land before receiving such a responsible post. Perhaps, too, Alexander had to be sure of his loyalty, for he was one of the few Gaels to be given land in and around the Easter Ross area among an influx of foreigners.

Although the Normans never conquered Scotland, as they did England, Anglo-Normans became landowners by invitation of the kings or by planned marriages with Scottish heiresses. The historian Marinell Ash tells us that 'Scotland was the country for younger sons and ambitious men, many of them of Anglo-French origin, who were attracted north by the chance of land and advancement.'

For example, William de Comyn, whose family had originally come from Flanders with William the Conqueror, had attended Alexander II's coronation with Farquhar. Through a judicious second marriage to Marjory, countess of Buchan he had inherited that earldom. Their friends the Mowats (de Monte Alto) may have held the area around Strathpeffer and Castle Leod before becoming the Lords of Cromarty in 1263. A branch of the de Vaux (Vass) family were in or about to settle in Lochslin castle in Easter Ross. The de Bissets were at Aird at the head of the Beauly Firth, the de Boscos at the royal fortress of Eddidour (Redcastle) in the Black Isle. Thomas Durward was sheriff of Inverness in 1226 and his son was granted the lordship of Castle Urquhart on Loch Ness. The de Freskins – originally Flemish merchants already in possession of Castle Duffus in Moray – had recently expanded into Sutherland. The Roses (Ros de Normandy) were at Kilravock near Nairn (and are still there), while the Grants (le Grand) were at Stratherrick south of Loch Ness. These were all incoming families who knew the rules of feudalism and the importance of supporting the crown if they wanted to keep their lands and titles.

Sometime in 1215 Farquhar must have returned to Applecross with the bewildering news of his promotion and the announcement that the family would have to move to the other side of the country. We have no means of knowing how old Eighrig was but if she and her sister were married in the 1220s she would have been about ten. The logistics of such a move would have involved endless discussion. When would be the best time to travel, bearing in mind the all-important harvest in Applecross, the weather conditions and the phases of the moon? Who would go with them and who stay behind to run the estate in Farquhar's absence? What in the way of possessions would they take and how were they to travel?

If Eighrig's mother was, as has been suggested, a descendant of Somerled from Argyll, this would not have been her first move, but the idea of leaving Gaeldom for what would have seemed to her the barbarous east of Alba must have filled her with dread. Old heads no doubt were shaken in foreboding, old tales remembered of monsters and giants lurking in the lochs and mountains, added to the more substantial threat of wolves and thieves. No doubt many tears were shed, many blessings evoked, many gifts and promises of prayers exchanged.

One decision had to be made. The time was fast approaching for William and Malcolm to be fostered. This custom that dated back into prehistory was, according to G. W. S. Barrow, 'an integral part of the Gaelic system of education' whereby sons, and occasionally daughters, of leading Gaels were taken into the homes of friends or less important members of the clan who could be trusted to protect and educate them according to their talents and future needs. The practice continued among the clan chiefs up till the early eighteenth century and there are many stories of the love between foster-parents and their *dalta* (foster-children).

Whether Farquhar was important enough to have been fostered himself or to consider his sons eligible for the custom is hard to tell. He may have thought it more important to take them with him to Easter Ross. He may have left Malcolm, his second son, later to be styled 'the Green', who was to inherit Applecross and the lay abbacy, in the custody of local relatives as insurance in case he or his eldest son perished. It is more than likely that William was fostered with a family skilled in the art of warfare for he was to follow his father's example in warrior service to Alexander III.

It is equally possible that William and Malcolm were still too young to be fostered from Applecross and that all four children accompanied their parents on the journey to Easter Ross.

CASTRUM DINKEUAL

There were three choices. To go by sea around the perilous north coast of Scotland, a voyage fraught with danger not just from storm but also from piracy; to go overland, or to go partly by sea and partly by horseback. Perhaps all three methods were used. Eighrig and her siblings may have gone with their mother by sea south through the Inner Sound into Loch Carron to wait for Farquhar who would have ridden over the bealach with the rest of his warriors to protect the herdsmen, servants and those cattle he had decided to take.

They would then have commenced the great trek east perhaps through Glen Carron to Achnasheen, down the long wet boggy plain of Strath Bran to Garve, thought to have been the scene of the battle where William the Brawny's warriors decapitated the elder Donald MacWilliam in 1187. Then on to Contin where they would have no doubt received a warm welcome from the priest at Preas Maree (Maelrubha's Grove), a little church and settlement founded by their own St Maelrubha. An analogy can perhaps be made with the covered wagons that rolled through alien territory to the American west. In Alba the journey was about a hundred miles from Applecross to Easter Ross, the terrain rough with no shelter from the fluctuations of the weather and the predations of wild clansmen. At Contin Farquhar would have ridden on to make himself known at the centres over which he was soon to claim superiority.

And what must Eighrig have made of this promised land as she rode on her tough little Highland garron through mountain passes and forest tracks, over innumerable bogs and finally down the side of the river Peffery towards the colourful patchwork of cultivated land and settlement surrounding Dingwall castle at the head of the Cromarty Firth?

All we know of Dingwall at this time comes from Matthew Paris's celebrated thirteenth-century map which shows *Castrum Dinkeual* beside 'a mountainous and woody region producing a people rude and pastoral, by reason of marshes and fens'. That it was marked at all in a map which shows only a handful of places, including the two Roman walls of Hadrian and Antoninus, is an indication of its importance. Its name, derived from the old Norse *Thing Vollr*, meaning 'court of justice', tells us that this settlement had once been the centre of the Scandinavian occupation of the north of Scotland.

Some believe on reading the Norse sagas that it was here in 1034 that the armies of Malcolm II and the Norse Yarl Thorfin met on the slopes of Knockfarrel and that Malcolm was wounded in the Coil an Righ (King's Wood) just below Knockbain farm. Thorfin entered Dingwall and ruled in its castle for thirty-seven years. The sagas boast of his grandeur, how he maintained his warriors during the winter seasons with the best of food and drink so that no one had 'occasion to go to a tavern' and how in the summer he sent out his fleet on looting expeditions. How he went to Rome to confess his sins, and returned first to Dingwall, then north to Orkney and thereafter lived a devout and peaceful life.

He brought many of his followers to Dingwall to settle and marry locally. His daughter, the beautiful Ingibiorg, married Malcolm III (Canmore) as his first wife before he fell in love with the saintly English Margaret. A century later David I, according to Fordun, built 'at great expense and richly endowed' a lazar-house (for lepers) near the castle. Little else is known of Dingwall, until 1226 when Alexander II created it a royal burgh, apart from the fact that its castle was occupied by a succession of governors appointed by the crown who were responsible for keeping the peace in those turbulent times.

It must have been the first town Eighrig had ever seen with its great wooden keep raised on an earth mound at one end and the lazar-house beside it, with the church of St Clement at the other end, with the Norse Gallows Hill to the west. She must have gazed with wonder at the cobbled High Street set out with market stalls and lined with small houses, each built with its gable-end facing the road and behind it a rig of garden enclosed within a wattle fence. Each plot would be separated from the other by pends or narrow lanes that led to the backlands, a jumble of even smaller cottages stretched along narrow roads lined with wattle fences, humming with life, hooded with smoke, and heavy with the stench of middens.

Excavation of towns like Perth have shown that the majority of the houses at that time were single-storey wooden frameworks with wicker walls daubed with clay or dung, mud or turf for protection against the weather. The walls were usually about five foot high and thatched with rushes or broom, heather or straw. As in Applecross, animals shared the same roof, occupying one end of the house which was cobbled and drained. Peter Yeoman tells us that one of the grander houses excavated in Perth had an internal lavatory tucked into a corner with an oak plank toilet seat built over a timber-framed pit.

Leaving the cattle and horses to graze the commonland in the care of their drovers, Farquhar and his wife would have gone to pay their respects to the governor of the castle. Meanwhile Eighrig and her siblings, astonished and excited by all they saw, may have explored the busy High Street under the watchful eye of a nurse and some of their father's henchmen.

Towns – burghs as they were called in Scotland – were creations of David I and his successors in the twelfth century. Those in existence before Eighrig's time were on land belonging to the king, associated with royal castles and established as markets for the surrounding countryside. In 1210 there were some forty burghs in Scotland, thirty of which were to be found in the east. Although Dingwall was not to have the full privileges and charter of a Royal Burgh until 1226, it would most certainly have been an important centre of trade in Eighrig's time.

She would have had to pick her way through the muck on the cobbles, careful to avoid a squealing pig chased by a pack of noisy children, the bandaged hand of a leprous beggar, a defecating dog, a woman yoked to a couple of heavy buckets of water, a travelling priest followed by his overburdened servant, lean ponies bent under laden panniers or bearing farmers and their wives with a tethered cow in tow. Norsemen, Gaels, Normans, farmers, craftsmen, labourers. Noise, stench, bustle and the occasional staring lad, as curious about her as she was about him.

She might even have witnessed a fire. Wooden houses were particularly susceptible and the first fire law dates from a thirteenth-century collection of *Laws of the Four Burghs*, which may go back to the days of David I. Each burgh had to have 'v, vi or vii ladderis efter the quantitie of the burgh. And that they be keipit in a redy place of the toun, and til that use and nane uthir . . . and of the samyn wise thre or four sayis [pails] to the common use, and vi or mair cleikis of iron to draw doun timmer and russis [rushes used as thatch] that are fyrit'.

Perhaps Eighrig was most impressed by the variety of goods for sale in the market stalls. An economy based on cattle saw to it that every part of the carcass was used to provide meat for the butchers, hide for the tanners and leatherworkers, lard for the candlemakers, horns and bones for the makers of cups, spoons, combs and finely carved knife-handles. There would be bread and bannocks on sale, honey combs, clay pots, metal and wooden goods, wool, materials and ale. She might have coveted a fine yellow silk shawl imported from Spain, or a set of five finger rings made by a silversmith in Perth, or a pottery jug with a face-mask imported from Scarborough or – a real luxury this – her first pair of leather shoes.

That evening, as she and Christina took their places for supper in the castle hall and chattered in hushed whispers to their mother of the wonders of the day, the lady of the castle might have smiled indulgently and told their mother that 'Eupheme and Christiane' – no longer Eighrig and Cairistiona – would have to learn to speak French, the fashionable language of the court, if they were to marry well.

A few days later they would leave Dingwall for the heartland of Farquhar's new territory, riding eastwards down the northern shore of the Cromarty Firth, stopping to visit the small parish churches and surrounding farmsteads, including Kil Clyne (Mountgerald), which was soon to be part of Euphemia's dowry. No less than twelve chapels, each a centre of cultivation and settlement, existed within the fourteen miles between the Dingwall area and Delny where the family was finally to settle.

THE NEW HOME

Although a handsome comparatively modern mansion house stands on the site, nothing today remains of Delny, the stronghold which was to be the principal seat of the earls of Ross until 1321, when Robert the Bruce granted Dingwall castle together with 'the lands, burgh and liberties of the same' and other lands to Farquhar's grandson, William, the third earl.

Deilgnidh in the Gaelic means 'place of prickles' and if the family arrived in May or June, which is likely, Euphemia's first impression must have been of a great green mound crowned by a wooden keep rising above a sea of golden whin. No mountains here, only the gentle rise of the muir to the north, grazing ground for cattle from earliest days, with the densely wooded Ardross hills to the northwest. To the south lay the long hump of the Black Isle, casting a dark shadow on the bright waters of the Cromarty Firth. Perhaps some of Farquhar's boats already lay at anchor in the bay, beyond which to the south-east stood the Sutors, twin sentinels to the narrow entrance of the Firth. No doubt one of the first stories Eighrig would be told was of the two shoemakers who gave their names to these crags, and who shared their tools by throwing them over the narrow channel between Cromarty and Nigg.

The type of motte-and-bailey stronghold that dominated the northeast of Scotland at that time originated in Normandy. These were constructed by labourers excavating a great round ditch or moat not just for defensive purposes but also to provide earth for the mound or motte on which the timber tower was raised. The whole site was surrounded by a courtyard or bailey defended by a timber pallisade and more ditches. The bailey would have been big enough to contain other wooden buildings to house Farquhar's servants and his cattle in time of siege. The lord of the castle and his family lived in the tower house itself set within another palisade which might have included a chapel or oratory. It was reached by a wooden staircase or steps cut into the side of the mound.

It's more probable that the original keep at Delny had been burned by the previous owners, the MacHeths, out of revenge for Farquhar's beheading of their chief. If so, it would not have taken Farquhar long to rebuild, using all the available labour in the neighbourhood. At York in 1068 a small motte-and-bailey was built in eight days.

It is also possible that Farquhar might have taken this opportunity to build in stone, as was soon to happen to Dingwall castle. If so, he would have extended the motte with layers of stone to create a suitable base for building a rectangular stone-walled enclosure which could have been roofed over as a hall house or left open to surround a wooden building within.

Farquhar's first task would be to find suitable stewards to oversee his territory which was probably already divided up into what were known in later documents as the five quarters of Ross. Some land he would have undoubtedly given to his warrior companions and relatives who had fought with him for the king. He would have confirmed territory like Ferindonald in the trustworthy hands of the Munros of Castle Foulis whose barony marched with Delny. The Munros, possibly of Pictish origin, seem always to have been supporters of the crown and had been firmly established on the north bank of the Cromarty Firth at least since the time of the first baron who died in 1126.

It seems possible that Eighrig and her family would have stayed with the Munros until Delny castle was made habitable, possible too that Farquhar made arrangements to foster one of his sons with Robert Munro, the sixth baron of Foulis who, like himself, was a Celt, a personal friend and a comrade-at-arms, but that has to be speculation. Meanwhile Farquhar was proving himself to be a powerful, shrewd and ambitious nobleman, more often away supporting Alexander II at court or on his numerous skirmishes than he was at home.

One delightful story recorded by Hector Boece describes how on one of the occasions when he accompanied Alexander to the English court, about 1227, he challenged a cocky French champion to single combat and beat him. For this gallant deed which pleased the 'Little Red Fox' but not the English court, he was awarded his earldom. It is fairly certain however that he was promoted at an earlier date. The story goes on to say that he had sworn an oath that, if he won the joust, he would establish a monastery in his earldom. On his way home he stopped at the priory at Whithorn in Galloway and there persuaded two Premonstratensian canons to come north to re-found a religious house on the site of an ancient Pictish monastery at Fearn near Edderton. Accounts differ but this was thought to be about 1223.

It seems likely that Farquhar would have accompanied Alexander when, according to John of Fordun, he went 'with some of the chief men of the kingdom' to meet King Henry III at York in 1220 to negotiate a marriage between himself and the English king's sister, the young Princess Joan. It may have been on this occasion or the following year, when Alexander became formally betrothed to the Princess Joan, that Farquhar won his joust, and with an earldom in his saddle-bag returned home in thanksgiving with the two canons of Whithorn.

Alexander's marriage heralded a time of peace and prosperity between the two nations which was accompanied by a great flowering of chivalry, religion, architecture and the arts on both sides of the border.

Eighrig was fortunate to be alive.

GROWING UP AT DELNY

Eighrig's life must have changed completely with the move to Easter Ross. The Norman influence superimposed upon such a rooted Celtic upbringing might have had two effects on an impressionable girl, either to make her inwardly ashamed of her unsophisticated Gaelic background and therefore eager to adopt new fashions, a new language and a new way of thinking, or else deeply resistant. Her pride in her father for his knightly achievements would perhaps have predominated, and whatever loyalties and longings she might have felt for her old home and the old customs, she would have submitted – for the time being at least – to his wishes. In later years, as a mother herself she would have remembered – as we all remember a happy childhood as the golden years – and brought her own children up to respect the Celtic language and way of life.

It has been said that one of the reasons why the French language did not become established in England was because so many Normans married Anglo-Saxon women. So it was in Scotland. Gaelic survived because it was the language of the nursery, the kitchen and the farm. Old French however was the language of status and the court. Although Gaelic would always be Eighrig's first language, she would most certainly have been taught French. Perhaps she and Christina were fostered by the wife of some Anglo-Norman knight whom Farquhar had met at court, who made her lessons enthralling by tales of romance between knights and beautiful ladies at the jousting tournaments in which Farquhar himself had been so successful.

And Eighrig would have become Eupheme to her new acquaintance, the old name remembered only by her nurse and servants.

Eupheme – from now on Euphemia – would also have learned how to embroider clothing, rich vestments for the canons and tapestries to adorn the walls of her new home. Anglo-Norman women of all classes were renowned for their needlework. The great Bayeux tapestry was made by women. No doubt the young Euphemia learned to sit for long hours weaving her dreams into her work.

And if she rebelled? No doubt she was beaten. According to Nicholas Orme in *From Childhood to Chivalry*, 'in practice, the corporal punishment of children was widespread in medieval society.' When in the thirteenth-century apocryphal *Story of Fulke Fitz-Warin*, Prince John hit a little friend with a chessboard, his father, King Henry II, ordered him to be beaten. Although *Piers Ploughman* was written a century later, the sentiments were not new when he makes Reason recommend the beating of children and quotes Solomon's famous proverb that 'He who spares the rod hates the child.' The threat of hell was real to Euphemia's generation and if she had been wicked she would have expected to be chastised by a loving father or indeed a diligent chaplain, in order to secure her place in heaven.

Farquhar's personal chaplain would henceforth play a dominant role in her life. In the church's eyes women were either virgins, wives or widows. Women were also mothers. Christ had come into the world through a woman. Therefore women were to be respected, but women were also responsible for the fall of man, therefore women were wayward, dangerous, in need of continual guidance and correction. A rigorous regime of fasting, prayer, confession and exhortation would have replaced the grind of daily chores in Applecross. Which was the harsher to the young Euphemia is impossible to say.

But there were good times, too. Perhaps she played on the beach at Nigg with her siblings, as Gerald of Wales and his brothers did, erecting towns and palaces, churches and monasteries out of sand in the mid-twelfth century. Or perhaps, like Scottish border children, she made houses out of sticks or a ship from pieces of broken bread, or a beautiful lady from a cloth adorned with flowers. Perhaps, too, she and her siblings, as children of a chief, enjoyed extra food. While adults existed on two meals a day, a dinner and a supper, better-off children were allowed a breakfast to encourage growth. This would have consisted of gruel and porridge with the addition of raisins or figs with milk or beer to drink.

There is little evidence to tell us what she would have worn. Before Farquhar became a knight he would not have worn the protective armour that came in with Norman influence. We know from a passage in Magnus Berfaet's Saga that when this Norse king conquered the Hebrides, 'he adopted the costume in use in the Western lands, and likewise many of his followers . . . and went about bare-legged having short tunics and also upper garments, and so many men called him "Barelegged" or "Barefoot".'

However, Farquhar would no doubt have taken to wearing plate armour, a helmet, leggings of mail, a mail shirt or aketon which was a tunic of quilted leather or linen. He would also have retained his saffron shirt which, as the bishop of Ross recorded, contained twenty-four ells of pleated linen stuffed with wool and 'smeared with some grease to preserve them longer clean among the toils and exercises of the camp'.

Euphemia would have learned, as a girl, how to make these costly garments. The bishop records that they were made with great care 'and a certain attention to taste was not altogether neglected, and they joined the different parts of their shirts very neatly with silk thread, chiefly of a red and green colour.' The only near contemporary reference to Scottish male wear comes from Guibert of Nogent's description of the First Crusade written in the early twelfth century where he describes 'the Scots, fierce in their own country, unwarlike elsewhere, bare-legged, with their shaggy cloaks, a scrip hang *ex humeris*, coming from their marshy homeland'.

What Farquhar wore at home is not so easily discovered but it may have been the *Feileadh Mor* (Big Wrap) better known as the belted plaid, a double width of material some twelve to eighteen feet in length, part of which hung like a kilt to his knees while the rest could be worn as a mantle round his shoulders or else fastened across one shoulder with a great silver brooch. He would have worn his hair long and uncovered, with possibly the front locks plaited to keep them out of his eyes. The flat bonnet did not come into use until the seventeenth century.

What Euphemia herself would have worn is even harder to discover. Much more is known of the clothing of Irish Celtic women at an earlier date when they were recorded in the *Tain Bo Fraech* as wearing purple tunics, green head-dresses and silver brooches. There are four words for gloves in old Irish and a woman in the *Voyage of Maeldun* is described as wearing gloves embroidered with gold thread. Euphemia would have had at least two dresses, one elaborate and embroidered for special occasions and the other plain for everyday. She would have worn a belt to which may have been attached a *ciorbhalg* (comb-bag) with a small metal mirror. She would probably have worn an undergarment made from linen or, as Farquhar grew richer, silk or satin. She would have had two mantles for winter and summer use. A sixteenth-century illustration published in Paris which may or may not be accurate shows '*la sauvage d'Ecosse*' wearing a voluminous sheepskin cloak, and neat laced shoes, tongued at the heel and the instep. This is about the nearest we can come.

As an unmarried girl she would have worn her hair long and loose, perhaps held back with a snood of coloured woollen thread, perhaps entwined with gold thread for important occasions. Euphemia's mother would have covered her head with a linen or silk kerchief. A manuscript drawing of the two women at the coronation of the eight-year-old Alexander III in 1249 shows how these head-dresses were worn with two edges fastened at the back of the head while the other two fell either side of the face, similar to a nun's head-dress which has survived to the present day.

Euphemia would already have begun her collection of jewellery, inherited, commissioned from local metal-smiths or brought back by Farquhar as loot from his campaigns. Rings, brooches, bracelets and ear-rings were worn by Celtic men and women, as Nennius recorded in ninth-century Wales and they most certainly still did.

Whether make-up was used by Highland women in the thirteenth century we don't know, but it is more than likely Euphemia learned to darken her eyebrows and tint her lips and finger-nails with *sugh-subh* (bramble or raspberry juice) as the great Celtic heroine Deirdre had done. She may well have used infusions of cowslip, elder-flower and the astringent leaves of wood violet for her skin, the water from boiled fir club moss as a hand lotion, or a honeysuckle wash if she had freckles or sunburn.

There is no reason to suppose that girls were less inclined to make the most of their looks then than they are today.

THE MONASTERY AT FEARN

The most memorable event of her girlhood at Delny would have been her father's foundation of a monastery only about ten miles as the crow flies from the castle.

The ultimate act of piety in Farquhar's Alba was to establish a community of monks. By so doing he would have bought himself and his family much time off the sufferings of purgatory and considered himself a safe candidate for heaven.

Monasticism began in the third century in the Egyptian desert where monks lived as hermits. In the subsequent centuries the movement expanded and spread until it reached Iona and Alba with the coming of St Columba in 563. In the early sixth century St Benedict established a monastery at Monte Cassino in Italy and laid down a rule for an ordered and communal life of work and prayer built around the daily choir offices. The superior was called an abbot.

By the tenth century St Benedict's rule was reformed at Cluny in Burgundy and became hugely popular in Europe and there were further monastic revivals in Normandy which affected England after the Conquest but had little relevance in Scotland. But by the end of the eleventh century a further revival in France was to have a huge effect in Scotland. Three men in particular were responsible for the new orders.

In 1084 St Bruno founded the Carthusian Order, a strict rule which stressed solitude and silence. The first 'Charterhouse' was established in Perth in the fifteenth century by James I. In 1109 St Bernard of Tiron founded the Tironensians near Chartres, while Robert of Molesme settled with a group of monks in the woods at Citeaux near Dijon. Their aim was to follow the Benedictine rule more closely and, under the influence of St Bernard of Clairvaux, they became known as Cistercians. Because they wore a cowl of unbleached wool they became known as White Monks.

Another popular religious order founded by St Francis of Assisi in 1209, the Greyfriars, were essentially missionaries. The Dominicans, or Blackfriars, followers of St Dominic of Toulouse, were instituted in 1215. Both orders reached Scotland in 1231 and 1230 respectively.

Then there were the canons, priests taking monastic vows and following the rule of St Augustine. Canons at that time meant ordained priests living in a community. Like the original Benedictines they wore black and were called Black Canons. One of these Augustinian groups was founded by St Norbert at Prémontré in France in 1120. The aim of the Premonstratensians was to combine a strict monastic life with pastoral work. St Norbert was a friend of St Bernard and copied many of the Cistercian ideals, and the colour of the habit. These were the White Canons whom Farquhar was to bring to Ross. As Abbot Mark Dilworth, Abbot of the Benedictine monastery at Fort Augustus writes in *Scottish Monasteries in the Late Middle Ages*: 'Expansion in Scotland must be among the most impressive in the annals of monasticism.'

David I (1124–53) set the example which was taken up not only by his descendants but by the lords of the Isles, the lords of Galloway, many bishops and earls. In the century up to 1230, thirty important monasteries were founded, belonging to seven different groups with over a dozen less important foundations. An astonishing expansion by any standard.

Whithorn, in Galloway, was the shrine of St Ninian. In 1186, Fergus, lord of Galloway, restored the bishopric, founded a priory, built a cathedral and brought in the Premonstratensian canons who served as its chapter. The province of Galloway had been taken over by emigrants from the Hebrides, the Isle of Man and probably Ireland itself in the eighth to tenth centuries and Farquhar, as a Gael, would have known Lord Alan, hereditary constable of Scotland, and his neighbouring lords. This may have been the reason why he looked to Whithorn to find two canons to establish his monastery at Fearn.

No doubt the two canons, dressed in their black cassocks, rochets, square-cornered white caps and long white copes with almuces of white fur carried over the right arm, filled the adolescent Euphemia with awe. She and her siblings would probably have met them briefly and listened enthralled to Farquhar's plans. They might even have been allowed a glimpse of the sacred relics of St Ninian, said to have been brought north by the two canons.

Abbot Malcolm would have wished his new monastery to resemble Whithorn as closely as possible and where Farquhar's men provided the labour, he would have supervised the building of the wooden chapel, refectory, dormitory and guest house. The original site near Ardgay by the edge of the Dornoch Firth and now impossible to locate was not a success. Between 1238 and 1242, the canons moved under a new abbot some fifteen miles east to New Fearn in the parish of Tarbat. The alleged reason was the hostility of local inhabitants who were said to be loyal to the old Pictish customs. The canons may have been too strict, too severe in their pastoral care, their ways too new. The ostensible reason for the move was for peace and quiet, but perhaps the real reason was for more and better land as the foundation grew in prestige and importance.

Fearn was the most northerly of all the Scottish monasteries. Its list of abbots included Patrick Hamilton who was burned as a heretic for his reforming sermons before the gate of his old college of St Salvator in St Andrews in 1527. Nearest to Fearn two Valliscaulian priories were to be established in 1230–1. This later order came from Val de Choux in Burgundy and Sir John de Bisset founded a house in Beauly which is now a ruin and in the care of Historic Scotland. Pluscarden in Moray, today a thriving Benedictine monastery, was founded by Alexander II in thanksgiving for the final defeat of the rebel MacWilliams. A grim event this, for the last surviving member of the family was an infant girl whose brains were dashed out against the market cross in Forfar. No doubt there was an element of penance as well as praise in the raising of this monastery which Euphemia would come to know as a married woman.

But Fearn abbey with its relics of St Ninian was not the only important religious site near Delny castle. Only a few miles north was the burgh of Tain with its six-mile girth and sanctuary dedicated to a popular local saint, Duthac, who lived about the year 1000 AD. This was already a place of pilgrimage in Euphemia's day and would eventually become one of the most important ecclesiastical centres in the Highlands.

It is probably true to say that Farquhar's dearest wish would have been to make Tain the centre of the diocese of Ross and build a new cathedral there to replace the small cramped kirk at Rosemarkie. However the bishop of Ross, whose seat was at Rosemarkie in the Black Isle, had other ideas and shortly before Farquhar's death in 1251, he obtained permission from the pope to build a grand new cathedral in Fortrose on what was probably church land.

But these were events for the future. There were other matters of more importance to Euphemia. First and foremost her betrothal.

FAMILY MARRIAGES

In a world which was small enough for everyone who was anyone of importance to know each other, Farquhar would have decided at an early stage in his children's childhood which lords were most threatening to him as rival landowners, which antagonistic and in need of appeasement and which most likely to bring honour to the family. Monopolies and take-overs were not necessarily managed by warfare. The balance of power was more profitably kept by carefully arranged marriages. Friendships between adjacent landowners and new relationships between once hostile families were cemented by mutual grandchildren. Thus sons and daughters were a valuable form of currency to be spent with great care.

This custom was not new to the thirteenth century but as old as marriage itself. Euphemia and her siblings would not have questioned it, but seen it as their filial duty, and trusted their parents to choose partners they could respect rather than love in the romantic sense for the future prosperity and honour of the family. Henrietta Leyser in *Medieval Women* writes that 'getting married was like finding a job: the working conditions were important, advice from those with experience was welcome and the testimonials of elders essential.'

He chose well for William. His bride's Flemish great great-grandfather, Robert de Comyn, had come to England with William the Conqueror who in 1069 created him Earl of Northumberland. These were the days when the Norman conquerors were hated by the English and he and two of his sons, one a bishop, were killed at Durham. The family survived however and in 1144 the earl's grandson Richard of Northallerton married Hextilda of Tynedale, a granddaughter of the Scottish King Donald III (Donald Ban).

Hextilda and Richard had five sons which was one of the reasons why there were to be so many Comyns. Their heir, William of Tyne-dale, married twice. His second wife was Marjorie, countess of Buchan in her own right, so he became earl of Buchan. He was probably a good friend of Farquhar, as he too attended court and like Farquhar accompanied the king on his journeys to England. He had three surviving children by his first wife: Richard whose son John became lord of Badenoch, Walter who in 1230 married Isabella, countess of Menteith in her own right, so became earl of Menteith, and Jean or Joan who married Farquhar's heir, William.

Jean Comyn was therefore a great-great-grand-daughter of a Scottish king, the sonless Donald Ban, through his daughter Bethoc, mother of Hextilda. The Comyns were so proud of this royal connection that one of their descendants based his claim to the Scottish throne on that relationship. Whom Malcolm married is not known. He was styled 'the Green Abbot' and he and his descendants inherited Applecross.

Farquhar somewhat cunningly divided his daughters between two of the most important families in the east and west. But before we look at Christina's marriage it is important to understand how the system was regarded in the Celtic west.

CELTIC SECULAR MARRIAGE

In his *Description of the Western Isles of Scotland*, written about 1695, Martin Martin wrote, 'It was an ancient custom in the islands that a man should take a maid to his wife, and keep her the space of a year without marrying her; and if she pleased him all the while, he married her at the end of the year and legitimised these children, but if he did not love her, he returned her to her parents, and her portion also; and if there happened to be any children, they were kept by the father.'

That great historian of Celtic Scotland, Donald Gregory, writing in the early eighteenth century, noted the status of two half-brothers to the lord of the Isles in the sixteenth century who were styled *frater naturalis* and *frater carnalis* but this did not imply *bastardus*. He believed that the terms were used to designate the children of what were called 'handfast' or 'left-handed' marriages, common in the Highlands and Islands. Article One of the *Statutes of Iona* (so-called) introduced by the crown in 1609 to control the power of the clan chiefs states that a marriage contracted merely for a certain number of years should be 'punist as foarnicatouris'. This was seen as proof that the practice of handfasting still existed in the seventeenth century.

The other great nineteenth-century Scottish Celtic scholar, W. F. Skene, also noting the incidence of apparently irregular succession, concluded that the Highland law of marriage was originally very different from the feudal, and that 'a person who was feudally a bastard might in their view be considered legitimate'. Skene also called the practice 'handfasting' which he believed 'consisted in a species of contract between two chiefs, by which it was agreed that the heir of the one should live with the daughter of the other as her husband for twelve months and a day. If in that time the lady became a mother or proved to be with child, the marriage became good in law' but, if there were no children, 'the contract was considered at an end and each party was at liberty to marry or handfast with any other'.

However more recent research by A. E. Anton points out that these descriptions of the ancient custom of trial marriage or 'handfasting' show a misunderstanding of medieval Canon Law. There was confusion between betrothal and marriage itself. 'The ceremony of joining hands became so closely associated with betrothals in medieval times that in Scotland and apparently in the North of England, the ordinary term for a betrothal was a handfasting.' When betrothal was followed by intercourse then a valid marriage resulted. A priest was not needed. Although the clergy disapproved, they recognised such 'common law' marriages which in Scotland were a way of life up until the Marriage (Scotland) Act of 1939.

The modern historian W. D. H. Sellar believes however that there is plenty of evidence to show that there were very unusual practices in existence long after Christianity laid down one rule of marriage for all. The clue lies in Irish law and custom. 'The ancient Irish law of marriage allowed for polygamy, concubinage and divorce, and customs reflecting this law were to flourish for over a thousand years after the introduction of Christianity.' Sellar tells us that Irish dynasties were polygamous from the earliest times and in spite of the growing power of the church throughout the medieval period and up till 1603, Celtic secular marriage was the norm.

Irish law was no haphazard arrangement, but a well-organised code first committed to memory and chanted by druids in the oral tradition, then written down by the monks. One of these codes, the *Senchus Mor*, was transcribed as early as the seventh century. It reflects the customs of an ancient society 'whose roots lay deep in the Indo-European past'. Briefly, it recorded that a man could have a first or chief wife, and also a second whose *raison d'être* was primarily to produce sons. Later the second wife came to be known as *adaltrach* or adultress, indicating strong Christian disapproval. If the *adaltrach* did not bear a son within a year, she could be dismissed. There were also various types of concubine less important than the *adaltrach* but whose children were also considered legitimate.

Divorce, too, was recognised and available equally to men and women. A woman could divorce her husband if he slandered or hit her or if he took an *adaltrach* against her wishes, or was insane, impotent or homosexual. A man could divorce his wife if she dishonoured him, procured an abortion, was unfaithful or a scold. Divorce could also be by mutual consent. These causes were all against the church's teaching.

The Irish laws included marriage of close kin. In 1101 a synod at Cashel forbade a man to marry his stepmother, or his step-grandmother, his step-daughter, his wife's sister or his brother's wife, again all against the code of Canon Law but evidence that such marriages were taking place. In 1172 Pope Alexander III complained to the English King Henry II, who was overlord of most of Ireland at that time, that the Irish married their stepmothers, and their brother's wives while the brother was still alive and 'that a man might live in concubinage with two sisters; and that many of them, putting away the mother will marry the daughter'.

Celtic secular marriage survived in Ireland because it reflected the way of life of an ancient clan-based society in a harsh and difficult environment. The laws were there not just to gratify a lustful warrior elite, but also to produce and protect their most valuable asset, children. Perhaps a comparison could be found with the multiple marriage practice of Mormon men who in the nineteenth century wedded the widows or orphaned daughters of those who had perished on the long trek west in order to protect and provide for them in an equally harsh environment.

As Sellar says, 'one would expect to find Celtic secular marriage also in Scotland' which had been conquered and colonised by Irish Gaelic dynasties in the ninth century. The parallels in law and society are to be found in every walk of life, including the Celtic church founded by the Irish St Columba. They existed throughout the eastern half of Scotland, at least as long as the influx of Norman feudalism in the twelfth century, and remained in force in the Western Highlands and Islands for a further five hundred years.

There is a tradition recorded by Andrew de Wyntoun in his *Chronicle* that King Malcolm III (*Ceann Mor*) himself was the son of an *adaltrach*. When his father, Duncan I was hunting near Forteviot he came across the beautiful daughter of a miller and fell in love with her. The child of that union was to be Malcolm Canmor.

The practice of Celtic secular marriage probably accounted for the claims to the crown put forward by the MacWilliam rebels who were descendants of Duncan II, king in 1094, and whose legitimacy is still a matter of argument. There are too many examples of unorthodox marriage customs continuing into the seventeenth century to dismiss the practice as unusual or unimportant. Sellar however argues that to call these marriages 'handfasting' is confusing. He suggests that 'Celtic secular marriage' or, as Article One of the *Statutes of Iona* put it, 'marriages contracted for certain years' is a better way to describe what was undoubtedly common practice.

As we shall see, Christina's marriage was the result of just such a union, allowable because Olaf's first marriage was a secular one.

CHRISTINA, QUEEN OF MAN

Like the other Western Isles, or the *Sudreys* as they were called in Norse, Man belonged to the Norwegians. However between 1161 and 1208 Norway had her own troubles at home and the islands were virtually ruled by warriors whose Gaelic inheritance was at least as strong as their Norwegian allegiance. In contrast to the feudalising influences that had taken over eastern and lowland Scotland, there had been a strengthening of Gaelic culture, the Gaelic language and, as G. W. S. Barrow states, a 'notably non-Scandinavian feature', the use of the title *righ*, which translates as king, for the principal chiefs. Thus the islands west of Kintyre, north of Skye and Lewis and including the province of Galloway, which for geographical reasons was also ruled by men of mixed Norse, Irish and Hebridean blood, all had 'kings'. One of these was the king of Man.

The Manx dynasty, though paying tribute to the kings of Norway, was as important as the house of Somerled in Argyll. Indeed Somerled himself had thought it important enough to marry Ragnhildis, a daughter of Olaf the Red of Man, though this did not prevent him from going to war with her brother, Godfrey II, and defeating him in 1156 and 1158. Although based in Man, the Manx kings also controlled Arran and Lewis, the Uists, Barra and Skye which made them Farquhar's nearest neighbours to the west of Applecross. They also ruled Glenelg on the mainland, less than twenty miles south of Applecross as the boat sails.

Godfrey II lived in Peel castle on St Patrick's Island off the west coast of Man where he died in 1187 and was buried on Iona. He had three sons, Reginald and Ivar who were probably born of a Celtic secular marriage and therefore not recognised by the church, and Olaf the Black whose mother was a grand-daughter of the king of Ireland. Before he died in 1187 he appointed Olaf, who was only eleven at the time, to be his heir.

As soon as Godfrey was dead, the Manx people sent for the adult Reginald, living on one of the islands, to become their king. Not unnaturally they considered Olaf to be too young. Reginald, who probably saw himself as the rightful heir anyhow, was delighted to accept. However he had a problem – what to do with Olaf.

The *Chronicle of Man* (perhaps not entirely reliable) recorded that 'Reginald gave his brother Olave a certain island called Lewis which is said to be more extensive than the other islands, but thinly populated, because it is mountainous and rocky and almost totally unfit for cultivation. The inhabitants live mostly by hunting and fishing.'

Olaf however complied and went to live in Lewis, probably with his mother, where he may well have been a slightly older contemporary and friend of Farquhar. However he soon found that the island was too poor to support him and his followers so he went to Reginald and begged him 'to allot me land somewhere in the isles sufficient for my own decent maintenance and that of my followers, for the island of Lewis which you gave me is unequal to my support'. When Reginald heard this, he promised to take advice on the subject.

But when Olaf came to hear Reginald's decision, the latter captured him, chained him and sent him to William the Lion who imprisoned him in Edinburgh. Of course, there was trouble. The sons of Somerled raided Skye, a Norwegian force plundered Iona, Man was attacked and Reginald hastily declared himself a vassal of King John of England, seeing him as a more useful ally than Norway. Then King William died and on his death bed ordered the release of all political prisoners. Olaf was set free and, after going on pilgrimage to St James of Compostela in Spain, returned in a mellow mood to make peace with his brother. Reginald welcomed him and arranged for him to marry his wife's sister Joan before sending them both back to live in the previously despised isle of Lewis.

Somewhere between 1220 and 1223 Bishop Reginald of the Sudreys (Sodor) and Man made a pastoral visit to Lewis. As he happened also to be Olaf's nephew, Olaf laid on a great feast for him which the bishop refused to attend declaring his uncle to be living in sin. 'Know you not that you lived long with the cousin of her who is your present wife?' The church did not allow the marriage of cousins. Olaf agreed that he had indeed lived with Joan's cousin but that she had only been a concubine. He probably meant that theirs had been a Celtic secular marriage not recognised by the church. But the bishop would not listen. A synod was called to settle the matter and as a result Joan and Olaf were forced to separate.

Farquhar must have seen an opportunity here to extend his influence in the west. He could not have planned this marriage for, until the church interfered, Olaf was already married. He may well have discussed the situation with Alexander II who, like his father, was determined to seize every opportunity to extend Scottish influence over the islands. However it happened, almost as soon as Joan was divorced, Olaf the Black married Christina. He was fifty years old and in need of an heir. She is said to have been sixteen.

Immediately there was trouble. Joan's sister, wife of King Reginald of Man, was outraged. She wrote secretly to her son Godred in Skye who collected a force and sailed to Lewis 'for the purpose of carrying out his mother's wicked desires'. Undoubtedly murder. Olaf and Christina, presumably living with him at the time, escaped in a small boat and fled to Farquhar, possibly in Delny but more likely to the sanctuary of Applecross while Godred plundered Lewis.

The Norwegian sheriff of Skye, Paul Balkeson, who refused to support Godred – no doubt he was a friend of Farquhar – was also forced to take refuge with Olaf and Christina in Applecross. Hearing that Godred was staying on the 'Island of St Colm' (thought to be Portree in Skye), Olaf and Paul collected as many warriors as would join them, borrowed a boat from Farquhar, attacked at 9 a.m. and murdered all who had not taken sanctuary in the church. They seized Godred, castrated him and although Olaf objected – Godred was after all his nephew – Paul insisted on putting out his eyes. This was all said to have happened in the year 1223.

Olaf's blood was up. No doubt encouraged by Farquhar who saw his grandchildren as future kings, he returned to Man with a fleet of thirty-two ships. Reginald was forced to accept that for the time being at least Olaf was in charge.

Reginald had his pride and his son's injuries to avenge so, joined by the father of his son-in-law to be, Alan of Galloway, he raised an army to oust Olaf. The Manxmen however preferred Olaf and gave Reginald a hundred marks to send him off to England. When Reginald squandered the money on his daughter's wedding to Alan's illegitimate son Thomas, the infuriated Manxmen accepted Olaf gladly as their king.

So in 1224 Christina became, unofficially at least, queen of Man. But for a long time life was no easier for her. While Olaf was away touring his island kingdom, Reginald and Alan of Galloway landed in the south of Man where they plundered the people and destroyed their churches. Olaf pretended to forgive Reginald, but there was too much bad history between the two brothers for the truce to last. Finally, they met on the field of battle at Tingwall in Man on St Valentine's Day 1229. According to the *Chronicle of Man*, Olaf attacked with such ferocity that he drove the enemy before him 'like a flock of sheep'. During the pursuit 'some ruffians overtaking Reginald slew him on the spot without the knowledge of Olaf'. A convenient error from Olaf's point of view. The assassins were never punished.

Olaf and his friend Paul and Paul's son then sailed to Norway for Olaf to be formally recognised as king of Man and the Isles only to discover that King Haakon had conferred that dignity on another man called Uspak (*Gilleasbuig*), one of Somerled's grandsons. The reason given was that Olaf had neglected the Hebrides. He was amazed and after four nights in Bergen set sail for Orkney. The Northern Isles were not at all happy with Haakon's decision either and there followed a series of skirmishes culminating in a battle at

Rothesay against the Scots. Three hundred Norsemen and Islanders were killed in the siege. Uspak died, having been hit by a huge stone. Olaf and Paul escaped assassination on several occasions and Olaf returned to reign as the undisputed king of Man and the Isles in 1231. Christina was now truly a queen.

There is a tailpiece however. When Alan of Galloway died in 1234 he left Thomas, the son of a secular marriage, and three legitimate daughters. The nobles of Galloway wanted to keep Galloway intact as a kingdom so first they offered it to Alexander II. But the king was determined to uphold feudal law which meant that the land should be divided between Alan's three sons-in-law. The Gallovidians then decided they wanted Thomas to be their king, so they rose in revolt and ambushed Alexander II whose army had got stuck in a bog.

Once again Farquhar came to the rescue. Arriving late, he and his warriors caught the rebels at the rear, and decapitated their leaders. Thomas was imprisoned in Barnard Castle guarded by John Balliol the husband of Devorgilla, Alan's second daughter. Balliol eventually inherited all of Galloway, as Dervogilla's sisters were childless. It was Dervogilla's son John Balliol who was to become the successful contender for the Scottish crown in 1229.

Olaf the Black died in 1237 at the age of sixty-one. He was buried at Rushen abbey, having left his throne to his eldest son Harald who must have been in his early teens when he inherited, Christina being about thirty.

One wonders what sort of marriage Christina shared with her elderly warrior husband. The first fact to recognise is that marriages between much older lords and child-brides were normal in the Middle Ages. Although Olaf the Black had a difficult time claiming his throne, there are indications that he may have not been unkind. His pilgrimage to Santiago de Compostela perhaps suggested a wider outlook and understanding of the world beyond the narrow boundaries of the Western Isles. His imprisonment in Edinburgh must have introduced him to the feudal system. Bearing in mind his constant campaigning, Christina cannot have seen much of him during the early years of their marriage. Enough however to give him four sons.

Harald Olafson ruled for eleven years until he was drowned off the Shetland Islands. His brother Reginald was assassinated after a year on the throne and Magnus Olafson (1250–65) was to be the last King of Man. Leod, the youngest was fostered by Paul Balkeson the younger, who must have been fond of him for he left him Harris, Trotternish, Waternish, Sleat and Snizort. He married a daughter of the Norseman, Mac Harald of Dunvegan in Skye. Thus Christina's son, Leod, was progenitor of the great clan Macleod. He is thought to have built a massive curtain wall around a rocky outcrop which was to become Dunvegan castle. His descendants live there to this day.

From the worldly point of view Farquhar chose well for his younger daughter. She was a queen, the mother of kings and ancestor of one of Scotland's proudest clans.

EUPHEMIA'S BETROTHAL

Farquhar chose a very different husband for Euphemia.

Freskin the Fleming was the name of another incoming feudal knight whose family was to become almost as successful as that of the Comyns. He was first heard of in the barony of Strathbrock (Linlithgow) in West Lothian when he was offered the lands of Duffus in the province of Moray by David I. He may have been the son of Ollec who held lands in Pembroke. It was probably Freskin who built the huge motte-and-bailey castle of Duffus which was to be Euphemia's home. The remains are still impressive today. We know that David I stayed there in 1150 when he supervised the building of the monastery at Kinloss, a daughter house of the Cistercian abbey at Melrose.

Freskin died before 1171, leaving two sons, William who inherited Duffus and Strathbrock and who was sheriff of Invernairn, and Hugo, who died without children. William died in 1204 leaving several sons, the eldest of whom was Hugo of Duffus and Sutherland, father of William, first earl of Sutherland, and Walter who was to inherit Duffus in 1224. Farquhar chose Walter for Euphemia and they were probably betrothed or 'handfasted' in the true sense of the term soon after her arrival at Delny.

How was a marriage such as Euphemia's arranged? Usually by the fathers concerned. George Duby in *Love and Marriage in the Middle Ages* states that 'marriage was a serious matter and thus a male affair'. However the young knight could put himself forward but never to the girl, always to her father or nearest male relative.

By the middle of the twelfth century the church had begun to see marriage as a sacrament rather than a civil contract. Although it piously hoped that the contract would be arranged with the mutual consent of the couple involved, the only way a girl could avoid marriage was by making a vow of chastity and joining a convent. In those days maiden-aunts did not exist.

The theory of marriage as a sacrament became one of the laws of the church under Pope Alexander III (1159–81) and by 1215 at the Fourth Lateran Council it was decreed that banns should be announced three times in church to make the marriage open to public scrutiny. It also included seven degrees of prohibition, one of which decreed that it was incestuous for the couple to have a common ancestor of seven generations, though later this was reduced to four. It insisted, too, that the marriages themselves be celebrated as far as possible in church.

Once the partners were chosen, complicated financial arrangements followed. A woman was expected to bring a dowry, her share of her family inheritance. This could be in goods, cash or land which she might have inherited from her mother whose dowry it had originally been. Christina's dowry may have been inherited through her mother and consisted of land in the west, but not so Euphemia's. The following undated charter is thought to refer to hers.

> Farquhar earl of Ros sends greeting to all his friends and people. Let those living in the present and the future know that I have given, conceded and by this deed confirmed to Walter of Moravia son of the late Hugh of Moravia two davochs of the land of Ros – namely Clon [Clyne] along its correct boundaries and with all its just appurtenances to be held by himself and his heirs from me and my heirs ... Wherefore I will and grant that the aforesaid Walter and his heirs should hold and possess the aforesaid land ... in woodland and in the open, in meadows and pastures, in moors and marshes, in ponds and waters, in millponds and fisheries, on road and ? as freely – peacefully – fully and honourably as anyone who holds and possesses land in the realm of Scotia as a gift from any earl – returning to me and my heir from there each year for every service and charge pertaining to us one pound of pepper on the feast of St Martin – and doing foreign service for his lord the King which pertains to the aforesaid land ...

Among the ten witnesses were the bishop, precentor, chancellor and two canons of Moray diocese and also William, Farquhar's heir. A davoch in the Highlands measured approximately 416 acres, but the measurement was not always constant, as it varied according to the soil and locality. It could be anything between one and four ploughgates and a ploughgate was about 104 acres. Over the years Clon became Clyne. It translates from the Gaelic *an claon* which means 'the slope', a descriptive title, for the land faces south and slopes gently down to the Cromarty Firth near Dingwall. From the early eighteenth century it became known as it is today as Mountgerald.

After the marriage settlement had been agreed the betrothal or handfasting ceremony took place in front of witnesses. This ceremony was legal after the age of seven, which was considered to be the age of reason, and the marriage could be solemnised after the bride reached the age of twelve and the groom fourteen.

A CHURCH WEDDING

At a date suitable to both families, but not during the fasting seasons of Lent or Advent, the wedding day was fixed. Euphemia would have been escorted to Duffus, or more likely Walter would have ridden over to Delny with his brother Andrew – recently appointed the bishop of Moray, who may indeed have married the couple – and other supporters.

A week of celebration would have included hunting, falconry, shinty, archery contests – a great favourite this with the clergy – and possibly trials of single combat. On these occasions the feudal and clan systems, though they differed in origin and expression, were not opposed in fact. Frank Adam in *The Clans, Septs and Regiments of the Scottish Highlands* writes, 'As the system of clanship, like that of chivalry, was calculated to cherish a warlike spirit, the young chiefs and heads of families tended to be regarded or despised according to their military or peaceable disposition.' Euphemia's wedding would have given the young men, both feudal and Celtic, ample opportunity to show off their swordsmanship, gamesmanship and valour.

While the men were showing off their skills the women would have been equally occupied preparing for the ceremony and the feast.

No doubt Euphemia dressed with extra care, watched her betrothed secretly through downcast eyes, willing him to excel in the sports, exchanging chaste kisses, accepting small gifts, perhaps even learning to fall in love. Though romantic love was neither expected nor required when marriages were arranged, women were as capable of passionate love for their husbands then as now. The twelfth-century letters of Héloïse to Peter Abelard are abundant proof of this: 'You alone have the power to make me sad, to bring me happiness of comfort . . . my love rose to such heights of madness that it robbed itself of what it most desired beyond hope of recovery, when immediately at your bidding I changed my clothing along with my mind, in order to prove you the sole possessor of my body and my will alike . . . farewell my only love.'

Euphemia's perception of love must have been influenced by the oral tradition of her race. Perhaps it lay somewhere between the hot passion of Skatha, warrior queen of Skye, for the god-hero Cuchulain, and Cuchulain's determined courtship and enduring love for Emer who was to be his wife. She might well have gone to the shrine of St Duthac in Tain, or perhaps to the holy well of St Mary at Balintore, to pray openly that she would be a worthy wife and secretly that he would be a loving husband. She would most certainly have been counselled by her confessor in the words of St Paul: 'Let the husband render to his wife what is her due, and likewise the wife to her husband. A wife has no authority over her body but her husband; likewise the husband has no authority over his body but his wife. You must not refuse each other except perhaps by consent for a time, that you may give yourself to prayer and return together again lest Satan tempt you because you lack self-control.'

On the day of the wedding the couple would have met at the door of the church where Walter would have announced his gift to her and given her as a token a piece of gold or silver arranged on a holy book or possibly a shield. After the priest had blessed the ring, Walter would have placed it on her finger. The wedding vows were made, probably in Gaelic, possibly in French. Interestingly enough the bride's vow of obedience was not introduced until the time of the Reformation (1560). Obedience was taken for granted.

The couple would then have entered the church to celebrate nuptial Mass in Latin. They would have knelt together under a pall or canopy for a further blessing and, if they already had children, which would not have been the case with Euphemia and Walter, these too would have gathered under the pall and thereby gained legitimacy.

Then followed the wedding feast which would have cost Farquhar almost as much as the dowry. Imagine the hall at Delny, lit and warmed on one side by a great peat fire. A long narrow table on trestles – the *hie burde* – was set up against one end of the room with benches, perhaps cushioned for the principal guests, either side of Farquhar's high-backed chair. Behind him might have hung a splendid piece of tapestry, perhaps partly woven by Euphemia herself.

The rest of the household and guests sit on benches at side tables with their backs to the wall to leave the front free for service. All except the servants have their heads covered, the women with kerchiefs, the men with hats as a precaution against 'flyes and other filth' contaminating the food. Table manners were, according to modern standards appalling. As late as the fifteenth century people were still being warned that it was bad manners to spit or blow the nose at meals without turning aside, that it was rude to catch fleas at table and scratch an itching scalp.

On this special occasion, the *hie burde* might have been laid with a linen cloth and lighted candles with the large salt-fatt (cellar) as the only other decoration. The division of the table into below and above the salt had not yet come into use. Inferior people sat at different tables. Wooden trenchers were used for plates, but if there were not enough of these, bread was used instead. Men used their own knives but forks were unknown. Euphemia would have been taught to use two fingers and her thumb. She would help herself from a central dish, a messy process, so there were basins of water and napkins provided.

The floor would be spread over with rushes or bent grass and the family dogs would lurk below to seize bones or other tid-bits dropped by their masters. Near the entrance a stand supported armour, spears and staves with perhaps a 'blawin horn' hanging on the wall. Apart from the boards and benches the only furniture would be a kist in which to keep dishes and napery when not in use. There might be a spinning wheel in the shadowy window alcove. But the food would be good and plentiful and the wine and ale flowing.

When William the Lion paid a friendly visit to Richard I of England in 1194 he asked that he should receive daily 'a livery of twelve royal

wastel-cakes and twelve royal simnel cakes, four pints of the King's
royal wine and eight pints of expensive wine, two pounds of pepper,
four pounds of cumin . . .' Pepper and spices were important disguises
for meats that were past their sell-by date. As well as cakes and wine,
Farquhar would have provided a variety of fowl, salmon and venison,
and one of his oxen roasted outside in honour of the occasion would
be served to all his retainers.

Whether there was ever a musicians' gallery at Delny is not known,
but there would most certainly have been music, poetry and singing
in honour of the newly-weds. Farquhar would have taken the opportunity to have his seanachie recite his genealogy to impress the
Flemish family. Dancing was part of the fun with the bridal couple
taking the lead. The wedding reel was always a riotous affair.

The priest would then have blessed the bridal bed which would
have been strewn with flowers and hidden charms and the bride
formally led there by her attendants to await her bridegroom, by
now well drunk, escorted by the ribald comments of his companions.

Next morning she was no longer a virgin and subject to her father
but a wife, the property of her husband, the lady of Duffus and
Moravia, with all the responsibilities of such a position.

A NEW HOME

In its flatness and fertility the parish of Duffus in Moray resembles
that of Delny in Easter Ross. It extends for some five miles along
the south shore of the Moray Firth to include the massive Iron Age
fortress of Burghead, already a ruin in the thirteenth century, and the
impressive Covesea caves 'very prettily scooped out by the frequent
washing of the sea' with their mysterious Pictish symbols. Stretching
about three miles inland, this green 'heart of Morayshire' consists
mostly of rich arable farming ground.

Fortunately Duffus castle was partially excavated in 1984–5 so
we know far more about it than we do of Delny. Built, as has been
established, by Walter's ancestor, Freskin the Fleming, whose son
William adopted the title de Moravia (of Moray), it is still an enormously impressive relic to this day.

The Statistical Account describes it as it was in the 1790s as
follows. 'Upon the north-west border of the Lake of Spiney [Spynie],

there are, standing upon an artificial mound, surrounded with a fosse and drawbridge, the walls of a strong castle called Old Duffus ... It is surrounded with orchards and forest trees, and, standing in the heart of a charming plain, presents, at every point of view, one of the most picturesque and beautiful objects which the country exhibits.'

Although the Duffus end of the loch has long since been drained the motte is still massive. In Euphemia's time its flat top would have supported timber buildings, protected by a wooden palisade erected around the edge of the summit. Halls, lodgings, a brewhouse, bakehouse, stables, workshops, and perhaps a chapel, all necessary to maintain a large important household, once stood here but sadly none has survived.

The castle was rebuilt in stone sometime in the fourteenth century, perhaps by Euphemia's grand-daughter Mary of Duffus and her husband Sir Reginald Cheyne (le Chien). Mary and Sir Reginald died without children in 1312 and the Sutherlands thereafter became lords of Duffus. An old woman remembered working there as a servant in the early 1700s, which was probably when the castle was last used. When Duffus House was built a short distance away, the castle fell into ruin. Little was found during the later excavations in the way of artifacts dating from Euphemia's time apart from a squashed 'bovine skull' and 'some sherds of straight-sided cooking pots'.

Though Euphemia's married home was on a beautiful site, it was exposed and cold, as the following description suggests: 'The castle had no chimneys, nor any window of glass. When the winds blew across the Laich [of Moray] they shut them with stout window boards, crowded round a fire of peats in the middle of the hall while the smoke escaped as it could and was welcome as communicating some feeling of heat to the upper chambers.' Though this description must have referred to the first stone tower, it cannot have been more comfortable in Euphemia's day. Nevertheless from its size – the motte was some 122m (400ft) long – and dramatic situation it must have made an impression upon the young bride. This was far removed from the farmstead at Applecross.

What were Euphemia's thoughts as she was escorted into the bailey and climbed the motte to enter her new home? Perhaps her first feelings were of overwhelming homesickness and a paralysing shyness. Applecross and Delny, her mother and her sister, her friends and family must all have seemed very far away. Perhaps she clutched the arm of her maid servant and murmured a quick prayer for help as she had been taught from childhood.

> God bless the pathway on which I go,
> God bless the earth that is beneath my sole ...
> Bless, O bless, Thou God of life
> Each day and hour of my life.

THE YOUNG WIFE

We know nothing about her first sexual encounter. Was Walter a grey-beard who took her greedily to gratify his lust and need for an heir, or a fumbling young man scarcely older than she who, according to the tradition of the times, had left the care of women in his seventh year to spend his time practising the martial arts or on the hunting field surrounded by men? Given that so much was invested in a marriage, it is not surprising to find that many young husbands like Philip Augustus II of France were unable to consummate their unions, and many girls were physically and mentally scarred, as in the case of dispensation granted to a youth by Pope Alexander for irreparably damaging his young bride.

Let us hope Euphemia's marriage was better than these. We can be sure that she would have taken her married status seriously and paid her 'debt' (*debitum*), the term used to describe the conjugal relationship as defined by St Paul, to the best of her ability. What was expected of her? There were three examples of saintly women whose lives she might well have known about, if not before her arrival at Duffus, certainly soon after, perhaps preached by her brother-in-law, Bishop Andrew, or by Walter's personal chaplain. Thirteenth-century women were continually subjected to homilies on how best to fulfil their wifely duties.

The first example was Queen Margaret, wife of Malcolm *Ceann Mor*, whose hagiography had been written by her confessor Turgot in 1093–5. Although Margaret was not officially canonised until 1250 she was already considered a saint and her shrine in Dunfirmline a place of pilgrimage. Margaret was well-born, beautiful, dutiful,

pious, charitable and chaste. Above all she was the mother of successful sons.

Perhaps the ideal example preached to Euphemia, would have been
Ida, countess of Boulogne, born around 1040, whose *Vita* had been
written in the early twelfth century by a Cluniac monk in the monastery she had founded. Ida, too, was beautiful and good, the daughter
of a wealthy duke, who married a man of equal rank, Eustace II,
count of Boulogne. He was attracted to her not just for her beauty
and moral character but also for the 'dignity of her race'. He had
previously been married to a sister of Edward the Confessor who
had died untimely. He badly needed an heir.

She proved herself to have all the virtues of a good wife. She was
submissive to her husband, diligent in her household duties, devout
as a Christian, chaste in her behaviour towards her husband's
knightly peers. Above all, like Queen Margaret, she was the mother
of successful sons. As Georges Duby writes, 'The sanctity of marriage
was indeed measured by the glory of the males who were its fruit
... It was a wife's privilege and function to form by the grace of
God, a link in a genealogy.' Moreover Ida was praised in the *Vita*
not for rearing her sons to be good citizens, but for having breast-fed
them herself, so that they were not contaminated by milk from an
immoral source.

On the death of her husband, she continued to be fruitful in a
new direction. With the permission of her relatives and the support
of her sons, she sold her personal possessions for money which she
used 'to give birth to spiritual sons: monks'. In other words she
founded a monastery. Ida's *Vita* taught Euphemia nothing she did
not know already, that it was a woman's duty to be dominated first
by her father, then by her husband and finally by her eldest son.
Should he not be available, then she became subject to the monks
whose monastery her family had founded.

The other example comes from earlier texts, dating from the
eleventh century. The heroine, Godelive ('dear to God') was the
daughter of a knight of Boulogne in the service of Ida's husband,
not so noble as him but well-born nevertheless. Her cult took root
in Flanders and she was particularly popular with ordinary folk.
Godelive was a devout virgin, but not beautiful in the conventional
sense as she had black hair and eyebrows. Fortunately her skin was
white, 'something which is agreeable and pleasing in women and

which is held in honour by men'. She had a host of suitors out of whom her father chose Bertulf, a Fleming from Bruges, because he was the richest. Not a good motive. Marriage purely for money was considered immoral.

After the betrothal Bertulf took Godelive home to his mother, who was living apart from her husband. On the journey Drogo records that the devil 'struck the mind of the newly-wed man, who started hating his wife'. In this he was fully supported by his mother. 'All mothers-in-law hate their daughters-in-law . . . they desperately want to see their sons married, but immediately become jealous of them and their wives.' His mother mocked Bertulf for choosing a dark-haired foreigner. ' "So there were not enough crows here – you had to go and track one down," she told him.' Sulking, Bertulf refused to take part in the marriage ceremony, so his mother took his role during the three days of ritual feasting, while he went off to stay with his father.

Godelive was mortified. She worked patiently at prayer and spinning while Bertulf did his best to get rid of her. She was put on a starvation diet while her servants were fed rich food. So, bare-footed and hungry, she ran back to her home, a serious sin which was to be her downfall. Her father immediately complained on her behalf to Bertulf's superior, the count of Flanders, who wisely consulted the bishop and he ruled that Bertulf must take his wife back. Reluctantly he agreed, but he refused to sleep with her. She did not care. 'I scorn the pleasures of my body,' she declared and devoted herself to good works and prayer.

Meanwhile Bertulf with two of his serfs was plotting revenge. First he pretended to repent, turned to her with feigned love and told her he had found a wise woman who would help unite them 'in staunch love'. Godelive agreed to go with the two serfs who in the middle of the night led her backwards from her bed in a parody of the wedding ceremony to the sorceress who strangled her and plunged her into water in a parody of baptism. The water however gained miraculous power to heal the sick and her cult as an innocent victim spread throughout Flanders, thus turning the story of an unhappily married woman into the life of a saint.

The three stories help us to understand how marriage was perceived among feudal families in the thirteenth century. First it was important to marry well, not for wealth but for honour, prestige and moral well-being. Secondly, marriage was a holy vow that, however unhappy, could not be undone by man. Thirdly, love, too, was desirable. Duby tells us that the love of a husband for his wife was called delight (*dilectio*), whereas that of a wife for her husband was called reverence (*reverencia*). In the eyes of the church it was important that a couple should be united in flesh as well as in mind. The love between them was as much a love of 'the body as of the heart'. The story of Godelive tells us that it even permitted the use of sorcery to achieve this end.

RESPONSIBILITIES

Although outwardly society was male-dominated in Euphemia's time, with women seen as symbols or as creatures of temptation with no desires of their own, yet within the castle walls the situation was more complex. While Walter and his peers were involved for the most part with the outward world of politics, battles, jousts, hunting and the organisation of their property, women, being forced to remain indoors, developed a power structure of their own. Within the castle walls in all matters pertaining to the household, the lady of the castle was in charge.

George Duby records that French chronicles show that at the end of the twelfth and in the early thirteenth century there were some real tyrants among the wives who not only terrorised their servants but also their daughters-in-law. It is not to be supposed that they were any different in Scotland. Euphemia's mother-in-law whose name has not been recorded may well have been alive when Walter took his bride to Duffus.

On the other hand Euphemia had much to learn. Duffus was a huge establishment and Euphemia would have been greatly in awe of her mother-in-law. The custom of the age would have taught her to respect her elders whom – just because they were older – she would have seen as betters. She may even have had a grandmother-in-law and though as the wife of the lord of Duffus – Walter inherited in 1226 – she would have taken precedence over his female relatives, natural courtesy would have taught her to respect her elders and learn all they had to teach, including the complicated genealogy of her new family.

In the days when documented history was almost non-existent, the oral tradition was of enormous significance. Those with the longest memories were not just useful for story-telling but also for repeating the history of the family. Genealogical memory was of supreme importance and the old respected for their powers of recall. That respect remained into and beyond death. Therefore however unwelcoming and difficult Euphemia's in-laws may have been, she would have kept her feelings to herself, and learned from her elders how to organise the household and servants with economy, efficiency and authority.

Perhaps the nearest we can get to understanding the immensity of Euphemia's task is by studying a set of rules laid down in the thirteenth century for the widowed countess of Lincoln known as Saint Robert's Rules. These rules – which could have come into operation during a lord's absence – covered all aspects of estate administration, the appointment and dismissal of servants, knowledge of the law and local customs, and an understanding of the various methods of farming.

Writing a century and a half later, Christine de Pisan, the first woman writer to be published by Caxton, and the first woman to write for other women recorded in *The Treasure*: 'Because barons and still more commonly knights and squires and gentlemen travel and go off to the wars, their wives should be wise and sound administrators and manage their affairs well, because most of the time they stay at home without their husbands, who are at court or abroad.' In the same manual she also warned against collapsing 'like a simple woman into tears and sobs' when she found herself in charge. No doubt Euphemia did her best, though there would surely be times when the administrative and personnel difficulties, not to mention the criticism of her new relatives, must have reduced her privately at least to bitter tears.

PREGNANCY

Euphemia would have seen her priority as a wife to have children. It must have been a great disappointment to her and to Walter that they only had one surviving son. So what happened? Did she have many children, all of whom where stillborn or died in childbirth, or was he her only baby? The year of his birth has not been recorded, but he was married in 1248. Assuming this happened when he was about twenty, he must have been born a couple of years or so after Euphemia's marriage.

If Euphemia found it difficult to conceive she would have resorted to all the methods available, Christian, superstitious and pagan, to help her to become pregnant. She might well have visited the *cailleach chearc* (henwife) the local wise woman for advice. Mrs Katherine Whyte Grant speaking to the Caledonian Medical Society in 1904 recorded the *cailleach*'s importance in the community. 'She is resorted to for love potions, for charms, for advice on setting out upon an expedition – in short, she it is who guides almost all affairs to a happy issue . . .'

She might perhaps have suggested that Euphemia had been 'over-looked' or ill-wished by someone envious of her position, and provided her with an antidotal incantation.

> Eye will see you,
> Tongue will speak of you;
> Heart will think of you –
> The Three are protecting you –
> The Father, Son and Holy Ghost.

The *cailleach chearc* might have given her a charm made out of coloured threads to wear around her neck or a potion made out of wild orchids which were regarded as powerful aphrodisiacs. She might have advised her to serve more *siunas* (lovage), a celery-like plant used to flavour stews and broths, but so powerful a love potion that, according to Mary Beith, 'medieval Spanish nuns were forbidden to grow it in their convent gardens'. Perhaps she suggested that Euphemia take out the family cradle and rock it – an act of sympathetic magic – in hopeful anticipation.

Advice would have come to Euphemia from all quarters. Those with an Anglo-Norman background might have told her to stroke the sides of a white bull garlanded with flowers like the infertile women of Bury St Edmunds. The chaplain might have advised her to go to one of the many holy wells and shrines – her own St Maelrubha had a dedication at nearby Forres. She would have attended Masses with the special intention of conceiving a son. Above all, she would have implored the Virgin Mary to have pity on her childlessness. Her Anglo-Norman relatives might have told her to invoke the support of St Margaret of Antioch, patron saint of would-be mothers, while together with her Celtic servants she would have called upon St Bride.

And then when the miracle happened – she would have seen it as such – and she knew she was pregnant there was a host of taboos and rituals to be observed in order that the child be born well and safely. She would have believed the old tales that a mother who walks slowly and has hollow eyes will give birth to a son, and measured her tread accordingly.

Bald's *Leechbook III*, a source for Anglo-Saxon medicine before the Conquest but still remembered in the thirteenth century, warned a woman not to eat anything too salty or too sweet, or to drink ale, or eat pork or anything fatty or to ride too much on horseback for fear of a miscarriage. Nor, Henrietta Leyser tells us, should she eat 'bull's flesh or ram's or buck's or boar's or gander's or that of any animal that can beget or the child will be a hunchback'. Her old nurse might have warned her against hares for fear her child be born disfigured.

Her mother might have sent her a special stone, such as the one that used to lie on the altar of St Ronan's chapel on the island of Rona near Lewis. It lay with five others in holes cut in a plank of wood some ten foot long. Each stone had a healing virtue and one was especially dedicated to giving a speedy labour.

Although the Beatons, an Irish family of hereditary physicians, had not yet settled in Scotland that is not to say that there were no medical practitioners to consult. Highlanders were as well-travelled as other races and no doubt Salerno, the eleventh-century centre for the transmission of Greek medicine, was as well known to them as to English physicians. By 1224 Salerno had become Europe's first officially recognised medical school.

In the eleventh century a woman called Trota of Salerno (Dame Trot of the nursery stories) was credited, perhaps wrongly, with three treatises on medicine which were in use up to the sixteenth century. Anglo-Norman and Middle English translations were certainly in use in England for the treatment of women. No doubt Anglo-Norman families in Scotland such as Walter's would have been aware of them too. *The Practice According to Trota* treatise on obstetrics contained advice on what to do before, during and after childbirth, the treatment of prolapse and polyps of the womb, the choice of a wet nurse and diet in pregnancy – no salt, garlic, onion or pepper for example.

Birth was an anxious time. Mothers were urged to go to confession before labour in case they died. There are no statistics for Euphemia's period but three hundred years later in England it is reckoned that one in every forty women died in childbirth and that as many as two hundred out of every thousand children died before the age of five. It cannot have been any better in thirteenth-century Scotland. Dame Trot's treatise described sixteen 'unnatural presentations' with which the midwife had to deal. She was advised to rub her hands with 'wild thyme oil, lily oil or oil of musk' before attempting to turn the infant or enlarge the cervix. In cases of danger to life, it was taken for granted that the mother rather than the baby was to be saved.

It is more than possible that Euphemia had several stillbirths or miscarriages both before and after the arrival of the precious son and heir. In which case, as we have already seen at Euphemia's birth, the midwife was there to baptise the dying infant. Clean water was at hand for the purpose. The church's ruling on neonatal baptism was, as Henrietta Leyser points out, 'awesome'.

But births were sociable occasions with usually more than one midwife present, as well as friends and family, though not as a rule men, unless possibly a priest. Witnesses were necessary in the case of a careless death or fraud. The midwife might bring some saint's relic with her as an aid to labour. Girdles were particularly coveted and used by both rich and poor alike. One hopes Euphemia had a natural birth with 'twenty pangs' as described by Dame Trot. We can be very sure that the birth of an heir brought great joy not only to his parents but the whole de Moravia family.

The infant would have been taken within a week of his birth to Duffus church for baptism perhaps by Bishop Andrew himself and, in accordance with the rites of the day, salt would have been put into his mouth, saliva on his ears and nostrils, oil on his breast and back before he was totally immersed in the font three times, once on the right side, once on the left and one face downwards.

In the presence of at least three godparents, two men and a woman for a boy, relatives and friends, Euphemia and Walter named their child Freskin after the progenitor of his race.

MOTHERHOOD

Freskin belonged to Euphemia until he was seven years old, during which time, according to the seventh-century scholar Isidore of Seville, whose works were well known in medieval Europe, he would have been considered an infant (*infantia*). From age seven to fourteen he was a boy (*pueritia*) and from fourteen to twenty-eight an *adolescentia*. In those first years of his life, perhaps the clash of cultures between his Hiberno-Celtic-Norse mother and his Scotto-Anglo-Norman father may have been more evident than hitherto.

Would she have breast-fed him? Certainly the church would have urged her to do so. Thomas of Chobham, writing in the twelfth century in a penitential available to confessors, considered a mother's refusal to breast-feed her child a form of blasphemy and scorned those women who claimed to be too delicate. 'Was she not [already] so delicate when she underwent intercourse and the labour of giving birth?' If the mother found it impossible 'she should at least wash and feed the baby so that she does not seem . . . to overturn nature through never deigning to go near her own offspring'. In spite of the emphasis on breast-feeding, the use of wet-nurses was common in the Middle Ages among aristocratic families perhaps due to a belief that a nursing mother should not have sex.

Henrietta Leyser writes that thirteenth-century mothers and nurses would have continually been subjected to sermons on how to rear their children, the need to feed babies with care and, for example, not to sleep with them until they were at least three years old for fear of over-lying them. They were to see that their cradles were safe, that they were never left unattended.

The first quarrel between Euphemia and her new family may have been over the practice of swaddling. Gerald of Wales (1147–1223) in his *Topography of Ireland* recorded that the Irish 'do not put their babies in cradles or swathe them'. This he saw as a sign of Irish barbarity. Indeed the de Moravia family may also have seen it this way and criticised Euphemia for her Celtic upbringing. Gerald of Wales added that Irish midwives did not 'use hot water to raise the nose or press down the face or lengthen the legs'. Today's conception of barbarous behaviour would undoubtedly favour the Celts.

Little Freskin would have had a nurse of his own whose job is described most touchingly in the *Encyclopaedia of Bartholomew the Englishman.*

> She kisses him if he is sick, binds him and ties him if he flails about, cleans him if he has soiled himself, and feeds him although he struggles with his fingers. She instructs the child who cannot speak, babbling, practically breaking her tongue in order to teach him speech more readily . . . She lifts him up on her hands, shoulders and knees, and relieves the crying child. She first chews the food preparing it for the toothless child so he can swallow it more easily . . . Whistling and singing she strokes him as he sleeps and ties the childish limbs with bandages and linens lest he suffer some curvature.

When a baby was weaned and out of swaddling bands, the thirteenth-century English knight, Walter of Bibbesworth, had more useful advice to offer. When a toddler dribbled, his mouth should be wiped with a 'slavering clout'. As soon as he started to crawl someone should follow him about to prevent him falling and getting dirty. At dinner-time he should be given an egg or a peeled apple. He should be encouraged to dress himself and learn how to do up his buttons.

He would probably have been taught the rudiments of reading and writing in Latin or French by the chaplain at a very early age. Although still in his mother's care, he would have learned to ride, groom and take care of his first pony. He would have played by the loch, gone fishing and boating with the other castle children. He might have had his first lessons in chivalry and the art of war, practising with a wooden sword and shield. He would have enjoyed the indulgence of his mother and the castle women, a little lordling spoiled and indulged by all, and why not? His childhood was to come to an end when he was seven, old enough to leave the care of women and enter his father's domain.

Whether he was fostered in the Celtic tradition it is impossible to say. Fostering was not unknown in feudal families. Nicholas Orme records that 'Both boys and girls might . . . be sent to other households as foster children or as servants to learn either good manners or a trade.' A compromise may have been reached whereby he was sent to another important household to further his education and his apprenticeship as a knight. If so, Euphemia must have missed him greatly, eager for news of him, anxious as any mother for his health and happiness. Or he may have remained at home with plenty of experts at hand to teach him all the necessary accomplishments of the day, hunting, jousting, dancing and music, reading, writing and Latin grammar.

A GODLY MATRON

Apart from rearing her son and the organisation of such a large and busy household, Euphemia would have taken a lively interest in the world about her, particularly the church.

The Moray bishopric had been founded in 1107 with its cathedral first at Birnie, then at Kineddar and Spynie. In 1203 Bishop Bricius, formerly prior of Lesmahago, and thought to have been a member of the Norman family of Douglas with connections to the de Moravias, was appointed to the diocese. It was his dearest wish, in keeping with the age, to build a splendid new three-towered cathedral at Elgin. He applied to Rome and received permission to found a chapter of eight canons based on the design of the choir of Lincoln cathedral. By the time he died in 1222, building had probably begun just outside the burgh of Elgin, though the see was not officially dedicated until 1224, during the early years of his successor, Andrew de Moravia, formerly parson of Duffus and Walter's brother.

In spite of his noble birth Bishop Andrew seems to have been a modest man. He had already refused the bishopric of Ross in 1213, preferring to remain as parson of Duffus which with his father (or brother – records differ) he had rebuilt. As bishop of Moray he increased the number of prebends to twenty-three, of which he held one, Duffus, and sat as a canon in the chapter with only one vote. He lived in Spynie palace, not three miles distant from Duffus, another defensive earthwork raised on the lochside which was thought to have been constructed by Alexander II's rivals, the MacWilliams c. 1187.

In the mid-thirteenth century the timber buildings were replaced with a stone tower which contained at least one window of beautifully painted glass, produced by the same glaziers employed at Elgin cathedral but this may have been during the time of Andrew's successors. The new cathedral was to have an unfortunate history. It was first accidentally burned in 1270 and again deliberately in 1390 by the Wolf of Badenoch, husband of Euphemia IV, but that is another story.

Euphemia would have taken a great interest in the building of Elgin cathedral, spending time embroidering rich vestments for her brother-in-law and the canons, listening with interest to the tales of progress or delay recounted by the bishop. She would no doubt have visited Spynie castle, gone to see the cathedral building in progress and had her favourites among the canons and other clerics.

She may also have entertained Alexander II when he came north in 1230 to found his priory for Valliscaulian monks at Pluscarden some seven miles south of Duffus. This would have been a huge logistical problem for her as Alexander would have brought a large retinue of knights and clerics whom she would have been expected to feed and house. He might even have brought his wife, the English Queen Joan, sister of Henry III, who sadly had no children. It would have been Euphemia's responsibility to entertain her and her women personally.

As Freskin matured she would have taken a lively interest in the plans for his betrothal and marriage in 1248 to Joanna, the heiress of Strathnaver, a descendant of Moddan, the Pictish *mormaor* of Caithness. With a Moravia cousin as earl of Sutherland, this was a shrewd and well-planned match which was eventually to bring the whole of Strathnaver to the Sutherlands.

Walter, whose name appears on many charters died in 1262/3. He was buried beside his father in Duffus church as the old chartulary records *'Iste versus habetur super tumulus eius in Duffus. Hic pater dormit tumulatus Hugoque beatus.'*

Euphemia was still alive and in her fifties, for a charter dated February 1263 signed and sealed by herself confirms a grant of her dowry lands 'that I have in consideration of divine love given and altogether renounced to God and to the Moravian church [diocese of Moray] . . . which I held in Ros as a dowry namely a third part of all the land of Clon beside Dingwall – which indeed was the land of my late master Walter – therefore I wish that the above-mentioned church and bishops should freely have my above-mentioned land and should possess it for ever for the maintenance of chaplains in the cathedral church of Elgin who will celebrate Mass of the living and the dead.'

Her death is not recorded. Perhaps she lived on at Duffus to see her two grand-daughters Mary and Christina born. Her son was to die in 1269 only seven years after his father, leaving his property divided between these two girls.

Christina, named perhaps after her aunt, the queen of Man, married William de Federeth, constable of Roxburgh in 1662. They had one son William de Federeth II, comte de Elgyn and Moray who died without an heir. Mary of Duffus, the older girl, married Sir Reginald le Cheyne II (Chein), another Norman heir thought to have been descended from Rainaldus Canis, recorded before 1182 in Creuilly near Caen in France. Reginald I, who may have owned Inverugie castle near Peterhead, was a nephew of John Comyn of Badenoch and sheriff of Kincardine before his appointment to the office of Chamberlain of Scotland between 1267–9.

Through Mary, Reginald II inherited a quarter share of the lands of Caithness. Their son Reginald III left two co-heiresses when he died in 1341 so that the Cheyne lands in Caithness as well as in Duffus passed to the Sutherlands and the Keiths of Inverugie.

Euphemia was probably buried with her husband in Duffus church.

SOURCES

Alexander Carmichael's *Carmina Gadelica* (Gaelic Songs) from whom the incantations, prayers and charms are taken was the result of forty-four years of work in the field of oral literature. Carmichael was born in 1832 on the island of Lismore. His work as a Customs and Excise officer took him throughout Gaelic-speaking Scotland, and the greater part of his collection was made in the Western Isles. He wrote, 'Three sacrifices have I made – the sacrifice of time, the sacrifice of toil, and the sacrifice of means. These I do not regret. I have three regrets – that I had not been earlier collecting, that I have not been more diligent in collecting, and that I am not better qualified to treat what I have collected.'

John MacInnes, writing in his preface to the 1992 Floris edition of the collection, declares '*Carmina Gadelica* is by any standards a treasure house . . . a marvellous and unrepeatable achievement.'

I cannot claim that Euphemia knew the exact words of the charms and croons I have quoted but the sentiments they reveal, that strong blend of pagan and Christian imagery, is perhaps the nearest we can get to understanding her perception of life.

p 29 The story of the Gaelic curse comes from Dr A. C. Gordon Ross's unpublished manuscript entitled *Chronicles of Ross* and is undoubtedly a poetic fiction.

pp 38–43 The rituals of the times and seasons described have several sources: 1) *A Collection of Highland Rites and Customs* copied by Edward Lhuyd from the manuscript of the Revd James Kirkwood (1650–1709) and edited by the folklorist John Lorne Campbell in 1975; 2) *Witches and Second Sight in the Highlands and Islands of Scotland* (1902) contains usages and superstitions taken from the oral tradition by the folklorist John Gregorson Campbell; 3) *The Folklore of the Scottish Highlands* (1976) by the Celtic scholar Anne Ross; 4) *Carmina Gadelica* by Alexander Carmichael.

p 43 The description of Alexander II's coronation comes from the *Chronica gentis Scotorum* by John of Fordun (c.1320–c.1387) a Latin scholar who may have been a priest in Aberdeen. His chronicle formed the basis of Walter Bower's fifteenth-century *Scotichronicon*, described as the most important source book of Scottish medieval history.

p 47 Matthew Paris lived and died in the Benedictine monastery of St Albans during the thirteenth century. His *Chronica Majora* is one of the most valuable sources for our knowledge of the period.

p 54 Both stories are quoted by Nicholas Orme in *From Childhood to Chivalry* (1984). The first is from the *Autobiography of Giraldus Cambrensis* (translated by H. E. Butler in 1937), and dates from the twelfth century. The second is from a list of children's games in the fifteenth century called *Ratis Raving* edited by R. Girvan for the Scottish Text Society, 3rd series, xi (1939).

p 54 Bishop John Leslie of Ross published his *De origine, moribus et rebus gestis Scotorum* in Rome in 1578. For a more detailed description of Highland dress consult. *The Costume of Scotland* by John Telfer Dunbar (1981).

pp 55–56 Mary Beith's *Healing Threads* (1995), an invaluable source book for the history of Highland medicine, rituals, charms and incantations, folk healers and learned doctors of the Highlands and Islands, also describes the make-up of herbal skin-preparations used by Scottish women.

p 59 and onwards. Part Three of Henrietta Leyser's *Medieval Women: A Social History of Women in England 450–1500* (1995) includes an informative and enthralling account of family roles in the High and Later Middle Ages.

pp 60–63 For a full description of early marriage customs see 'Gaelic Scotland: Marriage, Divorce and Concubinage' by W. D. H. Sellar. *Transactions of the Gaelic Society*, Inverness, Vol LI.

p 63 G. W. S. Barrow's *Kingship and Unity, Scotland 1000–1306* gives a lucid, readable and reliable portrait of the period.

pp 64–68 The Chronicle of Man is described and discussed in 'The Kingdom of Man and the Isles' in the *Transactions of the Gaelic Society*, Vol XII.

pp 69, 86 The charters are written in Latin in the *Registrum Episcopatus Moraviensis*, edited by C. Innes and published by the Bannatyne Club, Edinburgh in 1837.

p 71 Some of Peter Abelard and Héloïse's letters written to each other in the twelfth century are quoted in *The Voice of the Middle Ages in Personal Letters, 1100–1500* edited by C. Moriarty, 1989. The tragedy of their all-consuming passion is well-known and nowhere better told than by Helen Waddell in her novel, *Peter Abelard*.

p 73 'Excavations at Duffus Castle' were carried out and written up by J. Cannel and C. Tabraham in *PSAS* Vol 124 (1994). Further descriptions come from *The Statistical Account of Scotland*, Vol XVI and in *Elgin Past and Present* by H. B. Mackintosh, 1914.

pp 75–78 The stories of Countess Ida of Boulogne and the unhappy Godelive are told in Georges Duby's *Love and Marriage in the Middle Ages*, 1994.

INTERLUDE

WINNING THE WEST

The first Euphemia, as we have seen, lived in a time of peace between Scotland and her neighbours, an age when art and architecture, religion and chivalry were able to flourish without threat of major conflict. Our second Euphemia was to be less fortunate.

Although the Scottish king was a vassal of the English throne in that he had sworn fealty for the lands he owned in England, and though from the English point of view Scotland was considered to be a vassal state, this was not a matter of much moment to the Scots. As Monica Clough writes, 'The interplay between England and Scotland at this period was not particularly hostile, more a matter of opportunist and feudal homage by the closely related royal houses.'

At the Treaty of York in 1237, at which Farquhar was present, the Anglo-Scottish border was for the first time agreed between Alexander II and Henry III. The Scots gave up their claims to the northern counties of England and the boundary was set on much the same lines as it has today.

Alexander had a more important agenda. He had brought Ross firmly under his own control through Farquhar of Applecross; Moray and Sutherland were in the hands of the descendants of Freskin the Fleming. Galloway was in the firm control of the Norman family de Balliol. The same feudal organisation was repeated throughout the mainland but the Hebrides were still in Norse hands. Just before his untimely death in 1249 Alexander had begun to build up his navy, patrol western waters and garrison the west coast. His son was to finish the job.

John of Fordun records that Alexander III was only eight years old when he was crowned in a spectacular ceremony that combined ancient Celtic traditions with the feudal ritual of crowning and anointing by the bishop of St Andrews. He sat on the Stone of Scone in the sunny open air, flanked by his young mother, Marie de Coucy and possibly the countess of Fife, in the presence of his barons and bishops, while his genealogy tracing him back to Scota, the daughter of an Egyptian pharaoh, was chanted aloud.

Henry III of England kept a close and kindly eye on the young king and when he was only ten, knighted and betrothed him to his eleven-year-old daughter, the Princess Margaret. Tactfully the young Alexander avoided paying homage to his future father-in-law by declaring politely that he had not had time 'for full deliberation on the matter with his nobles'.

Years later in 1272 when he and Margaret, as honoured guests, attended the coronation of Henry's successor, Edward I, he was content, as his father had been, to do homage to the new king for his English territory only. 'To homage for my kingdom of Scotland no one has right except God alone, nor do I hold it except of God alone.' So far so good.

Queen Margaret is recorded as being beautiful, modest and good, but she also had a mind of her own. One day while strolling along the banks of the Tay with her courtiers, she pushed one boring and boastful young squire into the water. Unfortunately he was carried off by the current and drowned. A bad omen. She herself was to die at the early age of thirty-five and all the royal children were to predecease their father.

Determined to oust the Norwegians once and for all, the young king's first act on taking control of his government at the age of twenty was to try to buy the Western Isles from King Haakon but in vain. He devised other means. While Walter Steward, earl of Menteith, ousted the Macsweens from Knapdale and Arran, William of Ross – Farquhar's son who had inherited the earldom in 1251 – devastated the Isle of Skye in 1262.

According to *Haakon Haakonson's Saga* he and 'other Scots burned down a town and churches, killed and slew very many peasant men and women. And they said also that the Scots had taken the little children, and laid them on their spear-points, and shook their spears until they brought the children down to their hands, and so threw them away dead. They said also that the Scottish king intended to lay under himself all the Hebrides.'

This act of barbarity had the desired effect of rousing the elderly Haakon to action. After crowning his son Magnus in his stead, he sailed from Norway with a huge fleet led by his own magnificent oak galley carved with a golden dragon prow. He met up with Christina's son, Magnus, now king of Man, at Kyleakin ('Haakon's narrows') where he was joined by other allies. Altogether he raised a fleet of some one or two hundred ships and about three to four thousand men. We don't know how many warriors Alexander had, though William of Ross was certainly one of them.

Weather and time were on the Scottish side and, after a bruising encounter at the Battle of Largs on the river Clyde, the Norse fleet withdrew and King Haakon died in Orkney some weeks after. Three years later in 1266 Magnus, now king of Norway, sold the Hebrides and Man (though not Orkney and Shetland) at the Treaty of Perth for 4,000 merks and a further 100 merks a year 'for the sake of peace'. That peace was further cemented in 1281 by the marriage of Alexander's daughter Margaret to Eric, Magnus' successor.

William of Ross was to receive the islands of Skye and Lewis for his support. He died at Earl's Allane in May 1274 and was succeeded by his eldest son William, third earl of Ross.

THE MAID OF NORWAY

When his heir died in 1284 Alexander realised that he would have to remarry immediately in the hope of producing a son. He chose Yolande, the lovely young daughter of the Count of Dreux. The king adored her. On 19th March 1286, after a meeting in Edinburgh Castle, he decided to ride home late that night to be with her at Dunfirmline palace. It was a wet night and a gale was blowing. In spite of the entreaties of his nobles he succeeded in crossing the Forth but on the other side in the stormy darkness rode his horse over a cliff at Kinghorn in Fife. His death after such a successful reign of forty years was deeply mourned.

[93]

When Alexander our king was dead,
That Scotland led in love and le [law],
Away was sonce [plenty] of ale and bread,
Of wine and wax, of game and glee:
Our gold was changed into lead.
Christ, born into Virginity,
Succur Scotland and remede
That stad (placed) is in perplexity.

                       Anon.

Immediately there was trouble. The heir to the throne was a child of three, Margaret, the daughter of the nineteen-year-old King Eric of Norway whose queen – Alexander's daughter – had died shortly after her baby was born. Six guardians consisting of bishops and nobles were chosen to control Scotland, but there were so many arguments among the leading families that Edward I of England, the child's great-uncle, was invited by the guardians to restore order. His price was, on the surface at least, acceptable. The infant Margaret, Maid of Norway, was to succeed to the throne under his care and she was to marry his son. At the same time Scotland was to keep her independence 'separate and divided from England according to its rightful boundaries, free in itself and without subjection'.

Then, in 1290, Edward seized the Isle of Man. Worse still, poor little Margaret, only nine years old, died in Orkney on her way to Scotland, surrounded by sweetmeats, in the arms of the bishop of Bergen. Thus the dynasty created in 840 AD with Kenneth Mac Alpin had come to an end and with it began one of the unhappiest periods in Scottish history.

THE COMPETITORS

There were thirteen claimants to the throne to be known as 'the Competitors'. Edward I saw this period of unrest as his opportunity to unify the island under himself as overlord. The English lawyers had always seen the Scots as vassals to England, though the Scots lawyers saw them only as vassals with regard to their English property. Prove it, said Edward and hinted that they might have to prove with the sword. The Scots reluctantly agreed to recognise him as overlord and he insisted that whoever won the throne must recognise him as superior. By June 1291 English constables held most of the key royal castles. William, third earl of Ross, was one of those who did homage to him at Berwick in the following August.

Edward then summoned a court of a hundred and four auditors who in 1292 met at Norham on the English side of the border near Berwick to consider the 'Great Cause'. Again William was one of them. Of the thirteen claimants nearly all were descended from the Anglo-Norman families whose grand- or great-grandfathers had married into the royal dynasty. Some claimed they were descended from the illegitimate children of William the Lion or Alexander II. King Eric of Norway put in a bid, as did Floris, Count of Holland, descended from a sister of William the Lion but with no documents available to prove it. John Comyn the Elder, the Red of Badenoch, claimed descent through Bethoc (Beatrice) the daughter of Donald Ban III.

The list eventually was narrowed down to two 'Competitors', Robert Bruce (grandfather of the future king) who was a grandson of William the Lion's brother David of Huntingdon through his daughter Isabel, and John de Balliol of Galloway, a great-grandson of David I through his older daughter Margaret and already a vassal of the English crown as he held Barnard Castle and Bywell in England.

Partly in recognition of medieval law but partly because it suited him, Edward chose the forty-three-year-old John de Balliol, his liegeman, to be the new king of Scotland.

Robert Bruce the Competitor resigned his earldom and his right to the throne to his eldest son, Robert Bruce the Elder, earl of Carrick. He in turn refused to do homage to Balliol and resigned his earldom to his son, Robert the Bruce who, as we shall see, had no intention of giving up either his earldom or his grandfather's claim.

'TOOM TABARD'

John Balliol's task was unenviable. The last king to be crowned on the Stone of Scone, he was off to Newcastle a month later to do homage to Edward who immediately began to exploit him. He interfered on every possible occasion. On the one hand he urged Eric of

Norway to reclaim the Western Isles because the Scots had not paid the agreed annuity, and on the other insisted Balliol support him in war against the French. Balliol dug his toes in, made a treaty with the French and assembled an army. This was exactly what Edward wanted, the excuse to invade Scotland. He knew the inexperienced poorly-armed Scottish warriors were no match for his professional soldiers armed with their deadly long-bows.

Meanwhile the Scottish army led by Earl William of Ross and the earls of Atholl and Menteith marched towards England determined to make a stand, and the long battle for Scottish Independence started with the capture of Dunbar castle. Edward was furious. He himself headed an army said to consist of four thousand mounted knights and twenty-five thousand foot-soldiers. Early in April 1296 he destroyed Berwick-upon-Tweed, ruthlessly slaughtering the citizens, then marched on to Dunbar. The two armies met on the high ground above the town. The Scots were routed with a loss of ten thousand men. Edward himself entered Dunbar to accept the keys of the castle.

William of Ross was one of the many prisoners taken to the Tower of London where he was to remain for the next seven years.

As Edward and his army marched north, King John Balliol, who had already renounced his allegiance to Edward and was said to be in hiding with the Comyns in Angus, surrendered himself in the hope of securing peace for his country. On 2nd July 1296 at Kincardine castle he was publicly humiliated, stripped not only of his royal insignia but also of his tabard bearing the royal arms. Hence his nickname 'Toom Tabard', empty surcoat, though this is also thought to symbolise his alleged inadequacy as a leader, and there is contemporary evidence that the style Toom Tabard was applied to Balliol during his lifetime. A certain English chronicler called Peter Langtoft, living in the reigns of Edward I and II, wrote scathingly:

> For boule bred in his boke,
> Whenne he tint that he toke
> With the kingedom;
> For he haves ovirhipped,
> Hise typeth is typped,
> Hise tabard es tome.

Copyright T. E. Gray

1. The Cross-slab at Applecross.

2. Matthew Paris Map of Great Britain.

3. The Royal Burgh of Dingwall.

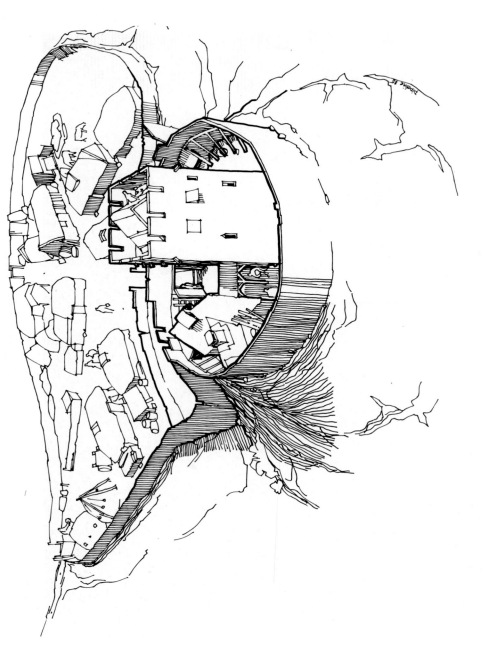

4. Reconstruction of Duffus Castle as the first Euphemia may have known it.

5. Duffus Castle today.

6. Fearn Abbey rebuilt in the 18th c. is still used as a parish church today. The ruined transept may have been where Farquhar, Earl of Ross, was buried.

7. Farquhar's (alleged) effigy in Fearn Abbey.

8. John Balliol offers homage to Edward I.

9. Urquhart Castle on Loch Ness. The English garrison was relieved by order of the second Euphemia in 1296.

10. Robert the Bruce. Pilkington Jackson's magnificent
monument at Bannockburn was unveiled in 1964.

11. St Duthac's Church, Tain. Its sanctuary was broken by William Earl of Ross in 1306.

12. Effigies of Celtic warriors from Kilmory showing
the padded *aketon* (surcoat) and iron *bacinet* (helmet).

(This translates as follows: 'Because of the breach that was thrust in his belly when he lost what he took along with the kingdom, and because he aimed too high, his cape is clipped and his tabard is empty.')

He was taken to the Tower of London and released in 1299 to spend the rest of his life in exile on his French estates in Picardy, where he died in 1313.

'HAMMER OF THE SCOTS'

Edward marched on in triumph. It was his intention to reduce Scotland to the level of a subject state like Wales. Following the route taken by the Roman general Agricola in the first century he proceeded north-east to Aberdeen, then north to Banff, no doubt determined to subdue the Comyns in Buchan and Mar whose family were allies of Balliol. He spent three nights in Elgin before turning south to Rothes. From there he sent out Englishmen to Badenoch, owned by the Comyns, and to garrison the royal castles at Nairn, Forres, Urquhart on Loch Ness, Dingwall and Cromarty.

Not however to Duffus. Like so many of the knights and noblemen who had lands in England, and who wanted to hold on to what they had in Scotland, Sir Reginald le Cheyne, who had inherited Duffus on the death of his father-in-law Freskin de Moravia, thought it expedient to support Edward. For his loyalty he was created guardian of Moray and given the castle of Inverness.

Having subdued the north, the 'Hammer of the Scots' then turned south to Perth, removed the Stone of Destiny from Scone which he took to Westminster Abbey, stole the Scottish regalia from Edinburgh, including the documentary records of the crown and the precious relic of the True Cross which St Margaret, Queen of Malcolm *Ceann Mor*, had brought to Scotland two centuries before.

At Berwick he called an assembly to receive the oaths of allegiance from the conquered Scots. One by one the nobles and bishops sealed their submission, fifteen hundred of them in what was to become known as the 'Ragman Rolls'.

'SCOURGE OF THE ENGLISH'

Perhaps it took a ruthless megalomaniac like Edward I to unite Scotland into a nation. Two men in particular were responsible for leading a rebellion against the occupying forces. One of these was Sir William Wallace, younger son of a Lanarkshire laird, who early in 1297 avenged the death of his wife and brother by slaying the English sheriff at Lanark. His skills were those of a guerrilla leader and his appeal largely to ordinary folk who, as opposed to the nobility, flocked to the struggle. Wallace – the 'Hammer and Scourge of the English' – was able to build up a national army which crushed Edward's forces at the Battle of Stirling Bridge in 1297. For this he was created guardian of Scotland.

The other great national figure came from the north. He was Andrew de Moravia, a descendant of Freskin the Fleming through a younger son. He had been captured at the Battle of Dunbar but managed to escape from prison in Chester to his castle at Avoch in the Black Isle where in 1297 he famously raised the standard for freedom. He and his followers worked their way south, capturing the castles taken by the English and gathering in strength to join Wallace at Stirling Bridge. Sadly, he was wounded in the battle and died in the Black Isle two months later, leaving Wallace to continue the struggle more or less alone.

The next battle at Falkirk in 1298 was a disaster. The Scottish foot soldiers enclosed in several *schiltroms* – (defensive palisades of sharply pointed wooden stakes bound together with rope enclosing some fifteen hundred warriors with spears) were no match for Edward's Welsh archers with their long-bows and deadly hail of arrows. The Scottish ranks were broken, the spearmen decimated, while the Scottish knights in the rear shamefully retreated.

Wallace escaped with his life but he was no longer guardian of the nation. He spent the next few years in hiding while trying to raise support on the continent for the Scots cause. Sadly, in 1305 he was betrayed by his valet for gold and caught in Glasgow in bed with his lover, or so the story goes. He was handed over to the English by Sir John Steward of Menteith, and on 23rd August taken to Westminster Hall where he was crowned mockingly with laurel leaves. Tried and found guilty of treason, he was dragged on a hurdle to Smithfield, half-hanged, then disembowelled when still alive. His decapitated head was mounted on London Bridge and his limbs exhibited in various towns including Perth and Stirling to deter other patriots.

But Scotland now had a martyr and a cause. Blind Harry the minstrel was not the first to declare: 'Rycht suth it is, a martyr was Wallace'. As Wordsworth was to write in *The Prelude* centuries later:

> Sometimes, more sternly moved, I would relate
> How Wallace fought for Scotland, left the name
> Of Wallace to be found, like a wild flower,
> All over his dear country; left the deeds
> Of Wallace, like a family of ghosts,
> To people the steep rocks and river banks,
> Her natural sanctuaries, with a local soul
> Of independence and stern liberty.

Even the English saw him as a hero, and the memory of his martyrdom persists right up to the present century and still has the power to stir the Scottish heart.

MURDER MOST FOUL

Support for the Scottish cause however also came from another source. Pope Boniface VIII issued a bull challenging Edward to prove that he had the right to rule the Scots as overlord. The English king was forced to agree a temporary truce to debate the matter but the war of words was inconclusive. In May 1301 the truce expired and Edward mounted a further invasion, which he was forced to halt in order to turn his attention to the French who were threatening to bring back John Balliol by force.

Another hero emerged. John Comyn (the Younger), the Red of Badenoch, attacked the English stationed at Roslin in 1303 with Simon Fraser, but now Edward was free to march north yet again. His army of seven thousand men advanced to Perth. On recapturing Brechin which had fallen to the rebels he marched on to Aberdeen and the north, following much the same route as in 1296, but this time he included the Comyn stronghold of Lochindorb in Badenoch where he stayed for several days before returning south to Stirling. Once again the Scots were forced to make peace. On the promise of their lives and lands, John Comyn and his followers capitulated, though they had to pay heavy fines. Edward needed their money and their support if he was to rule the country.

Then on 10th February 1306 the Red Comyn, Scotland's hero, was murdered, perhaps in a fit of drunken anger, within the sanctuary of the Greyfriars church in Dumfries. The murderer was Robert the Bruce, earl of Carrick, a man who, like most of his peers, had changed sides no less than five times before coming to the conclusion that he was the rightful leader of an independent Scotland. Did he murder the Comyn knowing that he was a Balliol supporter who would have opposed a Bruce's bid for the throne? Or was it all a dreadful accident? There are many theories but no one knows the exact truth. As a result Bruce was excommunicated by the pope, he enraged Edward and started a blood-feud with the Comyns and all their Balliol allies, particularly in the north of Scotland.

'GOOD KING ROBERT'

Whatever the truth behind the slaying, Robert was now forced to take the initiative. He captured Dumfries and other surrounding castles then hurried north to Glasgow where he collected the supportive Bishop Wishart, and rode on to Scone to be crowned king of the Scots on 25th March 1306, just six weeks after the murder.

The ceremony was performed by Isabella Macduff, aunt of the earl of Fife, whose family had always installed the Scottish kings. Oddly enough she was also the countess of Buchan married to another John Comyn, a relative of the murdered lord, and Bruce's sworn enemy.

Bruce's subsequent campaign to free Scotland was perhaps made easier by the death of the 'Hammer of the Scots' in 1307. Edward II was less ambitious. Nevertheless it was to take another seven years before the Scottish victory at Bannockburn in 1314, followed by another fourteen until the Treaty of Edinburgh and Northampton in 1328 which gave Bruce Scotland 'free, quiet and entire, without any kind of feudal subjection'. At least for the time being.

This then is the troubled background to the story of our second Euphemia.

SOURCES

John of Fordun's account of the coronation of Alexander III in Vol I of his *Chronica gentis Scotorum* is amplified by M. D. Legge's scholarly article entitled 'The Inauguration of Alexander III', *PSAS* Vol LXXX.

Several books have been written about Clan Ross which are listed in the bibliography. *The Earls of Ross and Their Descendants* by Francis Nevile Reid is the most comprehensive and certainly the most useful as it includes the early source references. It was published in *The Scottish Antiquary* and privately reprinted (fifty copies only) in Edinburgh by T. & A. Constable in 1894.

p 93 According to the *Kalender of Ferne*, William, second earl of Ross died at Earles Allane, a place which is untraceable today. The Inverness genealogist Alastair Macleod suggests that Earles Allane may translate from the Gaelic as the earl's 'rock' or stronghold and could mean his castle at Delny.

R. Nicholson's *Scotland, the Later Middle Ages* (1974) gives a clear and readable account of John Balliol and the Competitors. Peter Langtoft's scathing verse is recorded in G. G. Simpson's article in Vol XLVII of the *Scottish History Review* entitled 'Why was John Balliol called "Toom Tabard"?'

PART TWO

———— ◆ ————

THE SECOND EUPHEMIA
Châtelaine of Delny

Who was Euphemia, wife of William, third earl of Ross? All we know is her name, but not her antecedents. Strange this, as she is the only woman connected to the earls, apart from Farquhar's wife, whose pedigree is not recorded. Why?

Without any evidence, Dr Gordon Ross suggested in his manuscript chronicle of the Rosses that she may have been Norse. This is just possible. William inherited the earldom on his father's death in 1274. He is known to have been one of the lords who acknowledged the little Maid of Norway as heir to the crown after the death of Alexander III's son and heir in 1284. He may well have been one of her mother's escorts to Norway on her marriage to Eric II in 1281. He may have fallen in love with a Norwegian beauty whose pedigree has not been recorded.

We also know that Euphemia II's grandson Hugh was 'travelling in Norway' at the time of his father's untimely death at the Battle of Halidon Hill in 1333 and did not come into his heritage until 1335. He may have been sent there for safety or fosterage with one of her relatives. Or she may have been English. She is quoted in *The Earls of Ross and their Descendants* as being 'a lady who warmly supported the English party'. However, as most of the nobility switched sides several times during the Wars of Independence, this is not necessarily significant. Alternatively, he may have married her for love. The third earl was certainly powerful enough to choose whom he liked. He seems to have been an only child (or only surviving child), born late in the marriage and therefore sole heir to what had become a vast territory.

The earl of Cromartie in *A Highland History* records that William's main revenue came from the five mains (farms) of Kinnairdie,

Balcony, Delny, Kessock and Kinellan with all the ferries and mills in the eastern lowlands of Ross. The mills were a source of huge revenue, even though the Law of Thirlage passed in 1284, which forbade private milling, was never properly enforced in Ross-shire. But, as in the days of his grandfather Farquhar, his chief source of wealth lay in his vast herds of cattle. The price for a good beast was at that time about nine shillings.

Out of Ross, William possessed estates in Galloway, Renfrew and Argyll. He was the superior (in the feudal sense) of Glenmoriston and Glen Urquhart with its castle on Loch Ness. In Moray and Aberdeenshire he was superior of a number of important baronies, and in Badenoch he held Inneurmerky, probably through his mother Jean Comyn. In the west, he owned Skye and Lewis while his uncle held the lands of Applecross.

We know from the *Kalender of Ferne* that he died in January 1322. If he lived his full three score years and ten he must have been born about 1252 and therefore in his early twenties when he inherited his earldom. He was however probably younger. The date of his marriage to Euphemia is not recorded but we know that their third son Walter was a scholar at Cambridge in 1306 which suggests the latter may have been born about 1290. Walter's eldest brother Hugh, who was to inherit the earldom, may then have been born c. 1285. Thus Euphemia was probably married aged about sixteen in the early 1280s.

Impressively talented, as will be seen, probably beautiful and likely to have been well-born, Euphemia seems to have been an ambitious woman with the skills of a diplomat and the wiles of an adventuress. William would have taken her to Delny castle as a bride. By 1280, after such a long period of peace and prosperity, life would have been extremely enjoyable throughout Scotland at that time and no more so than in Easter Ross.

LADY OF THE HOUSE

The castle would now have had stone walls large enough to house a good part of William's considerable entourage. Among his Celtic kinsfolk and clan members, William was *ceann-cinnidh*, the head of his race, and Euphemia the *ban-tighearna*, the lady of the house 'surrounded by a bevy of maids of honour, daughters of chieftains sent to be educated, all learning and maintaining the standards and ritual of a stately little court'. Unless he was elderly or incapable of military leadership the chief was also *ceann-cath*, the war-leader, and his entourage of warriors and servants much as it had been in Farquhar's day, only larger and probably more formal.

The most important posts, often hereditary, still included the seanachie, who wore long robes on ceremonial occasions and recited the clan history whenever appropriate; the bard composed poetry and satire for recitation at feasts and festivals, while the harper (*an clarsair*) was responsible for the music. There were also the treasurer (*an fhear sporain*), the herald (*am bladier*), the banner-bearer (*an brataich*), sword-bearer (*an gille mor*), henchman (*an gille coise*) who stood fully armed behind his master's chair, the cup-bearer (*an cupair*) who tested his wine for poison and his personal bodyguard (*an luchd-tighe*) who consisted of the finest youths of the clan trained in the art of warfare.

Other offices included the quartermaster (*am fear fardaiche*) who was in charge of the internal economy of the household. He was responsible for arranging lodgings for the chief and his attendants when they travelled, a taxing task, and his reward was a share of the hides of the cattle killed for feasts or captured during a raid (*creach*). The forester (*am forsair*) watched over the hunting grounds in exchange for a croft and grazing in the forest. There were also a number of lesser posts, including a servant whose duty it was to carry his chief over fords and rivers when he was travelling on foot (*an gille-cas-fliuch*) and the cock-man or warder who guarded prisoners. There were grooms, running footmen, cooks, and a number of women servants.

A private chaplain and possibly a scribe would also have acted as tutor to the children. Whether William had his own jester (*an cleasaiche*) is not known, but it is certainly possible. The Gaels and indeed all medieval folk, including the monks, enjoyed a good joke and a clever riddle. The Gaelic language with all its subtleties is particularly appropriate to humour and satire which could often be savage.

This multitude of servants did not all necessarily live in or around the castle. Many held crofts and farms in exchange for their services but they were always available and present when their chief required them and on important clan occasions.

The language spoken at Delny would have been predominantly Gaelic, though French was still very much in fashion, particularly at court. English in its Scots form was becoming more common among the merchants in the burghs though it was full of French and Gaelic words. Visiting English clerics and educated men who perhaps did not have the Gaelic could have held a conversation in Latin.

As wife of the head of such a household, Euphemia had huge responsibilities. Entertainment was on a lavish scale and the guest-list would have included not only royalty, clan chiefs, bishops and knights but also their personal entourages. William was, as we shall see, very much an absentee husband and apart from the vast estates whose administrators she would have had to deal with, there were numerous cases of grievance and crime to adjudicate and five of her own children to rear with those of neighbouring chieftains to foster through adolescence into adulthood.

THE EARL'S DIARY

It is interesting to see how often William is recorded as having been away from Delny, leaving his affairs largely in the hands of Euphemia and his steward.

On 1st August 1292 he was at Norham as one of the auditors at the trial of the Competitors for the crown, and in the following January (1293) he was at Westminster witnessing John Balliol's fealty to Edward I. Later in the year he was in Argyll and Skye where his lands were formed into the sheriffdom of Skye. For the next few years he was occupied in organising an army of resistance against Edward I and in May 1296 he was taken prisoner at Dunbar and committed to the Tower of London. As we have seen he was kept a prisoner there for seven years.

About 29th September 1303 he was released under an escort and guard to join Edward in Scotland. The document survives and gives a valuable insight into travel conditions and necessities of the day. The escort party consisted of Sir Francis le Vylers, his squire, a clerk, a marshal, a cook and four sergeants, with fourteen horses and fourteen grooms. William was allotted two palfreys, two sumpter horses and four grooms. 'At each town where the earl rests at night he shall have fire and light in his chamber. Two horse and two footmen shall keep watch all night in his chamber, and six of the townsmen outside.' The expense of the journey included fodder for the beasts, shoeing William's four horses (2d), his grooms' wages (6d), the clerk's outlay for arranging the retinue, and making twenty pounds of wax into torches and candles (10d).

The travellers set out from London on 30th September 1303 and they reached St Albans that night where William's supper included soup at 1d and young roast pigeons at 3d. The total bill for everyone came to 12s 7d. Next day they reached Dunstable where they enjoyed butcher meat, six hens, larks for 1d, almonds, herrings and three flagons of wine. That same day they arrived at Newport Pagnell where in addition to bread, meat, poultry, herrings, eels and pikerells they also bought a hundred eggs for 4½d, mustard to store, vergus (soured fruit-juice), gingibo and lard for the cresset (torch). The hired beds cost 2d.

On Wednesday 2nd October at Northampton they bought two pounds of candles, salt, eggs and milk for soup, a hundred herrings, bran for a sick palfrey and litter for beds and horses at 15d. They had to pay for mending the fur of William's cape at a penny and filling new saddles for his palfrey and sumpters. At Suleby they were given hay by the local abbot in addition to the usual necessities. They reached Leicester on the 4th October and Nottingham the next day, where shaving and washing for the earl cost 6d. Dinner on Sunday at Blyth included five partridges. On Monday they reached Shireburn having breakfasted at Wentbury, bought hay and bread for the horses at Doncaster, hired a hackney to carry William's harness as one of his sumpters could go no further, and ate pears.

At York on 8th October they feasted on red and white wine, geese, lampreys, roach and perch. They stayed in York for four nights where the cook prepared sixty fresh herring, haddock and codling, onions bought for a farthing, butcher meat for Sir Francis, pork and mutton, apples and pears, white peas for soup, salmon and ale. Fur was also purchased for the coverlid of the earl's bed at 6d. Then on to North Allerton by way of Thirsk where the earl's washing cost 6d.

At Durham on Sunday 13th October they dined on young pigeons and larks for breakfast and dinner. It cost 3½d to ferry William's horses and baggage across the Tees at Nesham. At Newcastle-on-Tyne, the earl's hood and furs had to be mended for 6d and a *hulcia* for his palfrey cost 16d. On to Morpeth, then Bamburgh and on Thursday 17th they reached Berwick. It cost 3d to cross the Tweed and 3d to carry William's baggage from the Tweed to the castle. The following day the London escort returned while William and his retinue remained for a further five days when the detailed account ends. Thus the journey had taken seventeen days.

William then joined Edward prince of Wales at Perth where his expenses were paid by the king for forty-three days at a cost of 2d a day. While there he visited Dunfermline on 6th December to collect a panoply of armour made for him by a certain Gefrei Merre. He bought two *gambessouns* (sleeveless leather or quilted garments worn under armour), a *pissone* and a *gorger* (neck-piece), a *chapel-de-fer* (iron helmet), a *bacinet*, a pair of *jamberis ov'les wampes* (leg armour), a pair of *poleyns* (knee-guards), and a *colret* of iron. He also bought second-hand a coat of mail from a certain Walter de Rye for a hundred shillings.

At the same time he bought a range of materials which included 20 ells of red *sandal* (silk) and 6½ ells of white *sandal*, 8½ ells of *celevermayl*, 9 of worsted, some silk and sewing thread. He also paid the wages of six *valez* to make up the material which took them eight days at 6d a day. His total expenditure of over £17 was to be paid for by the English king. He duly received some compensation but was still owed £6 by he time he reached Perth.

In Perth we are told he was reconciled to the English king through his son Prince Edward and sent home to Delny in February 1304. Later that year he was away again for there were two further petitions for payment of expenses for an expedition to the 'foreign isles' presumably Skye and Lewis.

These are William's known expeditions. There must have been more which were not recorded. That Euphemia managed to keep his vast estates intact during his long periods of absence and imprisonment demonstrates above all her skills of organisation and diplomacy.

THE COUNTESS AND THE KING

Whatever her feelings may have been over her husband's capture, Euphemia would have seen it as her duty and indeed her priority to protect his life at all costs. Equally it was important to hold on to the family territory to the best of her ability for his heir. How was she to do it? Perhaps by direct appeal to the English king. It is possible, though cannot be proved, that she visited him during his three days' stay at Elgin from 26th–29th July 1296.

This event must have been the talk of the north. Elgin had never seen the like before, nor indeed since. Edward brought with him an army of thirty thousand footmen and four to five thousand horsemen who camped in a field outside the town. He resided at the castle and there he received homage and surrender from most of the local nobility. Although Euphemia is not mentioned by name, at least three men styling themselves 'de Ros' swore fealty over the three days' visit. They may have taken Euphemia's good wishes to the king for, while the castles of Dingwall and Cromarty, Inverness and Urquhart on Loch Ness were thereafter occupied by English knights, Delny was not.

Although there is no proof, Dr Robert Ross believed there was some sort of liaison between the king and the countess and that he went so far as to send her a Valentine. It is perfectly possible that there was some flirtation in the courtly sense between them, not as Dr Ross suggests in London, but possibly in Elgin.

Edward I was a man of contradictions. In the *Song of Lewes*, he is compared to a leopard, brave like leo the lion, but also as unreliable as a pard. Quick-tempered, single-minded and as tenacious as a ferret, he was also extraordinarily handsome. At 6ft 2ins he was head and shoulders taller than most men, with blond curly hair in youth that must have been nearly white when, at the age of fifty-eight, he may have met Euphemia. Still vigorous, upright, with good eyesight, he is said to have had a drooping left eye inherited from his father and an appealing lisp. He was also formidably intelligent.

He adored his first wife, Eleanor of Castile, a cultured woman who not only produced twelve children but also travelled with him on many occasions, even when he went on crusade. He was devoted to his children, particularly his daughters whom he spoiled with expensive gifts. He enjoyed chess, music, falconry and campaigning. His tomb in Westminster abbey is inscribed with the famous words *Edwardus Primus Scotorum Malleus*, the 'Hammer of the Scots'.

Perhaps Euphemia saw that the best way to preserve the safety of her husband and the future of her children was by amusing the king, by charming him and, above all, by persuading him that she was a woman he could trust. Not easy, for he was no fool but she must have succeeded. Perhaps indeed she genuinely admired him, for he had all the qualities to attract a woman.

Whatever happened, she was allowed to keep her castle, and in addition receive 'a hundred pounds worth of land for her support out of the earldom of Ross and if the lands are not sufficient, that she receive the surplus at the exchequer of Scotland . . .' Dr Ross sees this sum as paying for a visit to London but of this there is no evidence. There is however plenty of evidence of her continued support of Edward. In a letter written to him in Latin dated 24th July 1297 signed by the bishop of Aberdeen, John Comyn, the earl of Buchan and the son of the earl of Mar, in which they give an account of putting down an insurrection in Moray, they particularly commend the countess of Ross for her assistance.

'When a coup had arisen some time ago in Moray and certain other lands adjoining it through the agency of Andrew, son of Lord Andrew of Moravia and certain others who wanted to upset the peaceful situation then obtaining, the uprising was in no way small . . . We sought out the guilty ones . . . which Andrew de Bath will report to you in greater detail . . . We have sent this messenger on behalf of the most noble countess of Ross that he would reach you with her advice in the establishment of peace and the implementation of the Royal Code of Justice for the future and preservation of our prosperity.'

Meanwhile Castle Urquhart on Loch Ness was, as we have seen, in the hands of an English garrison and very short of supplies. A second letter to the king dated the following day (25th July) and written on behalf of the English commander there told Edward that 'certain evil men, insensed by me, moved over to Andrew of Moravia's castle in Avoch. He wrote to A— and to the great Reginald le Chen [our first Euphemia's grandson] asking him to come to Inverness on the very next day . . . but I tell you that he didn't come even at the end of the day.' However the commander had also written to our second Euphemia asking for her help. 'I looked out from a part of the castle and I saw some townsmen from Inverness and the earl of Ross's son which the countess had sent . . . to help you because she realised that danger, by no means small, was threatening me as no help was likely to come from other clans.'

Euphemia's army was enough to hold back the attackers who

would have understood Euphemia's tricky situation. They withdrew for long enough to allow the necessary provisions to enter the castle.

This was enough to satisfy the commander whose letter continued, 'The church gives praise for this deed. If it is your pleasure, think the countess deserves honour and a safe position ... Equally by restoring your safety the earl of Ross's son saved the day and begs that he may petition his Majesty asking that you consider him worthy.'

Euphemia herself was also to petition the king. Although undated, with holes and illegible words in the parchment, it is thought to have been written immediately after the Urquhart event. It indicates clearly how with flattery and affectionate words she managed to keep in with the king in order to protect her husband and at the same time not entirely offend the local clansmen.

To the most excellent Lord and Ruler to be revered, to the illustrious Edward, King of England, Lord of Ireland and Duke of Aquitaine, your humble and devoted Euphemia, countess of Ross sends greetings, the wish for your good health. She is ready and prepared to carry out your commands and precepts with full obedience.

To your most illustrious Majesty in whom all my hope and well-being in all my difficulties resides I give my most sincere devotion to you and have done since the beginning of your reign ... I beg you to favour those who took my side lately, you being without doubt worthy of all success in your undertakings ... Moreover whatever your clerk ... has told you about my part in the affair, I will be able to acquit him from dissimulation. May your gracious good opinion of the earl still prevail.

As a result, on 28th August her eldest son Hugh who must still have been a teenager at the time was granted safe conduct by Edward prince of Wales to visit his father for a short time at the Tower. This permit was endorsed by Edward I before 'crossing the seas'. Possibly as a result of that visit, the sheriffs were ordered to pay 6d a day each for the maintenance, not only of the earl but of the other eminent Scottish prisoners of war held in the Tower.

WARDEN OF THE NORTH

William and Euphemia were reunited at Delny after seven years as we have seen in February 1304. No doubt there was great rejoicing in the castle with the killing of many a fatted calf. No doubt too William listened to Euphemia's account of her stewardship with pride and gratitude. She had saved his life and above all she had preserved his *duthus*, the inherited lands of which he was so proud.

His conduct must have continued to satisfy the king who had paid another visit to Elgin, staying this time in the manse of Duffus in June 1303. Two years later Edward appointed him warden and justiciar of Scotland north of the river Spey and governor of Dingwall castle, while the earl of Atholl (who had been captured at the same time but released earlier) was made warden of the lands between the Forth and the Spey.

Then in 1306 Robert Bruce murdered John Comyn and had himself crowned king of the Scots at Scone in the presence of his four brothers, Edward, Nigel, Thomas and Alexander, three bishops and the earls of Atholl, Menteith and Lennox, but not the earl of Ross.

William was the son of Jean Comyn, and therefore a cousin of the murdered man. He must have been outraged, as indeed, for different reasons, was Edward himself who sent the earl of Pembroke north to quash Bruce and his supporters without mercy. The two forces met outside Perth and Robert was routed, forced to flee westwards to Argyll. But there was no escaping the Comyns. Only a few weeks later he was attacked by a thousand foot soldiers under the chief of clan MacDougal, a nephew of the murdered man, and was on the run again.

Meanwhile Elizabeth, his queen, and his daughter Marjorie (by his first marriage) and his sisters Mary and Christina were all escorted by his brother Nigel to Kildrummy castle, seat of the earls of Mar beyond the Grampians in Aberdeenshire for safety. Christina, Bruce's sister, as widow of the earl of Mar was also Bruce's sister-in-law as his first wife Isabella, mother of Marjorie, was a Mar. It seemed the obvious place to go.

When word came in August 1306 that Edward prince of Wales and the earl of Pembroke were on their way to besiege Kildrummy, the royal women, under the protection of the earl of Atholl were forced to take to their horses again and ride north. Eventually they hoped to reach Orkney but made the mistake of passing through Ross territory and claiming sanctuary at St Duthac's girth in Tain, only a few miles from Delny Castle.

Sir Nigel Bruce stayed to defend Kildrummy, said to have been the noblest of all the northern castles modelled on the great chateau de Coucy near Léon in France. After a brave defence, he was betrayed by the local blacksmith who, bribed by the promise of as much gold as he could carry, fired the castle with the red-hot blade of a plough-coulter. His reward of gold was melted and poured down his traitorous throat. Sir Nigel Bruce was beheaded.

Meanwhile William violated the sanctuary of St Duthac. He captured the royal party and imprisoned them in Dingwall castle where they were detained for some time before being sent south for Edward to deal with as he saw fit. The earl of Atholl tried to escape by sea but was driven ashore in Moray, captured and executed in London on a gallows thirty feet higher than the norm in an act of contempt for his noble birth.

Some have thought that William's act of violation was a cowardly deed done out of fear of offending Edward, and with good reason. Life was now easier for the earl after so many years of hardship and he would not have wanted to go back to the Tower, this time to be hanged or beheaded. Euphemia may have used all her wiles to persuade him of the importance of placating Edward who had time and time again proved himself to be an implacable enemy. Also she had a son at Cambridge university who might well have been taken hostage. However, William was probably equally motivated by anger at Bruce's murder of his kinsman. If his mother, Jean Comyn was still alive she too would most certainly have urged him to vengeance.

Edward's fury at Bruce was demonstrated by his uncharacteristic treatment of his womenfolk. Chivalry towards women, however disruptive their menfolk, was the royal norm, but not in this case. He first ordered that they all be confined in cages, then relented as far as the queen was concerned. Elizabeth de Burgh was the daughter of the earl of Ulster, a loyal supporter of the English king, so instead she was detained at Burstwick Manor in Lincolnshire where her servants were forbidden to smile 'or be riotous'.

Marjorie was to have been put in a lattice cage in the Tower of London but as she was only twelve years old Edward relented sufficiently to give her and Christina into the care of Lord Percy. Mary Bruce, however, was imprisoned in a cage at Roxburgh castle while the countess of Buchan, who had crowned Bruce, was also encaged for four years in the tower at Berwick. Food, drink and other necessities were allowed at a cost of 4d a day and privvies were provided but no Scotsman was tolerated near the two women.

But Bruce was not daunted. His mother had been a Gael and so it was to the west he escaped, travelling between the islands of the Inner Hebrides perhaps to find safety with Christian MacRuari, a relative and heiress in her own right. He may even have gone to Orkney under the protection of another sister who was married to the king of Norway, or to Ulster where two of his brothers had escaped to raise support for his cause.

Perhaps it was here that he watched the spider struggle to spin its web, a fictitious tale told to enhance his reputation for indomitability. By now Bruce the murderer, was fast becoming Robert the king, national hero of the Scots.

Early in 1307 he was on the march again, backed by the bishops and an Irish force. Many Scots, united in loathing for the English occupying forces, flocked to his banner. He was determined by guerrilla tactics to rid every occupied castle of its English commanders and at the same time destroy the power of the ubiquitous Comyns.

But Edward was equally determined to destroy him, and once again marched north at the head of a powerful army. Although indomitable in spirit, he was a sick man. He died in great pain from an undiagnosed disease at Burgh-on-Sands near Carlisle on 7th June 1307 and was succeeded by his son. Edward II, though a brave fighter, lacked his father's will and competence. His campaign was unsuccessful and he withdrew his army.

This was Robert's chance. With a force of three thousand men he marched north to rid himself of the Comyns for good. His forces reached the borders of Ross and Sutherland, slaughtering cattle and robbing the granaries to supply his troops. He offered William of Ross a temporary truce. The earl allowed himself to be persuaded by his vassals, 'good men, clergy and others' who, like him, realised that their lands would suffer if they refused to make peace with the Bruce. But at the same time he wrote to the new king of England, perhaps urged by Euphemia, to explain why he had done so and to ask for assistance.

'Know, dear lord, that we would have on no account made a truce
with him, if the keeper of Moray [supporter of Bruce] had not been
absent from the country, and the men of his province would not
respond to us without his orders in order to attack our enemies, so
that we had no hope except from our own men.'

Robert went on to destroy the Comyns and devastate their castles.
He also broke the power of the MacDougals at the Battle of Inverurie
in 1308 by which time nearly every castle in the north was back in
Scottish hands. William honoured the truce and on 31st October
1308 surrendered to Robert in full, and swore fealty to him at Auldearn near Nairn. Robert not only forgave him his treatment of
his womenfolk, but also gave him the coveted Dingwall castle as a
hereditary property with the lands of Ferrincoscy in Sutherland. At
the same time, William forgave Bruce the murder of his cousin, so
no face was lost on either side. It is said that the two men became
close friends and that Bruce was his guest on at least one occasion
when he visited the earl's hunting lodge at Kinnellan near Strathpeffer. In the same year, possibly at the same time, a marriage was
solemnised between William's son and heir, Hugh, and Robert's
sister, Maud, whose wealthy dowry was 'the lands of Nairn with
the burgh'.

Naturally, it suited Bruce to have the powerful earl of Ross on his
side, and Robert was fast learning that diplomacy won more than
the sword. At the same time one wonders why the king should have
been so magnanimous to William who had acted in what can only
be described as a cowardly fashion to his queen, his daughter and
two of his sisters. Did Euphemia whisper in his ear, did she charm
him as she had charmed the late King Edward?

Possibly, but there may have been another reason, apart from
expediency, for the switch from enmity and anger to support and
friendship. That reason had to do with Bruce's beloved brother
Edward, the earl of Carrick and two of Euphemia's children.

EUPHEMIA'S FAMILY

William and Euphemia had five children whose upbringing was
largely, as we have seen, in the hands of the countess. Hugh as a
very young lad had led a half-hearted skirmish on behalf of his

mother to relieve the English garrison at Castle Urquhart. He had also visited his father in the Tower of London and was no doubt outraged and angered at his father's humiliation. Because of that experience he may have grown to admire the Bruce and his fight for freedom. His wedding to Robert's sister Maud may have been more than a marriage of convenience, but it certainly cemented the new alliance. He was to have three children by Maud (and four by his second wife one of whom was to be Euphemia III).

Hugh inherited the earldom on William's death in Delny in 1322. He continued to fight for Bruce and Scotland's freedom, finally dying for the cause at the Battle of Halidon Hill near Berwick in July 1333. His body was found wearing the shirt of St Duthac, a sacred relic said to possess miraculous powers. On this occasion the powers failed. In an act of contempt the shirt was returned to Tain by the English with 'many offensive epithets on the great god Duthoch'. No more was heard of it.

In keeping with his policy to placate all parties, William married his second son, Sir John de Ross to Margaret Comyn. This marriage may have been arranged long before the truce with Bruce. Indeed, Margaret may have been originally betrothed to Hugh in childhood and given to John when the more eligible Maud came on the scene. She was the younger niece and co-heiress with her sister of the earl of Buchan and brought her husband the barony of Kingedward and other lands in Banff and Aberdeenshire. When Sir John and Margaret died without children, the barony went to his eldest nephew, Hugh's heir.

Euphemia and William's third son, 'the amiable Walter', was sent to Cambridge university to train possibly for the church in 1306. The medievalist Alexander Grant tells us that theology at the universities was 'a minority specialist subject. Most students studied arts or law.' He may have been preparing for high office in the church – bishops were often law graduates – or perhaps he had a love of learning for its own sake. English knights were becoming more literate and Dr Grant suggests that this was probably true of the Scottish nobility too. It is said that Robert the Bruce read French romances to his companions during his period as a fugitive. Walter became a knight like his brother.

While at Cambridge he received a gift of ten marks from Edward I on 4th June 1307 just three days before the king died. Was this a reward for family loyalty to the English crown? Had Euphemia petitioned him in her son's favour? But Walter was also a close friend of Edward Bruce.

John Barbour in his great epic life of Bruce while describing the Battle of Bannockburn in which Walter was killed wrote movingly of that friendship:

> Schyr Walter of Ross ane other
> That Schyr Edward the kingis brother
> Luffyt and had in sic daynte
> That as himself him luffyt he.
> And quhen he wyst that he was ded
> He wes sa wa and will of reide
> That he said makand ivill cher
> That him war lever that journey wer
> Undone than he sua ded had bene

(Sir Edward, the king's brother, loved and held [him] in such esteem as though [he were] himself. When he knew that he was dead, he was so miserable and at a loss that he said, in a sad mood, that he would rather that the day was undone than that he had died like that.)

Barbour goes on to explain that the reason why he was so fond of Walter was because 'he loved [Ross's] sister as his mistress and held his own wife, Dame Isabel, in great distaste.'

'Ross's sister' was Euphemia's eldest daughter, Isabella. On 1st June 1317 a dispensation from Pope John XXII in Avignon granted her permission to marry Edward Bruce. It seems they were connected within the third and fourth degrees of affinity. Despite the late date of the document, Edward and Isabella may have been married in 1308 as part of the treaty between William and Robert. Or they may only have been betrothed.

The other Isabel, quoted as Edward's 'wife' was the sister of David, earl of Atholl. She may have been his wife in a Celtic secular marriage for her son, Alexander, later the earl of Carrick, was styled illegitimate. Edward was King Robert's heir until he, Edward, was killed at the Battle of Dundalk in 1318 trying to establish himself as king of Ireland.

So it seems that before the treaty between Robert and William of Auldearn there were strong links of friendship and love between Bruce's family and at least two of Euphemia's children. These links may well have contributed to the formation of the treaty in the first place and to the establishment of peace in the Highlands. When Robert called a parliament in St Andrews in 1309, out of the twenty-eight attending, twenty of them were noblemen from north of the Forth-Clyde valley.

Euphemia's younger daughter Dorothea married into the thoroughly Celtic clan of Macleod. Her husband Torquil, second baron of Lewis, was a great-grandson of Farquhar, through his daughter Christina, queen of Man.

Thus the marriages of Euphemia's children brought not only prestige and prosperity to the family, but also took them into the realms of royalty itself.

FINAL DAYS

Whether William and Euphemia moved into Dingwall castle or stayed in Delny is not known. Perhaps they decided to remain in the old home and let Hugh and his bride Maud Bruce move into the bigger establishment. Certainly Dingwall was to become the principal seat of the earls of Ross from this time onward.

William's name continued to appear in various documents until his death in 1322. In 1312 he sealed an agreement between Robert and the king of Norway. Although he may not have been present at the Battle of Bannockburn himself, his was one of the twenty-one clans who turned out in force to fight for the king. Sir Walter was, as we have seen, killed, but Robert's victory was outstanding. It is said that the equivalent of three million pounds' worth of booty was collected on the battlefield.

The victory of Bannockburn did not end the fighting between the two nations however. In 1320, as an old man, William's name appears as one of those who sealed a letter to the pope – the famous Declaration of Arbroath – asserting the Scottish right to independence, thought to have been drawn up by Bernard of Linton, abbot of Arbroath and chancellor of Scotland: '. . . so long as a hundred men remain alive we will never in any way be bowed beneath the yoke of English domination; for it is not for glory, riches or honours that we fight but for freedom alone, that which no man of worth yields up, save with his life.'

As Ranald Nicholson has written, 'This still stands as the most impressive manifesto of nationalism that medieval Europe produced.'

William was dead by 1328 when the Treaty of Edinburgh and Northampton was signed. This gave Robert the kingdom of the Scots 'free, quit and entire, without any kind of feudal subjection'. The king is said to have died of leprosy the following year. History remembers him as 'Good King Robert', the saviour of the nation.

A WOMAN OF HER TIMES

When or where Euphemia died is not known but she emerges from the few documents that remain as a survivor.

Whether she had a brief flirtation with Edward I because she was genuinely attracted to him or because she saw it as expedient seems unlikely. She may never even have seen him. She was not alone however in trimming her sails to every wind of change. Most of the nobility, including Bruce himself, acted in the same way in order to preserve their lands, not to mention their heads. It may have been that in the end she too was caught up in the wind of nationalism that was to sweep in a great gale through Scotland during her latter years.

Always she emerges as a charming manipulator. After so many years in control of his affairs, the earl may have relied on her advice more heavily than was normal for the times. It may have been at her instigation that he violated the queen's sanctuary at Tain, her advice again that urged him to make peace with Bruce.

She lived through a harsh and difficult period in her country's history. Perhaps it could fairly be said that her actions reflect what was most important to her as a woman, the preservation of what she loved most, her husband, her children and her home and, having made sure that these were secure, her country itself.

SOURCES

pp 107–108 Frank Adam's definitive description of a Highland chieftain's household comes from *The Clans, Septs and Regiments of the Scottish Highlands* first published in 1908 and revised in 1964 by Sir Thomas Innes of Learney who maintained that Adam thought that the clan system was dead, but that the clan spirit survived. Not so, says Sir Thomas. 'In law and social organisation the clan *system* is still quite alive. No legislation destroyed it . . . Too often it is the clan *spirit* which is, I would not say dead, but in a very anaemic condition.' Today the clan spirit flourishes again with hordes of descendants from all over the world attending the various clan gatherings throughout the Highlands every year.

pp 108–110 The earl's travels are recorded in J. Bain's *Calendar of Documents Relating to Scotland*, Vol II, nos 508, 1395, 1631, 1632 and F. Palgrave's edition of *Documents and Records Illustrating the History of Scotland*, no. 18.

p 111 The English monarch's complicated genius is fully described in *Edward I* by M. Prestwich, 1988. A pioneer of legal and parliamentary change, pious, uxorious, devoted supporter of the crusades, both peacemaker and warrior in Europe, conqueror of Wales, Edward never quite managed to subdue Scotland to his eternal chagrin. What he did achieve was to awaken in that nation a spirit of independence and a love of freedom which has never been extinguished.

pp 112–113 The documents and letters quoted come from J. Stevenson's *Documents Illustrative of the History of Scotland*, Vol II, and J. Bain's *Calendar of Documents Relating to Scotland*, Vol II and Parliamentary Petitions, Record Office, London, no 9146.

p 112 Urquhart castle on Loch Ness stands strategically on a headland south of Glen Urquhart. It has had a long and troubled history. The Iron Age timber-laced fort was superseded by a Norman motte-and-bailey in the twelfth century. In the thirteenth century it was granted to the Durward family, then passed to the Comyns of Badenoch before Edward I's army occupied it in 1296 and again in 1303. Robert the Bruce regained it in 1308. Today the impressive ruins are dominated by its seventeenth-century tower. Maintained by Historic Scotland, the castle today is one of the most popular tourist sites in the Highlands.

p 118 Robert Bain, in his *History of the Ancient Province of Ross* (1899), records the event of St Duthac's miraculous shirt with some relish. His volume reveals that he had little respect for the earls, the pre-Reformation church and all forms of superstition.

Much the most reasonable and often amusing account of the whole period comes in the earl of Cromartie's *A Highland History* (1979) which was planned and partially written during his period as a prisoner-of-war in Germany. As a Mackenzie, and latterly chief of the clan, he had access to a host of charters, papers, letters and a wealth of clan lore.

However Dr Alexander Grant's *Independence and Nationhood, Scotland 1306–1469* (1984) gives a balanced, detailed and probably more accurate portrait of the times.

p 120 The Declaration of Arbroath was the most important of three letters written to Pope John XXII in the name of the king, the bishop of St Andrews and the community of the realm. Previous popes had agreed with Scottish independence but Pope John preferred the English claims and in 1319 had excommunicated King Robert, summoned him and four bishops to answer accusations of rebellion, and released the Scots from allegiance to their king. The Declaration put forward the Scottish point of view. After detailing the origins of Scotland as a nation and stressing the patronage of St Andrew, the letter goes on to describe Edward I as a tyrant and Robert I as one 'who has brought salvation to his people through the safeguarding of our liberties'.

It was sealed by eight earls and thirty-one barons but impressed the pope not at all. Nor did the papal attitude change until 1328.

INTERLUDE

THE BOY KING

When King Robert the Bruce died in 1329, he left one legitimate son, David, born as late as 1324, and a grandson, Robert the Steward, son of his daughter Marjorie who had died in childbirth in 1316.

David was therefore only five years old when he inherited Scotland and no match at that age for the English Edward III who has been described by Stewart Ross in *Monarchs of Scotland* as 'the most able and distinguished of the Plantagenet monarchs'.

At the age of four David was betrothed to Edward III's sister Joan. After her death in 1362 he married his mistress, Margaret Logie, and when she too had no children tried without success to divorce her to marry his current mistress. He died suddenly at the age of forty-six, heirless to the last. This was an enormous misfortune for him which he never quite believed could be possible. He was probably unable to have children.

David's reign divides neatly into three parts. The first seven formative years from 1134–41 were spent in a sophisticated French castle. Eleven years of his youth from 1346–57 were spent in England absorbing English traditions and ways of government, while for the final fourteen years of his life he ruled Scotland.

In spite of the Treaty of Edinburgh and Northampton, the English people had never accepted the fact of Scottish independence, nor had Edward III supported the marriage of his sister to the youthful Scottish king. The promised return of the Stone of Scone, stolen by Edward I, and the relic of the true Cross looted from Holyrood, was rudely prevented by a London mob.

Like his grandfather, the 'Hammer of the Scots', Edward III supported the Balliol claim to Scotish kingship rather than the Bruce dynasty. When Edward Balliol's supporters defeated the Scots at the Battle of Dupplin Moor near Perth he attempted to rule for three months as King Edward of Scotland. But the Scots for the most part were loyal to David Bruce and drove the Balliol south. Edward III then intervened personally.

The Battle of Halidon Hill was fought near Berwick in 1333 and the Scots were routed in one of the greatest disasters in Scottish history. Six earls, seventy barons, five hundred knights and unnumbered spearmen were killed, while the English losses were estimated at merely fourteen men.

Hugh, fourth earl of Ross, led the reserve to attack the wing which Balliol himself commanded but was driven back and killed, as we have seen, in spite of wearing the miraculous shirt of St Duthac.

The young and vulnerable King David went into exile at Chateau Gaillard in France where he remained enjoying a life of feasting and jousting while his subjects continued to struggle on his behalf in the Second War of Independence.

THE STRUGGLE CONTINUES

Two teenagers, both of whom had fought bravely to resist the English, were appointed joint guardians of Scotland in 1334. One of these was Robert the Steward and the other John Randolph, the new third earl of Moray. They soon quarrelled however, as Robert, David's heir-presumptive, probably thought he should have been sole guardian. The following year Edward III invaded Scotland and Robert Steward was forced briefly to submit while John Randolph was taken prisoner. Both these men were to be husbands of our third Euphemia.

An old hero emerged in the figure of Andrew de Moravia, recently ransomed from imprisonment, who by using Robert the Bruce's tactics of guerrilla warfare rather than pitched battle regained most of David's kingdom. The French too supported Scotland and when in 1337 the Hundred Years War broke out between England and France, Edward could no longer concentrate to the same extent on Scotland. When Sir Andrew de Moravia died in 1338, Robert Steward again became guardian of Scotland. Gradually all the English-held strongholds except Berwick were recaptured.

In 1241 David returned to his kingdom aged seventeen, but only for five years. When the French asked the Scots to assist them by tying up English troops in the north, David's army was defeated at the Battle of Neville's Cross in 1346. John Randolph – by now married to the third Euphemia – was killed and David himself taken a prisoner.

Nevertheless the king had shown himself to be a brave warrior. In spite of an arrow stuck in his face, he knocked out two of his captor's teeth before his arrest. His nephew, Robert the Steward, was portrayed as having ridden off and abandoned him on the battle-field. This was probably one of the reasons why David was never happy to have him as his heir.

For the next eleven years, David was a prisoner in England, living a not uncomfortable life as brother-in-law to the king, while the Steward resumed his guardianship of Scotland. Edward III decided that the best way to win Scotland was firstly by forcing the Scots to buy back their king for a huge ransom, secondly by occupying the major Scottish castles, and thirdly by insisting on English over-lordship and the succession if David died without an heir.

The Scots decided however that their independence was more important than their king's freedom. After years of haggling, Edward reduced his terms and in 1357, David was released on the promise to pay 100,000 merks in ten instalments as ransom money and to provide twenty-three hostages to guarantee the sum was paid. Once free, David was able to stall Edward with spasmodic payments and hints of what might happen should he die without an heir. By 1368, it seemed that at least the 'auld inimie' could no longer bully Scotland into losing her independence.

Meanwhile David ruled ruthlessly and effectively, especially where the exchequer was concerned. In spite of the ravages of war, the expense of the ransom payments and the misery of the Black Death, he left Scotland financially better off than it had ever been. Nor was he afraid to punish those nobles who acted above themselves.

When he died his nephew, the fifty-four-year old Robert the Stew-ard, inherited the throne as Robert II. The widowed Euphemia Randolph was his queen.

PART THREE

◆

THE THIRD EUPHEMIA
Queen of Scots

A DINGWALL CHILDHOOD

Euphemia may have spent time at Delny but she was probably
brought up in Dingwall castle which tradition has placed among the
largest and most important strongholds north of Stirling.

Although no documentary evidence exists for this royal fortress
in the fourteenth century and the walls have long since gone, local
tradition maintains that by this time the buildings covered more than
an acre of ground, enclosing a courtyard, with four towers, one of
which to the north-east was the principal defence with a domed
underground dungeon. From the base of this tower a tunnel – which
is thought still to exist – provided a secret and safe means of escape
to the south. Outside the walls there was an acre of stableyard to
the west and a huge girnel where the grain rents were collected and
stored.

The family lived at the west side of the main block and it was
here that Euphemia and her siblings were raised with periods spent
not only at Delny but also possibly at Balcony castle in Evanton,
Lochslin in Easter Ross and Balloan at Tarbat Ness. Ross abounded
in small castles and tower-houses, many of them centres of baronies
owned by the earl and occupied by vassals, unless he chose to spend
time there himself. Part of the summer months may well have been
passed in his various hunting lodges.

Castles grew insanitary with continual occupation and time was
needed for them to be cleaned up and made habitable again. Water
was supplied by a well situated within the walls, while the only
drainage consisted of privvies or small closets situated at the corners
of the tower-houses with a chute to the outside world. The various
floors were reached by chilly spiral staircases built either within the
thickness of the wall or in an outside turret. Although windows were

still narrow slits, glazing had become more common in the upper storeys. Robert the Bruce had installed glass in his castle at Cardross near Dumbarton, and perhaps his sister wanted it in Dingwall. Flooring above the great hall would have been old Scots pine wood resting on beams.

Conditions within the castles had improved since the first Euphemia went to Delny and Duffus. Although the floors were still strewn with rushes and scented herbs, and tapestries still covered most of the walls, wooden panelling in oak and pine, often painted, had become fashionable. The Earl of Cromartie tells us that furniture now included 'large heavily draped beds, cushioned settles, carved or metal-bound chests and metal holders for rush lights, and wax or tallow candles, the former being reserved for special occasions, the hall and lady's bower'.

Writing a hundred years later, the Spaniard Pedro de Ayala, commented of the Scots that 'all the furniture that is used in Italy, Spain and France is to be found in their dwellings. It has not been bought in modern times only, but inherited from preceding ages.'

Euphemia's father, Hugh, fourth earl of Ross, married twice. His first wife was, as we have seen, Lady Maud Bruce, King Robert's sister, whom he married in 1308 and by whom he had three children, William his heir, Sir John de Ros, and Marjorie who became the second wife of Malise, earl of Strathearn, Caithness and Orkney.

Hugh's second wife was Margaret, daughter of Sir David de Graham of Old Montrose and his wife Muriel de Bisset, co-heiress of John Bisset of Lovat, at the head of Loch Ness. She brought him the Lovat estates where her forebear had founded Beauly priory. The Graham family must have been well known to the Ross earls. Patrick Graym of Kincardineshire had sworn fealty to Edward I, been present when King John Balliol paid him homage, was duly disgusted by Edward's arrogant behaviour and was killed at Dunbar in 1296. There he was described by the English as one of 'the wisest and noblest of the Scottish barons'. His successor Sir David de Graym became a loyal supporter of the Bruce who allowed him to exchange his lands in Dumbarton in the west for those of Montrose in the east. His youngest son David through his marriage became Lord of Lovat. He was Margaret's father.

Exactly when Hugh and Margaret were married is not known, but well before 1329 when a canonical impediment was discovered long after they had had children. A dispensation was granted by Pope John XXII to legitimate their four children, Hugh, Euphemia and her younger sisters Janet and Lilias.

Euphemia may have been born about 1322, the year her father inherited the earldom, and life must have been pleasant at Dingwall as long as Bruce remained on the throne. Possibly her education reflected her position. *Maitresses* or mistresses for girls were now common among noble families in fourteenth-century England. The Scots, never behind the times when it came to education, no doubt also saw to it that their daughters were taught well enough to head the households of the highest noblemen in the land. Euphemia would have been taught enough to manage estates, as her grandmother the second Euphemia had done, in the inevitable absence of her future lord.

Chaucer in *The Physician's Tale* offers some advice to these 'maitresses ... that lordes doghtres han in governaunce' He describes them as older women employed either because they have always been virtuous or for the opposite reason that, having 'knowen wel ynough the olde daunce', they were now reformed characters. Above all, their duty was to encourage virtue and in addition, according to Nicholas Orme, 'general teaching on dress, behaviour, singing and dancing, with technical help from clergy in religious topics, minstrels with music and grooms with horses.'

Music would have played an important part in her upbringing. Gerald de Barri, a chaplain to Henry II of England in the late twelfth century, wrote flatteringly of Scottish music. 'Their skill [Irish harpists] is beyond comparison above that of any nation I have ever seen, for theirs is not a slow and sullen kind of melody, like the instrumental music of the British to which we are accustomed, but swift and abrupt, yet sweet and cheerful in its sonority ... It is thought by many indeed that Scotland has not only reached the level of Ireland, but in science and skill of music has far surpassed it, so that men now seek that land as the true fountain-head of the art.'

Euphemia's life in the castle would have been a very public affair, surrounded at all times by her father's clansmen, retainers and servants. On the other hand her parents and nurses would have taken every precaution to protect her innocence and to supervise her time so that she had no chance of becoming intimate with young men before her marriage. Nicholas Orme writes that this exposure to company on the one hand and seclusion on the other 'formed a pair of contrasting principles in medieval education for girls'. Again in *The Physician's Tale* Chaucer describes with approval a noble girl who was so modest and retiring that she pretended to feel ill when invited to feasts and dances. In his opinion it was soon enough for a girl to learn boldness when she was married.

Above all Euphemia would have learned her Christian duties and the importance of hearing Masses for the salvation of the living and the redemption of the dead. As Abbot Bower wrote in *Scotichonicon*, 'hearing the Mass devoutly built up credit against the dangers of dying unconfessed, reduced the devil's power, temporarily suspended the ageing process, protected against sudden death or blindness, improved digestion and facilitated childbirth'. She would have known that a soul's suffering in purgatory was relieved by the priest's special intention when saying the Mass. She may even have had her own cherished Latin prayer-book.

Would she have learned to read? Enough perhaps to follow the Mass. But probably not French, English or Gaelic. Nor is it likely that she was taught to write, though she would have learned to sign her name. It was more important for women to speak and sew well. Besides there was no need for her to become literate. There were scribes to write letters, chaplains to read the Gospels and story-tellers to inform, entertain or terrify during the long dark winter nights. Even if she had the aptitude and desire to be literate, there was prejudice against learned women. Nicholas Orme quotes a French poem popular in fourteenth-century England which states, 'Do not chose a wife for her beauty or because she is lettered for such persons are often deceivers.'

Above all, Euphemia's thoughts would have centered on whom she would one day marry. That was, after all, to be her career, to bring honour to her father by being an obedient and chaste daughter and to enhance the power and prestige of her husband by becoming a dutiful and fruitful wife. No doubt she joined with her sisters and the other castle girls in the Hallowe'en games of divination, visited the local seer or wise woman, slept with charms beneath her pillow to discover her fate.

As if she had any choice.

The Third Euphemia

BETROTHAL

Euphemia was probably about seven when her step-uncle King Robert the Bruce died, and the troubled times returned. However life goes on and by now, with the late king's approval, her husband had probably already been chosen for her. He was John Randolph, second son of Sir Thomas Randolph, lord of Nithsdale in the south-west of Scotland and first earl of Moray, a gallant lad a little older than herself who had inherited his knightly qualities from a brave and brilliant father.

The origins of the Randolph family are uncertain but it is probable that they were descendants of Ralph fitz Dunegal, a lord of Upper Nithsdale in the mid-twelfth century who came to prominence when the lords of Galloway disappeared. Sir Thomas was a step-nephew of the Bruce and another close associate of the Ross earls. He too had had a chequered past, having been present at Robert's coronation in 1306 and, when captured by the English, served Edward I for a while in order to keep his lands. When he was subsequently captured and imprisoned by the Scots he berated the Bruce for his policy of guerilla warfare which he considered ungentlemanly.

But just as the Bruce had pardoned the earl of Ross, so too he forgave his kinsman Randolph and in 1312 gave him the earldom of Moray, a vast territory which marched with the earldom of Ross from the north-west in Glenelg as far east as the head of the Beauly Firth. This territory, held in exchange for the service of ten knights, made Randolph as powerful a nobleman as the earl of Ross himself, answerable only to the king.

Indeed when Robert I died, it was Earl Thomas who saw to it that the king's heart was solemnly buried in a lead casket in Melrose abbey and Thomas who, until he died in 1332, became Guardian of Scotland for the young King David II. A strong leader, on one occasion he is said to have decorated the curtain walls of Eilean Donan castle in Wester Ross with the heads of fifty victims as an act of warning and retribution.

He left four children. His eldest son, Thomas, his heir was killed at the Battle of Dupplin the year after his father's death. His second son John inherited the lordship of Nithsdale and the earldom of Moray in 1333 and his two daughters Agnes and Isobel both married distinguished men. John was chosen for Euphemia, thus uniting the two most important families in the north.

Betrothed but not yet married, Euphemia must have been eleven or twelve when her father was killed at the disastrous Battle of Halidon Hill in July 1333. Six of the Scottish earls (Ross, Lennox, Atholl, Carrick, Sutherland and Strathearn) died in the carnage, as did the boy King David's new guardian, Sir Archibald Douglas. As we have seen, the Scots were obliterated by the enemy archers, while the English losses were only fourteen men.

Fortunately, Euphemia's half-brother William, now fifth earl of Ross, was safely in Norway at the time, but the outcome of the battle must have been a devastating loss, not just to herself, her family and the clan, but also to the whole of Scotland. The hated English were back with their puppet ruler, Edward Balliol, 'the Winter King', temporarily on the throne.

Fortunately, too, the young earl of Moray, John Randolph, was not killed. In command of the first division of Scots warriors, he managed to escape from the battlefield to France but he returned later that same year to David II's court at the great rock fortress of Dumbarton. There it was decided that it was safer for the boy king to find protection in France and during his absence John should act as a joint Guardian of Scotland. He was only seventeen or eighteen years old at the most, but there was no one else suitable. The flower of Scottish chivalry had been destroyed on the battlefield. Euphemia must have been very proud of her dashing heroic fiancé as she prayed fervently and heard Masses for his safety. She may well have fallen in love with him, or at least with the idea she had of him.

His co-guardian was another seventeen-year-old lad, Robert, the son of Walter, sixth High Steward of Scotland and Marjorie Bruce. Thus he was the grandson of Robert I, uncle of the ten-year-old King David and heir-presumptive to the Scottish throne. The two young knights soon quarrelled. Robert, orphaned of his mother when he was born by Caesarian section when she died in childbirth after a riding accident, and of his father at the age of eleven, had been raised as heir to his grandfather for the first eight years of his life. He was now heir to his younger uncle. Tall and handsome, he is said to have been warm-hearted with charming manners and an eye for a pretty woman. No doubt he thought that he should have been sole guardian.

John of Fordun in his *Chronicle* describes him as a man 'who was then not governed by much wisdom'.

According to Dr Boardman, John Randolph was 'clearly the more dynamic of the two' in the struggle to rid the country of the Balliol and preserve the Bruce dynasty. On one occasion he and a friend had discovered the Winter King at Annan and forced him to flee in his shirt on an unsaddled horse with only one boot on his foot. How Euphemia must have enjoyed that story.

The quarrel came to a head at a parliament held in Dairsie near Cupar by Robert and John in 1335 over the ownership of some territory in the north. The joint guardianship was dissolved. Edward III invaded Scotland in support of the Balliol and got as far as Inverness, burning the towns of Elgin and Aberdeen and devastating the countryside.

A new guardian was appointed in the great Sir Andrew de Moravia of Avoch and Bothwell, third husband of the Bruce's sister Christina. He is remembered as 'strong, self-controlled, just, devout and merciful'. John was with his brother-in-law the earl of March and Dunbar when the count of Gallere (Guelders), an ally of Edward III, landed in Lothian on 30th July 1335. Together they attacked and drove him into Edinburgh where he made a stand on the Rock, killing his horses to create a protective fortress of their bodies.

The count was starved out and surrendered. John who according to Fordun 'was beyond measure courteous and soft-hearted towards his foes, feeling sure that he would thereby give pleasure to the king of France, from whom he had lately parted, let the aforesaid Count of Gellere and his men go back free and scathless, without ransom or any other burden, and restored the booty which had been taken from him . . . And, the better to show his good-will, he accompanied him in person to the marches; but he was over-taken unawares by the onslaught of the garrison of a castle, taken by those churls, and thrown into prison.'

Thereafter John had a wretched time. First he was taken to Bamburgh castle and from there, via York and Nottingham, to Windsor. In May 1336 he was removed to Winchester and the following September shipped from Southampton to the Tower in chains. Five years later in February 1341 he was liberated, and went to France, perhaps to recuperate. He returned to Scotland in 1343.

Meanwhile Euphemia remained in the comparative safety of Dingwall, fearful for John's safety and for the future of her country.

BLACK AGNES OF DUNBAR

Dunbar was once again the scene of siege and battle and in 1337 it was the seat of the earl of Dunbar and March who had married John Randolph's sister, Black Agnes, so called 'be ressone scho was black skynnit'. While March was away from home Dunbar was besieged by Sir William Montagu, earl of Salisbury and the earl of Arundel.

Dunbar castle, perched on a rocky cliff overlooking the North Sea not far from the mouth of the Firth of Forth, was strategically important as it provided a link between the south of Scotland and France where David II was living. No one was more aware of this than Agnes and no one more determined that it should not fall to the English.

The *Liber Pluscardensis* records the story.

For half a year they [the English] were there, assailing the castle with divers engines [mangonels], but they could do nothing against it. Nor was any other captain in command there but the countess of March, commonly called Black Agnes of Dunbar, who defended the besieged castle most laudably . . .

She herself, in mockery of the English, would in the sight of all dust with a fair cloth the place where a stone from their engines had struck the ramparts.

Edward III was so enraged by her bravado that he sent a strong force to assist Montagu but this was broken up by the Scots before reaching Dunbar.

After this the earl of Salisbury, who took very ill the severe defeats inflicted by the Scots lords on the English troops who were coming to his aid, and wishing to attack the said castle more powerfully, had constructed a certain engine called a Sow, and brought it up to the walls of Dunbar Castle. Which when Black Agnes saw, she said to the earl, 'Montagu, for all the power that thou may ere long time pass, I shall gar thy Sow farrow against her will.'

And with that she made a very large engine in the castle, flinging huge stones, which flying night and day from the walls, shattered the said Sow and almost all who were within it, broke the heads of many, and forced them altogether to give up the attack: and she captured and brought into the castle all their siege-gear with their engines and provisions.

Montagu however kept two Genoese galleys in the harbour which prevented Agnes from receiving necessary supplies by sea. Fortunately, a certain Sir Alexander de Ramsay ran the blockade one night and managed to bring back a supply of provisions from the fortress on the Bass Rock. Next morning Black Agnes mocked the hungry earl with a gift of 'fine white bread and noble wine'.

But the earl was not finished with the countess. He bribed a porter 'for a great sum of gold, to open to him, under cover of night, one of the secret posterns of the castle, so that he might enter with his men. With the consent of the countess, who feigned not to know of it, this was arranged, and one night (when the gold had been received) the said postern gate was opened, as had been promised.'

Montagu was about to enter when one of his followers suspecting a plot, dragged him back just in time, but 'found himself inside the door, which was closed at once by the falling of that sliding door which in French is called *portculisse*. So the earl escaped ... and Black Agnes standing on the wall, called out to him mockingly, "Adieu, adieu, Monsieur Montagu!" ... After all this news came from the king of England that the mortal war between him and the king of France had been revived ... so he withdrew without ceremony taking no leave of his hostess.' The seige had cost him £6,000.

According to Sir Walter Scott in *Tales of a Grandfather*, the minstrels took the story to their harps. He wrote: The following lines are nearly the sense of what is preserved:

> She kept a stir in tower and trench,
> That brawling boisterous Scottish wench;
> Came I early, came I late,
> I found Black Agnes at the gate.

COUNTESS OF MORAY

Meanwhile Scotland had entered a tragic phase in her history with famine and starvation stalking the countryside so much so that 'a certain Crystyne Klek practised cannibalism'. Nor would she have been the only one to do so. John of Fordun wrote that in 1337 central Scotland was for the most part reduced to a wilderness.

Robert Steward, still only twenty-two, became guardian again in the following year. He continued to clear Scotland of the enemy with the help of some unusual allies. One was a brilliant soldier of fortune, once a priest called William Bullock who in 1338, after serving Balliol, changed sides to support Robert and brought him Cupar in Fife and helped him capture Edinburgh castle. Another was a sea-captain called Currie who by trickery helped in the capture of Edinburgh castle and a third, a French knight called de Garancières who with an expeditionary force sent over by the French king (Philip VI) helped him take Perth. Stirling castle fell soon after. At long last the dreadful 1330s were over and Robert believed it safe enough to bring the young king home.

David, now seventeen, landed at Inverbervie on 2nd June 1341, a handsome youth more French than Scottish in language and outlook after spending eight of his formative years in the sophisticated French court. He stayed at Kildrummy castle with his aunt Christina Bruce where Robert officially handed him the reins of government. Among his appointments he confirmed Robert in his earldom of Atholl.

When John Randolph returned to Scotland in 1343 he made him justiciar of Annandale and Mar and one of the wardens of the Marches. It may have been at about this time that John and Euphemia, now just over twenty, were finally married. Where they lived it is impossible to say. It may have been in one of the Moray castles, of which Darnaway – some dozen miles from Duffus – was the most important and which Sir Thomas had probably built when Bruce created him earl.

Originally a royal manor and hunting lodge Darnaway was famous for its forests of oak trees which belonged to the king. The roof of Dornoch cathedral was constructed with Darnaway oaks in 1291 and Edward I during his second visit to Elgin in 1303 granted the parson of Duffus twenty oaks to repair his church.

Not surprising then that the great medieval hall with its carved hammer-beam roof is still known as Randolph's Hall. Although this was reconstructed nearly fifty years later in 1387 by a later earl of Moray (John Dunbar), it probably owed its name to the great Sir Thomas or possibly his son.

On the other hand, Euphemia may have spent more time in the island castle of Lochmaben in Dumfries-shire. This peel tower had been built by the English in 1298 and had changed hands several times before being taken back by the English in 1333. As warden of the Marches John may have driven the English out and occupied it himself during the few years that remained to him.

Or he may have had another fortress in Nithsdale which stood somewhere on the long and beautiful river Nith which rises in the most westerly of the southern uplands in east Ayrshire to empty itself into the Solway Firth near Dumfries. From such strongholds as these John would have been able to carry out his raids on the north of England on behalf of the king. No doubt Euphemia waited at home anxious for his safe return for these were dangerous days.

PUBLIC RIVALRY AND SECRET SORROW

Although the chronicler Andrew Wyntoun had high praise for Robert, Dr Boardman thinks it unlikely that there was much love lost between him and David II. Robert who had been brought up as we have seen to think of himself as heir to his grandfather had virtually ruled the kingdom during his younger uncle's absence and now had to hand back power to a Frenchified lad with a passion for jousting, dancing and gaming. David, too, must have been deeply resentful of his nephew's superior years, his experience, and the fact that he already had sons. The situation cannot have been easy for either of them.

John Randolph, on the other hand, had no such jealousies. Called by Stephen Boardman 'warlike and chivalric', he became a close companion and fellow warrior with the king in his border raids on the English. He obviously shared his young king's passion for 'the knichtly game'. There was still less love lost between Robert and John. The other nobles took sides between them. The violent Douglas of Liddesdale sided with Robert, while Sir Alexander de Ramsay, who had come to the aid of Black Agnes, sided with John. No doubt Euphemia heard her husband complain of the Steward and took sides as passionately as the others. David's obvious favouritism of John must have exacerbated the situation.

In addition the condition of the country could not have been much worse. Food was scarce, the greater towns still in ruins, murrain destroyed the cattle and the important wool trade was ruined. John of Fordun records that in 1344 fowl pest broke out in such epidemic proportions 'that men shrank from eating, or even looking upon, a cock or a hen, as though unclean and smitten with leprosy; and thus ... nearly the whole of that species was destroyed.'

Euphemia had her own private worries. She was not pregnant. Perhaps this forged another bond between John and David. Neither of them had produced an heir, or indeed any children as far as is known. David had, as we have seen, married the English Princess Joan who was thought to have been barren but as he already had fecund mistresses none of whom had given him a child the fault was probably his.

Robert meanwhile already had a thriving family by secular marriage to Elizabeth Mure of Rowallan in 1336. She was the daughter of Sir Adam Mure, a vassal of the Steward who lived only a few miles north of his castle of Dundonald in Ayrshire.

In order to conceive, Euphemia may have made a pilgrimage to one of the shrines specially dedicated to the relief of infertility. The Holy Pool at the foot of Dun Fhaolain (St Fillan's hill-fort) at the east end of Loch Earn, may have been too distant, but during a visit to their Moray property she might well have stopped at the *Clach-bhan* (wife stone) near the Linn of Avon between Braemar and Tomintoul with its phallic symbolism. Her prayers however remained unanswered.

Although it was recognised as early as the eleventh century by the Bolognese lawyer, Gratian, that the purpose of a good marriages 'is threefold: fidelity, offspring and sacrament', Euphemia may well have seen herself as barren and therefore a failure as a wife. Indeed John, too, may have seen her as such in his anxiety to father an heir. The earldom was entailed in the male line, and although John had two nephews through his sister Isabella's marriage who were later to claim the earldom, they were not Randolphs. Without an heir, the earldom would revert to the crown.

The church, too, would have taken an interest in this situation as in every other aspect of life. According to canon law a woman's virginity could be inspected by worthy matrons in the same way as the Virgin Mary was inspected by her midwife Salome, according to a medieval play based on one of the apocryphal Gospels.

It was recognised of course that men could be infertile as well as women. *The Practice According to Trota* included a diagnostic test of infertility which could be used for both sexes. In Thomas of Chobham's manual for parish priests he advised the physical examination of a man's genitals by 'wise matrons'. 'After food and drink the man and woman are to be placed together in one bed and wise women are to be summoned around the bed for many nights. And if the man's member is always found useless and as if dead, the couple are well able to be separated.' Enough to put any husband off, one would have thought.

According to Henrietta Leyser these cases were rare but some were recorded in detail both in York and Canterbury. It is unlikely that John and Euphemia would have gone so far in their desire to have a child. With John constantly away at court or skirmishing with David on the English border their time together was considerably less than the marriage's probable three year's duration. It was now nearing its end.

In 1346 Philip of France, whose forces had been defeated by Edward III that August at Crecy and who was now besieged at Calais, begged his ally David to cause a diversion in the north. At the head of a sizeable force, David and John together led an army across the Tweed and marched for Durham.

Thus Edward's warriors stationed in the north of England, instead of joining their king in his siege of Calais, were forced to confront the invader. Led by the archbishop of York and Queen Philippa herself, who is said to have addressed the forces before the fight, the two armies met near Durham at Neville's Cross in October.

David and John's choice of site 'in a full anoyous place where nane, but hurt, mycht lyfft his hand' was, according to Wyntoun, a tactical error. Once again the English archers found an easy target and the result was another disaster for the Scots. David fought bravely enough but was taken prisoner with a serious arrow wound in his face. He was forced to ride through the streets of London on a tall black charger on his way to the Tower. The earls of Fife,

Menteith, Sutherland and Wigtown were captured with him. Menteith was executed for treason, but Fife was spared as he was related to the king.

Robert and the earl of Dunbar and March (Black Agnes' husband), who together commanded the left wing, had the better site where, according to Andrew of Wyntoun, their forces had 'rowme to stand in fycht'. But Robert was blamed, perhaps unfairly, by the chroniclers for having taken his men 'hame to Scotland' and 'got away unhurt'.

Sadly, John was killed. The marriage was over and Euphemia left a widow, an extremely eligible widow, probably still under the age of twenty-five.

For the next eleven years and for the third time Robert once again became guardian of the kingdom.

THE WIDOW

In the late medieval period estates and titles were usually inherited by the owner's sons in order of seniority and failing these, as was often the case in those precarious times, by their daughters. If there was more than one daughter, the estate was shared between them making them co-heiresses and thus highly desirable as brides, for their titles and property went to their husbands. Increasingly however it became the practice for estates to be entailed in the male line which meant that more distant relatives could inherit, thus keeping the property within the same family or clan. If there were no heirs the title and estate reverted to the overlord or the crown, as happened in the case of Moray. There being no heirs, the earldom reverted to the crown and David II allowed Randolph's brother-in-law, the earl of March and Dunbar to use it.

However, as Randolph's widow, Euphemia had certain rights which amounted to keeping her own dower and to the life-rent of a terce or third of her husband's estate which she could dispose of as she pleased. Henrietta Leyser estimates that at least ten per cent of medieval English households were in charge of widows. In Scotland the percentage in the mid-fourteenth century must surely have been a good deal higher.

How was an aristocratic and wealthy widow regarded in those far off days? First of all with respect and charity, according to biblical decree. But also, like Chaucer's Wife of Bath, they might be seen as greedy for money and sex. Above all they were a desirable property for several reasons, their dower, their inheritance and their capacity to have children.

Euphemia's mother, Margaret Graham, widowed in 1333, remarried twice. She probably waited until her three daughters, Euphemia, Janet and Lilias, were settled before her remarriage in 1341 to John de Barclay of Kippo in Fife. Widowed again, perhaps at Neville's Cross, she was married for a third time in 1348 to John de Moravia. Her credentials were not only her dower but also the proof that she could conceive. Euphemia's sister Janet also married twice, Monymusk of that Ilk and secondly, with Euphemia's support, Sir Alexander Murray of Drumsergorth in 1375. Lilias married William Urquhart, heritable sheriff of Cromarty.

David II, desperate for an heir, had many lovers. One of them, Katherine Mortimer, was murdered on the road to Soutra in 1360. After the death of Queen Joan, who had spent most of her time in England anyhow, he married another of his mistresses. She was a widow called Margaret Drummond, Lady Logie, whom he chose probably because she had already had children. When Margaret had none by him he forced a divorce on her in 1369 in order to marry yet another of his lovers, none other than Agnes, a relative of Black Agnes of Dunbar, and sister of the current earl of Dunbar and March. Like Margaret before her, she also had produced children for her previous husband, and David who was only forty-seven still hoped to father a Bruce heir. A few days before giving her 1,000 merks for her trousseau, he died on 22nd February of the same year, before the marriage could take place.

So Euphemia was desirable from the point of view of her birth, wealth and connections, but not as a prospective mother. This was perhaps one of the reasons why she did not marry for eleven years after the death of John.

Where did she spend her widowhood? Possibly she stayed on in the family castle in Nithsdale or Lochmaben or perhaps moved to that great fortress of Ruthven or Lochindorb in Badenoch near Kingussie. This is thought to have been her widow's inheritance to which, as we have seen, she was entitled under Scots law. Equally, she may have made Darnaway in Moray her principal home.

Apart from the danger of living too near the English border and the devastation of the countryside by war, there was another excellent reason for her to live in the north. The dreaded punishment of plague.

THE BLACK DEATH

In common with the rest of Christendom she would have seen the terrible death toll that had swept through Europe as 'a sign of God's displeasure with sinful humanity, and to teach other survivors that order, meaning and redemption were still possible'. Perhaps too, when she heard travellers' tales of its devastating arrival in Weymouth in August 1348, and its rapid spread to London by November and on to East Anglia and the north in the following spring and summer, she saw this as righteous retribution on the people who had killed her husband. She would have heard of the Flagellants who, clothed in long cloaks, tall black hats, their backs naked and bleeding below their cowls, flogged themselves continually with three-tailed lashes in the belief that God would be so moved by their suffering that he would end the pestilence.

She would have been told terrifying stories from travelling merchants of the dreaded signs to look out for, buboes, blotches, boils and pustules all over the body. She would have shuddered at the tales of hundreds of daily deaths, of the countless unburied bodies with none to pray for their souls in purgatory. She might even have heard ghastly tales of the Tartar commanders who catapulted the corpses of plague victims into the Genoese city of Kaffa. When the survivors escaped by boat they took the plague with them.

She would not have known that *yersina pestis* is a bacterium that usually infects rats, mice, voles and even rabbits. When they die their infected fleas abandon their bodies for the nearest host. The most likely explanation for the bubonic Black Death of 1348 and subsequent human bubonic plagues is that the black or brown rat (*rattus rattus*) ubiquitous in Europe, was a ready victim to the spreading plague. The typical flea of that rodent ensured subsequent human infection. Once bitten by an infected flea the cells around the bite die thus creating a black blister. This was the first dreaded sign, the 'token' of the plague. The infection quickly spreads and the lymph modes swell to the size of an apple or an orange. Within four to six days the patient has a high temperature, headache and delirium.

Within ten days sixty per cent of those infected are dead. *Yersina pestis* could also be coughed or breathed on to those close by, turning their infection to pneumonic plague. Those that caught the disease this way nearly always died.

But Scotland was not to escape after all. In 1349 twenty-four canons from St Andrews cathedral died of the disease. John of Fordun recorded: 'In the year 1350, there was, in the kingdom of Scotland so great a pestilence and plague among men ... as had never been heard of by man, nor is found in books, for the enlightenment of those who come after. For to such a pitch did the plague wreck its cruel spite, that nearly a third of mankind were thereby made to pay the debt of nature ... Men shrank from it so much that through fear of contagion, sons, fleeing as from the face of leprosy or from an adder, durst not go and see their parents in the throes of death.'

Over the next hundred years there were to be seven further outbreaks in the country. In fact Scotland did not suffer as badly as England. Fleas, according to Dr Grant, need a warmer climate to thrive and were 'most dangerous in towns and concentrated settlements ... nevertheless the Scottish population must have fallen significantly.' If, as has been estimated, there were about a million Scots in the years before the plague and if over the successive outbreaks there was a loss of about a third or the population, it was not until 1500 that the country regained the million mark.

Hard times indeed, not only in Scotland but throughout Europe, so hard that it was some time before Scotland again became involved in war. Robert spent part of his time negotiating for the return of the king known to the English court as 'Monsieur David de Bruis qui se dit roy Descoce', and the rest of his time establishing the Stewart dynasty in Scotland.

ROBERT THE STEWARD

After David's capture at Neville's Cross one of the first things Robert saw fit to do was to legitimise his nine children born of his marriage to Elizabeth Mure. He was only twenty when he had married her in 1336 probably in a hurry because she was pregnant and he occupied with trying to drive out the English.

Both he and Elizabeth believed their marriage to be valid as did everyone else but, as in so many similar cases, it was discovered that they were related in the fourth degree, though the evidence for that does not exist today. It was also discovered that Elizabeth was related to a former mistress of Robert's, which neither of them might have known about at the time. It's possible too that their marriage may have been secular in the Celtic tradition and thus not recognised by the church.

Whatever the cause, his supplication to the pope for a retrospective dispensation was supported not just by David but also the king of France, the seven Scottish bishops and parliament. John, their eldest son, became his heir, and thus David's heir after Robert, or so it seemed.

Then David returned briefly from captivity in November 1351 having negotiated his own settlement in which he agreed that if he died childless, a son of Edward III would inherit. Outraged by such an idea, parliament led by Robert, rejected the proposal and David was forced by threat of war to return to captivity in England. There he remained until 1557 when the cripplingly expensive ransom Treaty of Berwick was finally agreed.

Meanwhile Robert continued to govern the kingdom. Elizabeth Mure died in 1353, possibly in childbirth. She must have been a year or so older than Euphemia. Even if she had married at the age of sixteen in 1336 she would have only have been about thirty-five at her death. But in those days that was considered elderly for a woman.

Some time afterwards in 1355 Robert proposed to Euphemia.

A POLITICAL MARRIAGE

This would seem on the surface at least to have been a political match from its inception. To understand why Robert chose Euphemia as his second wife we need to know what happened to Euphemia's half-sister, Marjorie. Sometime before 1334 she had married as his second wife the powerful Malise, eighth earl of Strathearn, Caithness and Orkney.

The first Malise was a Celt whose family name is a direct translation from the Gaelic *Maelisu*, and means 'tonsured servant of Jesus'. He fought for David I in the twelfth century and won for himself the earldom of Strathearn, second only in precedence to that of Fife.

The eighth Malise had also inherited the earldom of Caithness and Orkney through his great-grandmother in 1329 when the Angus earls of Caithness and Orkney had died out in the male line. But Malise was attainted for treason when found guilty of surrendering his earldom of Strathearn to Edward Balliol in 1333. He also resigned his Caithness earldom and retired with Marjorie safely to Orkney. His earldom there was held under the Norwegian crown.

However he granted William, earl of Ross, his brother-in-law, the choice of husband for Isabel, one of his five daughters, and declared her to be heiress of Caithness. William arranged her marriage to Sir Henry St Clair who became earl of Caithness and their son in due course also inherited Orkney.

After Malise was attainted David II had appointed Sir Maurice Moray to be earl of Strathearn but, as he had been killed without a son at Neville's Cross, the earldom had become vacant. With Robert as guardian of Scotland and owner of the adjacent earldom of Atholl he saw himself as the ideal candidate for the vacancy. Dr Boardman writes, 'The only significant opposition to Robert's position in the earldom after 1346 [Neville's Cross] was likely to come from William, earl of Ross.' He was, as we have seen Malise's brother-in-law and Malise no doubt wanted his earldom back. Dr Boardman sees a reconciliation of the conflicting interests of Robert and Earl William effected by the Steward's marriage to Euphemia.

It was a clever move. It also gave Robert the right to Euphemia's property as the widow of John Randolph which seems to have included the lordship of Badenoch. The fact that she had borne no children was no obstacle from his point of view. He already had three surviving sons and five daughters.

Had Euphemia a choice? Undoubtedly. Her brother was powerful enough to have prevented the match if that had been her wish – or indeed his. She must have known of Robert's weakness where women were concerned. Seemingly she was content to marry the man who had quarrelled with John, who had later escaped the battlefield where her husband had been killed.

It's possible that she may have fallen in love with him. Bower describes him in his younger days as 'beautiful beyond the sons of men, stalwart and tall, accessible to all, modest, liberal, cheerful and honest'. He is said to have had all the Stewart charm. He obviously enjoyed the company of women and they his. He kept a mistress,

Lady Murray of Tullibardine at his castle in Rothesay where he was staying when news reached him of David II's death. By her he had at least one son. There was also Mariota Cardeny, daughter of the lord of Cardeny and Foss in Perthshire and possibly the widow of a Donald Macnaughton, chief of the Macnaughtons of Argyll. Her son Donald's career in the church, influenced by Robert, brought him the deanery of Dunkeld. With eight illegitimate sons – the daughters are not mentioned – and eight children by Elizabeth Mure all to be provided for he was surely not looking for more.

Euphemia may well have been attracted to him. There was only one impediment. They were related in the third degree of affinity and the fourth of consanguinity. The affinity was that Robert and John shared common ancestors in the earl and countess of Carrick but the consanguinity has not yet been discovered. Pope Innocent VI granted them dispensation on 2nd May 1355.

After so many years of widowhood Euphemia must have grown used to managing her own affairs and making her own decisions. Apart from the anxieties of plague and the poverty of Scotland, her days would have passed not unpleasantly, attending Masses, providing charity for the poor, supporting the local clergy, ordering her own property and perhaps visiting her family in Dingwall.

Second marriages were not allowed the full nuptial blessing accorded to first weddings and were quieter affairs altogether. But from the Wardlaw Manuscript *History of Clan Fraser* (which is not always reliable) we learn that Euphemia was escorted south in some style to her marriage by her maternal uncle, the lord of Lovat at the request of the earl of Ross and for this privilege he was created lieutenant of the North.

Euphemia was probably taken to Robert's 'modest but impressive castle of Dundonald' in the heart of his own family territory in Ayrshire for a comparatively quiet and private celebration.

THE STEWARD'S WIFE

The Stewards traditionally claim descent from Kenneth Mac Alpin, the first king of Scots in the ninth century, but it is considered more likely that they were Bretons who first settled in Shropshire after the Norman Conquest. A younger son, Walter fitz Alan, was one of the many Anglo-Normans to seek a fortune under David I and was awarded not only vast estates in Renfrewshire but the office of high steward to the royal household, which title and office were made hereditary by Malcolm IV. Over six further generations the Stewards' territory had expanded to include most of the eastern shore of the Firth of Clyde in order to protect Scotland from seaward attacks from the lords of the Isles. The family reached a pinnacle of importance when Robert's father, Walter the Steward, married Robert Bruce's daughter and their son Robert became heir presumptive to the throne.

It is more than probable that Robert and Euphemia knew each other well, indeed that Euphemia had been an acquaintance if not a friend of his first wife Elizabeth Mure. As John's wife living in Lochmaben, they were not many miles from Dundonald and probably met on social occasions. Dr Ross suggests that Euphemia, having no babies of her own, took a keen interest in Elizabeth's children but of this there is no proof. It is certainly true however that with the marriage she inherited a lively bunch of step-children, most of them teenagers and some very young. This may have been part of Robert's attraction for her, perhaps one of the cards he played to win her – his large motherless family in need of a woman's love. Aged between thirty and thirty-five she may have felt her barren state as a reproach. With Robert's little girls in her care she could fulfil her maternal role.

Almost immediately she became pregnant herself. One can only imagine her joy. She was to have four children, two sons and two daughters to add to Robert's brood, all of whom were to be raised in the Steward strongholds of Dundonald, Rothesay and Renfrew.

Peter Yeoman tells us that 'Dundonald stands today as a marvellous example of a late fourteenth century tower house, built by Robert II.' The tower-house was not built until after Robert was crowned. The original concentric castle erected on a hilltop which Euphemia would have first known was far older, thought to have been constructed between 1240 and 1280 by Alexander the Steward. During a pilgrimage to Santiago de Compostela he had visited the Norman stronghold of Couch-le-Chateau and copied its design.

Castles had their moral symbolism as well as a defensive purpose, as Ailred of Rievaulx explained in a sermon preached in the twelfth century. 'In a castle there are three things that are strong, the ditch, the wall and the keep . . . what is a ditch except deep ground which is humility. The spiritual wall is chastity . . . and we build the keep of charity.'

In Robert's time a pair of D-shaped towers formed the eastern entrance, while an identical pair provided the western defences behind which was built (probably) a chapel. Four lesser towers, which may not have ever been completed, linked the walls to the north and south, while there were two great gatehouses facing east and west. Rothesay castle on Bute was probably built by Alan le Steward who conquered that island in the late twelfth century. A defensive circular site with four towers it was virtually impregnable. Of Renfrew castle sadly nothing at all survives.

In these castles Euphemia and her ladies, nurses for her children and possibly some laundresses were the only women out of as many as a hundred and fifty males. These were knights, squires and other fighting men, senior officials, of whom the two stewards were the most important, the one managing the estate and the other the household. Under them a legion of lesser servants were responsible for the day-to-day running of such a large community. The castle functioned like a miniature township with its estate office, law court, church and prison, barracks and family home. There were cooks, pantrymen, brewers, poulterers, chandlers, tailors, barber-surgeons who took out teeth and shaved the knights. There were also grooms, blacksmiths, carters, and messengers. Within one of the towers, the *donjon* as it was called, the most secure place within the castle, Euphemia and her women would have lived.

Inside the walls too she might have had a garden for flowers and relaxation, perhaps close to a kitchen garden which supplied herbs and vegetables for the table.

EUPHEMIA'S GARDEN

Although next to nothing is known of Scottish horticulture in the fourteenth century there is evidence that Robert I, during the later years of his life, appreciated his garden at his castle of Tarbert in Kintyre. However more than enough documentation survives in English and European art and literature, in monastic records and encyclopaedias to show that gardens were cultivated and enjoyed throughout the Middle Ages.

Albertus Magnus, for example, was a Dominican monk of German origin who was writing about vegetables and plants in 1260 and Bartholomew the Englishman was a Franciscan whose encyclopaedia, compiled about 1240, contained a description of the three types of garden most commonly cultivated. It was widely read.

First there was the herber. This was a small enclosed garden, square in shape with four borders arranged around a lawn, with minor variations on the same pattern, the sort of garden which appears in so many medieval illustrations. Herbers were essentially small so that they could be incorporated within the castle walls and they were usually placed under the windows of the main bed-chamber.

According to Albertus Magnus, 'Care must be taken that the lawn is of such a size that about it in a square may be planted every sweet-smelling herb such as rue and sage and basil and likewise all sorts of flowers, violet, columbine, lily, rose, iris and the like.'

He suggested 'turf benches' be grown between the lawn and the beds with trees or vines to provide agreeable shade. These trees should have perfumed flowers but should not be planted on the middle of the lawn otherwise spiders' webs might 'entangle the face of passers by'. There should also be a fountain of water in a stone basin in the centre. 'It is delight rather than fruit that is looked for in a pleasure garden.'

If Euphemia had a herber at Dundonald she would almost certainly have had a kitchen or utilitarian garden for 'food and medicinal plants as well as plants for strewing on the floors . . . quelling insects and other household purposes'. Colewort a form of kale, would have predominated, with leeks and parsley, garlic, chives and onions, peas and beans. Salad plants would have included borage, mints, hearts-ease and chickweed, French cress, red dead nettles, primrose buds, violets, dandelions and daisies. Plants used for soups and pottage included marigold, mallow, lupin and sage. Drinks were made from infusions of rosemary, camomile and horehound, while fennel, mints, wormwood and mugwort were strewn on the floors.

As Sylvia Landsberg writes in *The Medieval Garden* 'in a holistic way gardens of the wealthy were understood to aid health.' It was believed that as we live predominantly on plants, diseases could be treated with their derivatives.

The old Greek teaching prevalent in the Middle Ages was based on the union of the four elements, earth, air, fire and water and the harmony of their attributes, coldness, dryness, heat and wetness. These were represented by the corresponding emotions of joy, anger, fear and distress. Illness resulted from an imbalance of these 'humours'. Thus the over-sanguine temperament – air – was the result of too much blood. The choleric nature – fire – produced too much yellow bile, while the melancholic – earth – produced black bile, and the phlegmatic – water – too much phlegm. The medicinal gardens grew plants that helped restore the balance of these humours. For example, Euphemia would have known that catmint, parsley, lovage, wild thyme and fennel were all hot and dry and therefore able to counteract symptoms of cold and phlegm.

In those days of recurring plague she would also have believed that various aromatic plants helped to protect against infection, such as roses, violets, mint and the like. She would have carried them about with her and perhaps had her women fill 'pots and pails and tubs' to decorate, scent and protect the great hall and her bed-chamber.

There would also have been a corner in her garden for narcotics such as mandrake, hemlock and poppies. Plants for making plasters like groundsel, chickweed, and mugwort to help heal infected wounds would be regularly ingathered, while poultices that soothed bruises were made of hot cabbage or leek overlaid with sheeps' wool.

It was essential for aristocratic women like Euphemia who headed large households to know which plants were efficacious and how to prepare them. There were always strangers at the gates, some sick and sore and in need of medical care, or chesty bairns within and without the walls. Just as the monasteries provided care for the ailing, so too did the great castles. Caring for the sick was seen as a godly act of charity and Euphemia would have organised such care with kindliness as part of her daily routine.

The third garden that Euphemia would certainly have had was an orchard planted outwith the castle walls and protected by wattle or wickerwork fences or hedges of hawthorn, sweet brier, hazel and willow. Apple, pear and cherry trees predominated and there would most certainly have been bee-hives, not only to provide honey – the only cheap sweetener available at that time – but also the all-important wax for the best candles.

Fish ponds, rabbit warrens, a park for falconry, perhaps a 'flowery mead' where wild flowers like meadow sweet thrived and could be harvested for strewing on the floor, or for medicinal purposes, were all part of the policies. Doocots, too, or *columbaria* were common in most important households. These dark towers could house up to a thousand birds and were a useful supplement to the medieval diet. Sylvia Landsberg has compared doocots to the battery-henhouses of today. Although destructive to crops, their droppings were considered 'top of the list as garden manure'. They were also kept for aesthetic reasons, for doves are beautiful to the eye, restful on the ears and symbolic not only of the Holy Spirit and the great Celtic saint, Columba, but also of love and peace in marriage.

THE NEW FAMILY

If the accounts are accurate Robert had thirteen legitimate and at least eight illegitimate children. Their upbringing and establishment in life was already one of his and now one of Euphemia's major concerns. There was also David's ransom to negotiate.

The Treaty of Berwick arranging for the payment in instalments of 100,000 merks and the delivery of twenty noble hostages was all but completed when the French once again asked Robert for military help, which unwisely he provided. Another disastrous defeat led to the destruction of Lothian by Edward III. When the French were also defeated by the English, Robert was forced to renegotiate and on 7th October 1357 David finally returned to Scone. In addition to the twenty noble hostages, three supplementary hostages were to be held in reserve among the leading noblemen of Scotland. Robert was named as one of them.

David ratified most of Robert's property gains made during his guardianship but theirs was always an uneasy relationship. On one occasion it led to open rebellion by Robert and his sons, and in 1368 and 1369 to Robert's imprisonment in Loch Leven castle, leaving Euphemia virtually in charge of his castles and his younger children.

Much of Robert's time both before and after David's return was spent in arranging politically advantageous marriages – medieval networking as it has been called – for his children, the better to establish the Steward influence in the country should the unthinkable happen and England claim the throne. It is interesting to note exactly how Robert with, no doubt, Euphemia's advice and support used his children to lay the foundation of the Steward dynasty and with it the future of the Scottish peerage.

His eldest son John married Annabella Drummond, King David's niece by his second wife. As heir to the throne after Robert, he was granted the earldom of Carrick as a personal gift from the king. This was the Bruce ancestral title and indicated perhaps that David recognised him as his heir. (Eventually he was to become king, taking the name of Robert III. John, having been the Balliol's name, was considered unlucky.) Robert's second son Walter before his early death married Isobel, countess of Fife in her own right, and thus became first of the Scottish earls.

His third son, Robert – much the most able and intellectual of all his children – married firstly Margaret Graham, countess and heiress to the earldom of Menteith, and secondly Muriel Keith, daughter of the marischal of Scotland. An immensely powerful and controlling figure, Robert Steward claimed the earldom of Fife in 1371 on his brother Walter's death and was later, in 1398, created duke of Albany. (As guardian of Scotland he was virtually to rule the kingdom for his elderly, and same say senile, father and thereafter his ailing older brother.)

Robert's fourth son, Alexander, as earl of Buchan became infamous as the Wolf of Badenoch. He was to marry our fourth Euphemia, countess of Ross in her own right. Her story forms the following chapter. David, Euphemia and Robert's eldest son, was given his father's title of earl of Strathearn when he was very young, while Walter, Euphemia's second son, married the heiress of Brechin and much later received his father's earldom of Atholl.

Among the girls, Margaret, Robert's eldest daughter by his first wife, Elizabeth Mure, married the powerful and ever-menacing John MacDonald, lord of the Isles. Marjorie married a Dunbar, brother of the earl, who was given the earldom of Moray which had been vacant since Randolph's death. Elizabeth married Thomas Hay, hereditary constable of Scotland. Isabella married twice, firstly James, the heir of the earl of Douglas, who on Robert's accession was unsuccessfully to claim kingship for himself through the Balliol line, and secondly John Edmonstone. Jean married three times, first to John Keith, heir of the marischal, and secondly to Sir John Lyon, ancestor of the earls of Strathmore and thus of our present Queen Elizabeth the Queen Mother, and thirdly James Sandilands of Calder.

Euphemia's eldest daughter, the beautiful Egidia who, it was said, could have been queen of France, chose instead to marry for love, the handsome and illegitimate Sir William Douglas of Nithsdale. Her younger daughter Jean married the first earl of Crawford.

Robert's illegitimate children, too, were all well catered for. John, for example, a son of Lady Moran, was made sheriff of Bute and became ancestor of the present marquises.

Thus the earldoms of Atholl, Carrick, Fife, Menteith, Ross and Strathearn were all to come into Steward hands, while the earldoms of March, Moray, Douglas, Crawford, the lordship of the Isles, with the offices of hereditary constable and marischal, were all closely tied to the same dynasty. Robert's single-minded pursuit of suitable partners for his children was perhaps due to the face that it was becoming increasingly unlikely that David would father an heir. Robert was determined that the throne should not go to England, or indeed to anyone else – there was to be a Douglas claimant – but to his eldest son. I don't suppose he thought for a moment that he himself would outlive the younger king. But in this case the unthinkable happened. On 22nd February 1371 David died in Edinburgh castle and a month later Robert was crowned king on 27th March 1371.

Meanwhile what of his queen?

THE QUEEN'S COURT

For some reason Euphemia was not crowned with Robert. Her own ceremony took place at Scone some months later. She was about forty-eight years old and Robert ageing at fifty-five. His energy and good looks were fast deteriorating and he was beginning to suffer from a serious eye complaint which, as he grew older, was to turn his 'red bleared eyes' to 'the colour of sandalwood'. Folklore blamed this condition on an accident during his birth by Caesarian section. Agnes Mure Mackenzie suggests that his ugly and painful eye disease may well have influenced his effectiveness as a ruler who needed all his wits and faculties in peak condition to control his children and his unruly nobles.

As queen, Euphemia would have moved from Dundonald with the court to Edinburgh castle, which by now was the main royal residence, much improved under the reign of David II. We know that Robert moved from castle to castle around the country and into the Highlands as part of his job, but how often she went with him, if at all, is not recorded. One of her most important occupations would have been to encourage and patronise the arts. Henrietta Leyser writes that 'aristocratic women were expected and encouraged to be connoisseurs and patrons of the arts' and who more able to reward artists, poets and musicians that the queen herself?

Although the golden age of Scottish literature was not to reach its full flowering for another hundred years with poet-priests like William Dunbar, Gavin Douglas and Henryson of Dunfermline, yet there had always been a strong bardic tradition which was fostered at court.

One writer whom Euphemia would certainly have known and patronised was John Barbour, archdeacon of Aberdeen, and author not only of the first masterpiece of Scottish literature but also of one of the finest. Barbour may have been born in Steward country about 1325. He was certainly a Steward man. He held the post of precentor of Dunkeld cathedral and was rapidly promoted to Aberdeen in 1356 as a piece of Steward patronage. During David's reign he left Scotland, perhaps strategically, spent time in France and may have studied at a French university before his return after David's death in 1371.

About a year later he began to write his great epic poem *The Bruce* for the new king, his royal patron, Robert II. A. A. M. Duncan, who has edited and translated the poem from Old Scots into accessible English, believes that the work which is very long cannot have taken less than two years to write 'and would not be surprised if it took five or six'. During the writing Barbour is thought to have spent most of his time at court, earning a salary of £40 a year working in the exchequer. After his return to the archdeaconry of Aberdeen he was granted a pension of a pound a year from the city's burgh payment to the crown 'for the compilation of the book of the deeds of the late Robert the Bruce'.

Duncan has called the work 'unique' as it was written in verse, Old Scots as opposed to Latin, and as 'a romance-biography not a chronicle'. He must have spent a good deal of time in research, questioning nobility and commoners alike and studying the myths and oral tradition of the day. It is more than likely that he consulted Euphemia. It was her grandfather, after all, who violated the sanctuary of Tain and arrested Bruce's womenfolk and that story is included. She may also have been responsible for the tale of her uncle Walter's great affection for Edward Bruce and the reason for it. Although women are barely mentioned in the poem, one of these is Isabella, Euphemia's aunt, whom Edward loved and the other, Isabel his unloved wife. This episode has the feel of a woman's sensibility about it and it is just possible that Euphemia was Barbour's source.

Patronage then would have played an important part in her life. People looked to the queen, as to the king, to influence their lives and no doubt she had her favourites. Courtly fashion was also important. We have no idea what Euphemia looked like. The formal illustration of her in her coronation gown embroidered with the three lions of the coat of arms of earls of Ross is taken from the sixteenth-century Seton Armorial and is not contemporary. She is given yellow hair, but this is undoubtedly artistic invention. However, much more is known of court fashion and women's dress in the fourteenth century than in previous ages.

Wool was still the basic material for clothing but after the fall of Byzantium in 1261, Spanish and Italian brocaded silks and velvet in rich colours dyed with cochineal became easier to obtain, though the price was high. The least expensive fabric produced by the Italian weavers was taffeta, called *sandal* or *cendal*, which was often used to line silk or woollen garments.

High quality linen, woven mainly by women, was used for underwear, shirts for men and long shifts for women. Babies were swaddled in wool that was lined with linen bands. According to J. Piponnier and P. Mane, 'rich infants wore very white linen, bound with red braid as recommended by medical treatises', while poor babies had to make do with greyish swaddling clothes made from hemp. Linen was also used for head-dresses for men and women in the form of close-fitting coifs or cauls. Women also wore linen veils, 'draped and decorated according to local fashion'.

Fur, too, was popular. At an earlier time in court circles fur was considered uncivilised as it was worn by savages. But used as a lining for a woollen cloak, visible only at the edges of the hem, wrist or neck, it was both fetching and fashionable. Beaver, fox, squirrel (miniver), marten and sable were all available but in Euphemia's time white or grey was the most exclusive. Bright colours, yellows, purples, blue-green (called perse) and azure were favourite colours, with scarlet at the height of fashion in Euphemia's time. Cloth of gold which interwove metallic threads with black was also a sign of affluence, while materials were heavily ornamented with metallic figures stitched to the fabric.

Because the church would have prohibited any emphasis on the female silhouette, extremes of fashions were confined to the head-dresses and sleeves. These latter hung so low in the twelfth century that they had to be knotted together to prevent them trailing on the floor. By the fourteenth century they were still full but a generation later they had become close-fitting to the wrist.

Long floating veils and wimples were still worn but could be replaced by a 'simple circlet made of jewels, ribbons or flowers, worn over plaited hair dressed to frame the face'. The *bourrelet*, originally a padded roll intended to protect the heads of children, had come into fashion for women. These were added to women's head-dresses and sometimes were developed vertically or spherically, or were occasionally split into two horns, a fashion deeply disapproved of by the church for obvious reasons.

For outdoor wear Euphemia would have worn the *houppelande*, 'a type of greatcoat with voluminous sleeves . . . always [for women] full-length and closed down the front; it sometimes had a train behind.' Sometimes it also a hood. *Houppelandes* were often decorated with small jewels or spangles hanging from rings. Her second-hand clothes or bales of cloth and rich accessories were considered suitable as gifts to godchildren and relatives, to serving women and other domestics who had pleased her.

Clothes, then as today, were seen as suitable objects for charity, for the church taught literally that it was an obligation 'to clothe the naked'. Euphemia's chaplain would have supervised the distribution of such gifts which would have gone firstly to cathedrals and local churches, secondly to the pilgrimage shrines and chapels and thirdly to the poor and needy. On Maundy Thursday it was the custom for twelve paupers, representing the Apostles to receive a suit of clothing.

Although no record remains of her will, one made by Sir James Douglas of Dalkeith written in French who died in 1392 (five years after Euphemia's death) gives an idea of the sorts of possessions she, as Robert's queen and widow of the earl of Moray, might have owned.

Her clothes would certainly have been not less grand than his 'garments both of cloth of gold and silk and other furred garments', or her jewelry less oppulent than his 'best ring with the sapphire which belonged to my lady mother and which she gave and granted me with her blessing'. He also had 'a gold ring set with a ruby endlong and on which is written "*Virtue ne puz avoir conterpois*"' and another 'gold ring with an emerald, and the posy round about beginning "*Remembraunce*"'. She would probably have possessed, at least one 'ouch [brooch] with a ruby in the midst' and at least 'ten buttons of gold and all the pearls I have, both set and unset, and one cross of the cross on which Jesus hung, and one relic of the hair of blessed Mary Magdalen and a golden circlet and one large *contreselat* of gold'. There was also a 'sapphire which purges the blood and has a case of gold'.

Perhaps too she owned valuable plate such as Sir James describes, as a 'gilt drinking cup' and 'twelve silver dishes, weighing twenty-one pounds eighteen shillings, and one silver charger weighing four pounds two shillings and twelve silver spoons weighing forty-eight shillings'. She might have possessed furniture like Sir James' 'best embroidered bed and the red bed with fetterlocks'.

Much of Euphemia's time, then, was occupied in adorning herself suitably for her role as queen, performing her Christian duties, hearing petitions, patronising the arts, practising charity, acting as necessary mediator between her quarrelsome step-children, raising her own daughters, supporting her sisters and their families, and the formal entertainment of courtiers, ambassadors, clerics and foreign knights from all parts of Europe. A busy life indeed.

But what was Euphemia's Scotland like?

THE QUEEN'S REALM

Scotland was virtually at peace with England during Robert's reign. The fourteen-year truce made between David II and Edward III which committed the Scots to paying 4,000 merks a year as part of David's ransom held. With the exception of one short but destructive invasion by the English king Richard II in 1385, conflict consisted mainly of some sea fights and border skirmishes, such as the moonlit battle between the Douglases and the Percys at Otterburn in 1388. The Scots however renewed the Franco-Scottish 'auld alliance'. Robert needed a powerful ally in case the English intervened.

John of Fordun describes the country as:

> strong and difficult and laborious to travel . . . To a man on horse-back the hills are impassable, save here and there: even on foot they are very hard to cross, for the snows lie there always, save only in the summer.

We know that throughout fourteenth-century Europe the climate had deteriorated and here is evidence that it was a colder country then than it is today.

Fordun continues:

> About the roots of the mountains the woods are huge, full of stags and roe-deer and other woodland beasts of many kinds. Often they give shelter to the cattle of the folk who live there, for they say that in these parts the beasts are used when they hear the shouts of men and women to flock hastily to the cover of the woods as if they were suddenly set on by dogs.

No doubt the poor beasts had learned by experience when to escape from local reivers and English invaders.

> The land of the sea-board plain is fairly level and fertile with green pasture and rich corn-land, fit for beans, pease and all other crops. There is no wine or oil, but there is much wax and honey. In the Highlands however the fields are poorer, save for oats and barley. There the country has ugly stretches of moor and bog. Yet it is full of pasturage for cattle: by the running waters the glens are bonny with grass. This country is rich in horses and wool-bearing sheep, abounding in milk and wool, and with manifold wealth of fish in sea, river and loch . . . It is namely above all for many kinds of birds. Noble falcons there are, of towering flight and splendid spirit, and hawks of the highest courage.

Though French was still spoken in court circles, Gaelic had by now been overtaken by English, heavily shot through with French words. Fordun explains that while Gaelic was still spoken in the Highlands and Islands, Teutonic or English was the language of the coast and the Lowlands.

As for the people themselves:

The coastal folk are homely and civilised, trusty, patient, mannerly, seemly in attire, courteous and peaceful, devout in worship but ready to resist a wrong from their enemies. Those of the Highlands and Isles are wild and untamed, given to reiving, loving their leisure, gentle and warm-hearted, comely in person but not so in their clothing, hostile and fierce to the English people and language and – because of their different speech – even to their Lowland fellow-countrymen. Yet are they true and obedient to King and country and easily made law-abiding if rightly governed.

Canon Froissart, a Frenchman from Valenciennes who visited Scotland during David's and Robert's reigns, left a foreigner's point of view.

In my younger days, I had been in Scotland as far as the Highlands [*la sauvage Ecosse*] and as at that time I was at the court of King David, I was acquainted with the greater part of the nobility of that country.

As Froissart travelled about on horseback accompanied by a greyhound, with his luggage strapped on behind him, he found the Scots to be 'bold, hardy and much inured to war ... The knights and esquires are well mounted on large bay horses, the common people on little galloways.' They carried no provisions 'for their habits of sobriety are such, in time of war, that they will live for a long time on flesh half sodden, without bread, and drink the river water without wine.' They enjoyed then (as they still do) porridge and oatcakes.

Under the flaps of his saddle each man carries a broad plate of metal; behind the saddle, a little bag of oatmeal: when they have eaten too much of the sodden flesh, and their stomach appears weak and empty, they place this plate over the fire, mix with water

[163]

their oatmeal, and when the plate is heated, they put a little of the paste upon it, and make a thin cake, like a cracknel or biscuit, which they eat to warm their stomachs: it is therefore no wonder, that they perform a longer day's march than other soldiers.

In Robert's reign (1385) Froissart records that the French army visited Scotland in force – 'five hundred to a thousand knights' – and did not enjoy the experience. There was not enough room for them to stay in Edinburgh, 'for there are not in the whole town four thousand houses', so they had to be billeted in neighbouring villages as far away as Kelso and Dunbar.
There was never enough to eat.

They had but little wine, beer, barley, bread or oats: their horses, therefore, perished from hunger, or were ruined through fatigue; and when they wished to dispose of them they could not find a purchaser who would give them a groat either for their horses or housings. [They complained bitterly that] they could no longer endure such difficulties, for Scotland was not a country to encamp in during the winter; and if they were to remain the ensuing summer, they would soon die of poverty.

They found their accommodation uncomfortable. The French knights 'had been used to handsome hotels, ornamented apartments and castles with good soft beds to repose on'. They complained that there was 'neither iron to shoe horses, not leather to make harness, saddles or bridles: all these things come ready made from Flanders by sea; and should these fail, there is none to be had in the country.'
They thought themselves hard done by for:

whenever they wanted to buy horses they were asked, for what was worth only ten florins, sixty and a hundred ... when the horse had been bought there was no furniture nor any housings to be met with ... [and worse]. Whenever their servants went out to forage, they were indeed permitted to load their horse with as much as they could pack up and carry [but they were invariably robbed] and sometimes slain, insomuch as no varlet dared go out foraging for fear of death.

Nor were they welcome in Scotland.

Some [Scots] began to murmur and say 'What devil has brought them here? or who has sent for them? Cannot we carry on our war with England without their assistance? ... Let them be told to return again for we are sufficiently numerous in Scotland to fight our own quarrels, and do not want their company ... They will very soon eat up and destroy all we have in this country, and will do us more harm, if we allow them to remain amongst us, than the English could in battle.'

The Scots farmers complained that the French had done them more mischief than the English 'by riding through their corn, oats and barley on their march, which they trod under foot, not condescending to follow the roads, for which damages they would have a rec-ompense before they left Scotland'. The landowners complained of the amount of trees cut down and 'of the waste they had committed to lodge themselves'.

So much for the Auld Alliance! But of course, as John Major wrote in his *History of Greater Britain* (1521), the French complained of exactly the same behaviour by the Scots who served in France.

A GLIMPSE INTO THE FUTURE

As Robert grew older his grip on government loosened, his control on rival dynasties such as the Macdonalds of the Isles and the Doug-lases in the Borders weakened. By 1384 he had been ousted from most of his functions as king by his son, the earl of Carrick, and the final years of his marriage and his reign were spent in his beloved Dundonald. During those later years, the failing and half-blind Robert, together with her children and grandchildren, would have been the queen's main concern.

Euphemia died in 1387, three years before her husband. She was probably buried at Scone, the traditional place of burial for the Scottish kings where Robert was later to rest. It was the custom for the body to be wrapped in a winding sheet somewhat similar to an infant's swaddling clothes according to the church's belief that the body as receptacle of the soul should be treated with respect but returned to the earth naked. Bishops and kings however who were buried in cathedrals or abbeys were usually dressed in their robes of office. Euphemia may have worn her coronation dress.

During the service the coffin would be covered with a pall, perhaps made of silk or cloth of gold marked with a great cross in a contrasting colour, though by the second half of the fourteenth century palls had become black. The habit of wearing black for mourning, rather than bright clothing, came from Spain and had reached England by the beginning of the fourteenth century.

But death is merciful. It is as well that she did not live to see what befell the descendants of her sons.

Her eldest, David, earl of Strathearn and later of Caithness married a Lindsay. He had one child a precious daughter whom he called after his mother. Queen Euphemia may have seen a great deal of this grand-daughter and namesake and grown to love her dearly. On David's untimely death in his early thirties sometime between 1385 and 1390, Euphemia Steward, aged fifteen or sixteen, became countess of Strathearn and Caithness in her own right. She married Sir Patrick Graham of Dundaff and had two children, another Euphemia and Malise who inherited the earldom. She also had a devious and greedy brother-in-law, Sir Robert Graham.

Euphemia's second son, Walter, who became earl of Caithness and Atholl must have been much younger for he did not marry Margaret of Brechin until 1378. They had two sons whom Euphemia would have known as youngsters. Sir Robert Graham, that man of black grudges and devious disposition, managed to persuade Walter Stewart that Robert II's first marriage to Elizabeth Mure was illegal and that Euphemia's sons were the true heirs to the crown. David, her eldest son, being dead, Walter therefore should have inherited the kingdom rather than Robert III and his heir.

The two conspirators and their accomplices attacked the new king, James I in the Blackfriars priory at Perth where he was spending Christmas. They wounded the queen and the women who were with her and dragged James out of the drain where he was hiding and murdered him. The conspirators were immediately seized. After three days of torture Walter – by now an old man – was crowned with a burning band of red-hot iron on which were inscribed the words, 'The King of Traitors'. His grandson, another conspirator, was executed a few days before him in Edinburgh in 1437.

An equally tragic fate befell Queen Euphemia's great-grandchildren. Euphemia Graham, sister of Malise, married Archibald, fifth earl of Douglas and guardian of the young King James II. When he died in 1439 their brash young son William, still in his teens, inherited the earldom. On 24th November 1440, William and his brother were dining with the ten-year-old king in Edinburgh castle when the head of a black bull was placed on the table. This was a token of death. Although the boy king pleaded hotly for their lives, Sir William Crichton, the ambitious keeper of the castle, had them seized and executed to break the power of the Douglas family.

But all that was for the future. Queen Euphemia's life was comparatively long for those days, as she must have been about sixty-five when she died.

Meanwhile there was another Euphemia Ross living in the north, the queen's niece by blood and soon to be her step daughter-in-law by marriage. Her life concerns us now.

SOURCES

p 131 A detailed description of the history, records and topography of Dingwall may be found in *The Romance of a Royal Burgh, Dingwall's Story of a Thousand Years* by N. Macrae (1923).

p 133 Gerald de Barri (c.1146–c.1220), also called Gerald of Wales (*Giraldus Cambrensis*), was archdeacon of Brecon. His many works include *Topographia* (a detailed account of Ireland), *Itinerarium* (a description of the topography of Wales), an autobiography and *De Principis Instructione* (an instruction manual for princes).

pp 136–137 *The Early Stewart Kings, Robert II and Robert III 1371–1406* by Stephen Boardman (1996) is one in a recent series of books by specialist authors which make the complicated historical period accessible both to a general readership as well as students and academics.

pp 138–139 The story of Black Agnes of Dunbar comes from the *Book of Pluscarden (Liber Pluscardensis)* Vol. II, edited by F. J. H. Skene (1877–80). This particular translation is taken from Agnes Mure Mackenzie's *Scottish Pageant, 55BC–1513AD*, a delightful anthology of bits and pieces from early Scottish history.

p 141 Andrew of Wyntoun (c.1350–c.1420) was a canon of St Andrews and prior of Lochleven and author of *The Orygynale Cronykil*, a history of Scotland in verse from the beginning of the world to the accession of James I of Scotland.

p 143 The quotation is taken from J. Murray's article entitled 'On the Origins and Role of "Wise Women" in Cases of Annulment on the Grounds of Male Impotence', *Journal of Medieval History* 16 (1990) and the subject further discussed in Henrietta's Leyser's *Medieval Women*.

pp 146–147 *Plague, Pox and Pestilence*, edited by K. F. Kiple (1997) and *The Hamlyn History of Medicine*, edited by J. Crane (1996) give graphic descriptions of the Black Death.

pp 152–155 Sylvia Landsberg, in *The Medieval Garden*, gives a comprehensive and fully illustrated guide to the plants and features used in the various types of garden from the small enclosed herber to the larger monastic infirmary gardens and peasant closes. She also describes the gardeners and horticulturists of the period.

pp 159–160 *Dress in the Middle Ages* by Françoise Piponnier and Perrine Mane (1997) draws on paintings, sculpture, documents, literature and surviving clothing to describe the garments and materials used by men and women in all classes of society.

pp 160–161 Sir James Douglas of Dalkeith's will is fully recorded in Agnes Mure Mackenzie's *Scottish Pageant*.

pp 163–165 Jean Froissart (c.1337–c.1410) visited England in 1360 and was received at the court of Edward III. His travels extended to Scotland, Italy and Belgium. His *Chroniques* cover the period 1325–1400 and three editions were issued during his lifetime. He is considered to be more of a literary artist than accurate historian but he gives a colourful portrait of his period. His work was first translated into English by John Bourchier in 1523–25.

INTERLUDE

William, the fifth earl of Ross, was as we have seen a nephew of Robert the Bruce and elder half-brother of Queen Euphemia. Indeed in a charter dated 1374 he was styled *frater regis*, brother of Robert II. He was also father of our fourth Euphemia.

He has been described as a 'man of fiery temper and hotter blood' who according to the Revd W. Taylor's *History of Tain* injured some woman and, when she threatened to complain to the king, nailed horse-shoes to her feet in order to hasten her journey. Although the tale is also ascribed to his half-brother Hugh of Rarichies and probably apocryphal, it perhaps gives an indication of how the earl and his brother were remembered in Ross-shire.

William was born c.1315. Because he was travelling in Norway when his father was killed at Halidon Hill in 1333, he did not come into his inheritance until the Friday before Whitsunday 1336, possibly when he was twenty-one. He may have been quick-tempered but William was also devout. According to the *Chronicle of Whithorn*, his foreign travels had made him aware of the poverty of the church in his own earldom. He was 'trublit of mynd with anguish that the Abby Kirk of Fearn the sepulture of his fathers' was built of 'clay and rouch stain alutterlie rewinous appearandlie' and that 'the dropis descending from heaven distilled in the challice, and upon the altar quhair the sacrament was ministered.'

With the encouragement of Abbot Mark Ross, son of a local knight, the earl called a council convened by the bishop and attended by all the diocesan clergy and important men of Ross. They agreed to rebuild Fearn abbey, and 'seven brethren' (monks) bound themselves to poverty 'and to beg and thig [borrow or entice] through the country, the abbot only to remain in the place for attending on the warke, now then begun, for beggin the said kirk there of hewen staines'. The building was finished before Abbot Mark's death in 1355 and Earl William (rather than the prior of Whithorn) chose his successor. He was 'Donald Pupill', an orphan reared by Abbot Mark, and 'a worthy person out of the bosome' of the abbey. Eventually, 'eftir many resonis and controversies', the new abbot's appointment was accepted by Whithorn.

Meanwhile on 17th August 1339 William had joined Robert Steward in his siege of Perth and was responsible for diverting the water from the fosse into a mine before storming the town and forcing the English governor to capitulate. Three years later, on 25th May 1342, William was granted a papal dispensation to marry Mary, a daughter of Angus Og of Islay and a sister of 'Good John of Isla', self-styled *Dominus Insularum*, lord of the Isles, who like most of his generation had changed sides from Bruce to Balliol several times. Eventually John swore allegiance to David II who confirmed him in his ownership of Islay, Gigha, Scarba, Colonsay, Mull, Coll, Tiree, Lewis, Morven, Lochaber, Duror and Glencoe. His first wife, the heiress Amie Nic Ruari, brought him Uist, Rum and Eigg, the lordship of Garmoran, Kintyre, Knapdale and Ardnamurchan. John who lived to be eighty-seven and Amie were the progenitors of the Macdonalds of Clan Ranald.

At the age of fifty John divorced Amie and married the young Princess Margaret, Robert Steward's (later King Robert II) eldest daughter in 1350. She can't have been more than fifteen, it was a political match arranged by the Steward who recognised and respected the power of her father. Their two sons became the progenitors of the Macdonalds of Keppoch, Loch Alsh and of Sleat in Skye. The lords of the Isles were an enormously powerful family who ruled in sophisticated splendour from their various castles, the main one of which was Finlaggan in Argyll.

William's marriage to Mary was therefore a highly desirable match from the point of view of both families and one which would prove to be of huge significance to the earldom of Ross. They had three children William, Euphemia and Janet.

In 1346 William committed the act which was to change the course not only of his family history but possibly that of his country. A few months after his marriage at a gathering arranged by Sir Thomas

Lauder at Urqhuart castle, William had granted a charter for ten davachs of land in Kintail to a relative of his wife, Ranald Mac Ruari of Garmoran. When Ranald also acquired the islands of Uist, Barra, Eigg and Rum, William was not pleased. He bore a grudge against Ranald for that reason and, according to the *Chronicle of Ross*, because Ranald had wanted to marry and was still in love with Mary.

Then, in response to the King of France's quest for a diversion, David II assembled an army at Perth in the autumn of 1346 to march into England. William with his followers responded to the call, as did Ranald with his following of seven men. They met at the nunnery of Elcho just outside Perth. Tempers were lost, and perhaps the feud was resolved in a duel. As a result Ranald was killed as Andrew Wyntoun records:

> The Erle off Ross wes thare allsua,
> That to this Raynald wes full fa;
> Tharefore he gert hym swa aspy
> In till Elyhok that nunry,
> Quhare he wes lyand then,
> He gert sla hym and his sevyn men;
> And to Ros with his menyhe
> Agayne in hy than turned he.

The Book of Pluscarden records that Ranald's men deserted to the islands, taking many other Highlanders with them, while William and his warriors 'withdrew to the mountains'. Meanwhile the army of Scots, depleted by the loss of so many warriors, marched south to be defeated at Neville's Cross where David II was taken prisoner.

In 1350, during David's absence but dependent on his approval, William – with his sister Marjorie's agreement – entailed his earldom in the male line and appointed his half-brother Hugh of Rarichies (Euphemia III's full brother) as his heir. He must have known then that his son William – who cannot have been more than six or seven years old at the time – was too sickly to survive. Nevertheless in 1354 the delicate lad was named as one of the twenty hostages guaranteeing the payment of David's ransom. When the king was finally released in 1357, the boy died before he could make the journey south. It seems that in 1358 William was one of twelve noblemen appointed to treat with the English for the payment of the ransom money. He received a safe-conduct pass to travel to England on 6th June of that year.

Although a wealthy catch, Euphemia was not now her father's heir to the earldom. This was no deliberate slight to Euphemia but rather a wish on her father's behalf to keep the earldom in the Ross family by leaving it to his half-brother, Hugh. The inheritance had been greatly increased at the death of his uncle Sir John de Ross who, through his marriage to Margaret Comyn, co-heiress of the earl of Buchan, had inherited half the lands of that earldom. Having no children of his own Sir John left his substantial territory in Banff and Aberdeenshire to his nephew.

But David II had not forgotten William's behaviour at Elcho, not just the murder but also the loss of so many fighting men to his cause. Shortly before 1366 – the date of the papal dispensation is 24th November of that year – he arranged for Euphemia to marry one of his personal favourites, a hero of the crusades, without her father's approval.

William was outraged. With the backing of Hugh of Rarichies he refused to contribute his share of David's ransom and other tax burdens. He also refused to attend the parliamentary sessions of 1366, 1367 and 1368, though he agreed to keep the peace and administer justice within his own territory. As a result David refused to recognise Hugh of Rarichies as heir to the earldom. He compelled William to resign all his possessions to the crown and issued a new charter forcing William to recognise Euphemia and her spouse as his heirs.

A few months later David was dead. How William must have rejoiced. His brother-in-law Robert II was now king, his half-sister Euphemia the queen. However his numerous complaints went unheard and he died an embittered man in his late fifties at his castle of Delny on 9th February 1371. His daughter Euphemia became countess of Ross.

This then is the historical background to the life of our fourth Euphemia.

SOURCES

pp 169–170 The history of the Premonstratensian foundation in Easter Ross is recorded by A. Scott in 'Fearn Abbey', *Transactions of the Gaelic Society*, Inverness, Vol. XXVIII.

pp 171–172 William's entail is recorded in *Origines Parochiales Scotiae*, Aberdeen 1850–55. His safe-conduct pass is recorded in *Calendar of Documents Relating to Scotland*, edited by J. Bain, Vol. III.

p 172 David II's refusal to recognise Hugh of Rarichies as heir to the earldom is recorded in *Shires of Aberdeen and Banff*, edited by J. Robertson and G. Grut, Vol. II.

◆

PART FOUR

THE FOURTH EUPHEMIA
Crusader's Widow and the Wolf's Wife

Euphemia's early childhood in Ross-shire cannot have been very different from that of her namesake and aunt, the third Euphemia who, when she was born, was countess of Moray. It is tempting to think that her birth may have coincided with John Randolph's death in battle in 1346 and that his young widow came back to her old home to mourn her husband and take some comfort from the arrival of the new baby. Indeed, she may have stood as godmother to the infant Euphemia which would account for the child's name.

With her mother a Macdonald of the Isles, and her father often referred to in charters as the lord of Skye, the young Euphemia's upbringing would have been thoroughly Celtic, her first language Gaelic. She may even have been fostered by her Uncle John of the Isles in his castle at his favourite residence, Finlaggan, and attended his wedding to Margaret Stewart in the early 1350s. There she would have learned the extent and sophistication of island hospitality. Fordun describes Finlaggan as more of a manor or mansion rather than a castle, though there was a stone castle built there in the thirteenth century. The policies covered two islands, Eilean Mor (big island) and Eilean na Comhairle (council island), situated in a freshwater loch in the middle of Islay and surrounded by some of the best farming land in the west. The site was at the height of its importance during the fourteenth and fifteenth centuries and would have been well known to the earls of Ross. Poets, bards and musicians mingled with the warriors and feasted on gold plates in halls ablaze with wax candles and drank from finely carved four-sided wooden cups.

A note of Lord John's clothes for the year of his second marriage has survived. They must have been very similar to those worn by Euphemia's father and his warriors when not in full armour. These

[177]

included a vest of woollen cloth, a pair of tartan plaids or, in this case, mantles in an assortment of striking colours and fourteen ells of yellow linen for his pleated tunic.

Perhaps Euphemia and her siblings were fostered nearer home by the Munros of Foulis. The two families had always been good neighbours. Charters from this period mention gifts from the earl to his close friend and neighbour Robert de Munro which include land, three suits of clothing a year, and 'ane pair of Parisian gloves'. Just the sorts of gifts that a chief might give to the foster-father of his children. Some years later (1369) Robert Munro was to lose his life in saving that of his friend for which Earl William granted 'his beloved cousin Hugh de Munro' certain lands 'for services rendered by him and by his father killed in the earl's defence'.

But there is another perhaps more obvious choice. Euphemia would have been about eleven when her aunt married Robert the Steward in 1355. Perhaps she accompanied her to Dundonald castle and thence to the court of King David in Edinburgh when he returned from his imprisonment in England a couple of years later. It's possible that at the age of thirteen or fourteen she became one of the queen's ladies, or, as Queen Joan spent most of her time in England she may have waited upon one of the king's mistresses, Margaret Logie for example, who was to become queen after Joan's death, in 1363.

It seems more than likely that she spent at least part of her teenage years at court otherwise David would have had no opportunity to negotiate her marriage to one of his favourites against her father's wishes. Had she remained within the fastness of Dingwall castle the king himself could have had little control over her future.

THE COURT OF KING DAVID

David came back to a Scotland which, as we have seen, had been governed by the Steward and the Steward's men for eleven years. Now as anglified as he had previously been French, the king had to stamp his own seal on the kingdom and he did it by slowly but firmly excluding the traditional nobles from his inner council and bringing in his own men. Gradually, according to Dr Boardman, he adopted 'a more aggressive and confrontational approach towards the assertion of royal rights and the promotion of royal favourites.'

To become a favourite of the king, it was necessary to show an interest and commitment to the crusades. Wyntoun in his *Chronicle* wrote, 'eftir his hame cuming [in 1357] he began and guvernit the realme richt weill and nobilly, and purposet to have gane to the Haly Land to fecht aganis the Turkis; but he deyt in the meynetyme.' Thus David's main administrator, Sir Robert Erskine, vowed to bear arms against the Saracens but was excused as the king needed him at home. David also tried, though without success, to marry off Isabella, countess of Fife, to Sir Thomas Bisset, another crusading knight. George and John Dunbar, now the earls of March and Fife respectively and brothers of David's mistress Agnes (later to be proposed as his new bride), were particular favourites as their father, captured with David at Neville's Cross, had died during a pilgrimage to the Holy Land. James Douglas of Dalkeith and the Lindsay brothers of Glenesk were renowned for their chivalry, as were their formidable half-brothers, crusaders supreme, Sir Norman de Leslie and his younger brother Walter, soon to become Euphemia's husband.

As Walter Bower wrote, David 'showed great and special favour and friendship to his knights and esquires of whom at that time there were many, who had enlisted and engaged in work of that kind; and he gave and granted them wide possessions and military honours.' To none was he more generous than 'the bald [bold] Sir Valter'.

Medieval aristocrats saw themselves as defenders of the faith as well as the working classes. Knighthood was an obligation as much as it was a privilege and there were rules of conduct well known throughout Europe. The *Epitoma Res Militaris* by the Roman Vegetius described the training of recruits, campaigning, fortifications, sieges and naval warfare dating from Roman times. By the thirteenth century it had been translated into French and was probably as familiar to the Scots nobility as it was to the English.

Training for knighthood began at puberty and consisted of strenuous exercise such as running, jumping, swimming, wrestling and stone-casting, the use of swords, spears and bows. Youths practised against a target called the quintain, learned how to ride, how to look after a horse, how to put on armour and equipment. The *Book of the Order of Chivalry* by Ramon Lull (d. 1316) encouraged the attendance of knights at tournaments which, like the football matches of today, attracted noisy partisan crowds. Euphemia no doubt enjoyed these displays of masculinity at David's court as much as the next girl, and had her favourites. Perhaps Sir Walter was one of them. Perhaps he tied her kerchief to his lance as he tilted at the quintain.

Hunting and hawking were largely but not exclusively aristocratic male pursuits. Although next to nothing is known about the participation of women in Scotland, literary sources elsewhere mention ladies who hunted like Hyppolita and Emilye in Chaucer's *Knight's Tale*. As Nicholas Orme tells us, 'women were certainly stationed to watch and shoot at game with bows, and they may well have followed the chase on horseback.' Archery, too, was a sport which could also be enjoyed by women, perhaps for hunting but certainly for recreation, and, of course, riding. Euphemia would have learned to ride as a child.

Chivalry however consisted of more than displays of jousting, horsemanship and swordplay. According to Lloyd and Jenny Laing in *Medieval Britain*, 'The chivalric code furthered an idea of social service without remuneration, and ideas of loyalty, virtue and generosity. It fostered *noblesse oblige* – privileges which carried with them responsibilities.' Chaucer has given us the best and most memorable portrait of a knight in his *Prologue* to *The Canterbury Tales*. 'Trouth and honour, freedom and curtesye', was his code. 'He never yet ne villainy ne saide, / In all his life unto no manner wight./ He was a veray, parfit geantil knight.'

Chivalry also promoted a new attitude towards women, the concept of romantic love which balanced physical lust with a more spiritual and romantic emotion. Courtly love grew from simple romance between unmarried couples into a sophisticated game that took two to play and focused on wives rather than virgins. It mirrored the feudal relationship between a lord and his vassal where the lady took the role of the lord and her lover became her vassal. There was never any shortage of partners. Women who were particularly admired had narrow shoulders and hips, small regular mouths and noses, a high unlined forehead and a pale untanned skin.

Feasting was very much part of court life and court cookery at Edinburgh would have been largely founded on French recipes which, the Laings tell us 'were based on three basic rules: never do anything simply, keep adding the spices and totally obscure the original flavour'.

There were usually three or four courses each announced with a flourish of trumpets. Soup or frumentie, made from boiled husked wheat and milk of almonds, came first followed by a main course which offered a selection of five meats, five birds – which might include heron, cormorant and curlew – a fish dish and four others. These might consist of a spicy custard made with veal, wine, cinnamon and eggs or a pie stuffed with hare or hedgehog. A second main course consisted of four meats, six birds and perhaps two fish dishes, with recipes such as a blancmange made with honeyed almond milk, meat or fish. No one ate the third course as it was usually too dark to see what was being served. Instead they ate wafers, fruit and spiced wine.

Table manners were beginning to improve, though it was to be another hundred years before the *Boke of Curtasye* appeared with its advice not to pick the teeth with a knife or drink with the mouth full, tell rude stories at table, lean on the elbows or slurp the soup.

Games would have played an important part in court life. For the long winter evenings Merelles, a board game similar to noughts-and-crosses, was popular. In Fox and Geese the counters representing the fox had to capture the geese pieces by jumping over them, while the geese tried to corner the fox. Chess and Tables, an early form of backgammon, and dice were all played.

Festivals such as Hallowe'en and Beltain were still celebrated in the old Celtic way with bonfires, dressing up, divination and a host of games but other traditions introduced by the French and English incomers had also become part of Scottish life. The approach of Christmas in the major towns was the time for the choristers and schoolboys connected with the cathedrals and abbeys to elect a Boy Bishop who led his 'imps' in procession through the windy wynds collecting generous tips. He first appears in the Dunfermline burgh records for 1303 and his rule extended from St Nicholas' Eve (6th December) to Childermas, the Feast of the Holy Innocents (26th December).

The Christmas season proper began on Christmas Eve and ended on Uphalieday or Twelfth Night, the Feast of the Epiphany. The period was known as the Daft Days, similar to the French *Fête des Fous*. At court a Lord of Misrule was appointed whose business it was to lighten the long winter month 'with fine and subtle disguisings, masks and mummeries'. In Edinburgh it was the custom for the merchants and burghers to present the king with Yuletide gifts of wine and velvet, with wax and spices for the queen.

Twelfth Night itself was celebrated at court with feasts, plays, pageants and revelries. Just how soon the King of the Bean was appointed at the Scottish court is not certain but it was surely before the end of the fifteenth century. This lord of the revels was chosen by means of a bean hidden in a cake. The finder could be a woman. One of the games played was called the Twelve Days of Christmas and involved paying forfeits. It survives to this day in the popular secular carol.

Just as in Applecross the Celtic saints were celebrated, so at court these now included French and English names. On St Valentine's Day – the feast of love – peacock eggs and decorated cakes were served to the courtiers who played Lady Anne, a guessing game after which couples paired off. Nowhere was the blend of Celtic, English and French tradition more apparent than in the festivals. Music too would have played an important part in court life. David, like his English brother-in-law Edward III, would probably have employed his own band of trumpeters, pipers, drummers and fiddlers to accompany the feasts and dancing. Life must have been exciting for a young girl at court with flirting, fashion, dancing, games and no doubt plenty of petty scandal to discuss.

Above all David's court was dominated by two supreme interests, jousting and the crusades. Champions had their supporters, just as the pop stars of today. And no champion had greater style, more service abroad, more favour at court than the crusader Sir Walter de Leslie.

TAKING THE CROSS

Stories of the crusades and the names of heroic crusaders must have been as familiar to Euphemia as the pages of her Gospel book. From the 27th November 1095 when Pope Urban II exhorted the chivalry of western Europe to support the Holy Places of Christendom, Scots had been involved in taking the cross. Through the seanachies of Ross Euphemia would probably have heard of Lagmann, king of Man and the Western Isles, who in the late eleventh century took the cross and died in Jerusalem. His was an act of penitence for blinding and mutilating his brother.

David I was a committed supporter. In his reign the military order of Knights Templar built chapels in the Lothians and Renfrewshire, while Alan Macquarrie in *Scotland and the Crusades* tells us that the Hospitallers also accumulated 'small parcels of land scattered over the length and breadth of the kingdom'.

According to John of Fordun, David I 'would have renounced his kingdom, laid down the sceptre, and joined the sacred army in the places of Our Lord's Passion and Resurrection if he had not been dissuaded by the counsel of prelates and abbots, the tears of the poor, the sighing of widows, the desolation of the common folk, and the clamour and outcry of his whole kingdom; he was detained in body, but not in mind or will.'

Euphemia would certainly have heard of her uncle King Robert II's illustrious Steward ancestors who joined the third crusade in which the city of Antioch was captured. She would have known, too, from her mother's ancestry of Ranald, son of Somerled of the Isles, who in the year he turned the Iona church into a Benedictine monastery 'received a cross from Jerusalem' (about 1203).

As a child in the Highlands, she may well have known the Gaelic poems composed by the two bards Muiredhach Albanach O Dalaigh and Gille-Brigde Albanach who both took part in the Fifth Crusade. Gille-Brigde in one of his poems (c.1219) described the journey from Acre to Damietta with great poignancy.

> . . . These clouds from the east are dark
> As they drive us from Acre;
> Come, Mary Magdalen,
> And wholly clear the air . . .
>
> Lady of the undulating hair,
> You have kept us all the autumn
> On the bright-edged Mediterranean;
> O modest one with the yellow locks;
> On the bright-edged Mediterranean;
> O modest one with the yellow locks;
>
> Brigid of the bright bosom,
> Though we have been sailing for some time,
> Our sailings here have been enough for me,
> Maiden of Europe, beloved one . . .

Although Muiredhach was Irish by birth, he settled in Scotland where his descendants became the hereditary bardic family of Max Vurich. One of his crusading poems is redolent with the homesickness which must have been felt by so many crusaders.

> . . . It would be as the reward of heaven tonight,
> If we could touch off Scotland of the lofty manors
> that we might see the haven . . .
> or whiff the air of Ireland.

As Alan Macquarrie writes, these poems 'provide a unique insight into the mentality of Scottish crusaders, whose movements often have to be deduced from legal documents or from laconic references in chronicles'.

By the middle of the thirteenth century the ritual in which the cross was blessed by the parish priest or a local monk before being sewn on to the crusader's clothing had become common practice. In 1244 the saintly King Louis IX of France, in thanksgiving for recovery from illness, himself took the cross. He was to be the greatest of all champions for the crusading movement and the French nobility flocked to the cause. Earl Patrick of Dunbar was Scotland's leading crusader at that time and it cost him a fortune. He had to sell his stud farm at Lauder to the monks of Melrose to help pay for it. Sadly, as Matthew Paris records, he 'who was regarded as the most powerful among the Scottish magnates . . . died signed with the cross in order to be reconciled with God and Saint Oswine.'

Euphemia would have known that Earl Patrick took with him, according to Hector Boece, 'David Lindsay of Glenesk and Walter Steward of Dundonald with one graete novmer of chosin men to support King Lowis in the said iornaye'. She would also have known that Walter's brother John died at the disastrous seige of Damietta in Egypt in 1249.

Another story well known in the Gaelic oral tradition may well have been told to Euphemia during her childhood in Ross-shire. It concerned Coinneach mac Mathghamhna, a member of Clan Mackenzie of Kintail in the mid-thirteenth century. Apparently he had the second sight and was banished by his father for his predictions told to him by birds whose language he could understand. He is said to have joined a ship and travelled to distant lands. Having grown rich from his ability to understand foreign languages, he returned to Kintail where in fulfilment of the original prophecy his father, not recognising him, waited on him as an honoured guest at table. A ship was built in Inverness in 1248 by a French nobleman, the count of Saint-Pol, so that he could join King Louis's crusade. Could the young seer have joined it? Alan Macquarrie suggests that there might have been a connection.

But the tales most popular at court and best known to Euphemia would have concerned the king's own forefathers. Robert the Bruce the elder, lord of Annandale, is said to have been one of the oldest of all crusaders. At the age of sixty-one in 1271 he set out with a retinue of local knights and squires for the Holy Land. His son Robert the Bruce the younger, described by Fordun as 'an extremely handsome and elegant young knight', set out the year before his father. Euphemia would have enjoyed the romantic story told about the young widowed Marjorie, countess of Carrick, who met him on his return to Scotland and imprisoned him at Turnberry castle until he agreed to marry her.

Their son Robert I was never able to fulfil his vow to take the cross. As he lay dying at Cardross he is said to have summoned the warrior James Douglas to his bedside and told him that he wished to send his heart instead of his body to the Holy Sepulchre.

> The good lord of Douglas syne
> Gert mak a cas of silver fyne
> Ennamylyat throu sutelte,
> Therein the kingis hart did he
> And ay about his hals it bar
> And fast him bownyt for to far.

A. A. M. Duncan's translation of John Barbour's verses from *The Bruce* is as follows:

'The good lord Douglas then had a case of fine silver made, cunningly enamelled; he put the king's heart in it and wore it always around his neck, then prepared himself to travel.'

Douglas and his retinue eventually landed in Spain where they were killed at the castle of Teba, fighting for the Spanish king against the Moors. The casket containing the king's heart was found on his dead body. Sadly, it never reached Jerusalem but was brought back for burial in Melrose abbey.

David II's passion for the crusades was therefore partly fired by his admiration for his ancestors, partly by his passion for chivalry and partly by his time spent in the French and English courts where crusading played a more significant role than in Scotland.

In 1359 a new enthusiast in the form of the young King Peter de Lusignan ascended the throne of Cyprus. He set out to initiate a new crusade in Europe. While David was on pilgrimage to the shrine of Our Lady at Walsingham in 1363 (no doubt to pray for an heir) news reached him that King Peter was in London so he hurried there in great excitement to meet him. Froissart recorded that the two kings (David and Peter of Cyprus) 'met and rejoiced greatly together; and the king of England invited them twice to dinners at the Palace of Westminster'. Although David could not go crusading himself, he persuaded many of his knights to take the cross. Two of those who joined King Peter's crusade were the Leslie brothers, Sir Norman and his brother Walter.

'THE GENEROUS KNIGHT'

The Leslie family was descended from a Hungarian called Bartolf (Bartholomew) whose son Malcolm had been given a grant of the lands of Leslyn in Aberdeenshire by David, earl of Huntingdon and brother of William the Lion in the second half of the twelfth century. They took the name of Leslie from their new land.

A descendant of Malcolm Leslie, Sir Andrew, who was one of those who had signed the Declaration of Arbroath in 1320, married Mary, co-heiress of Abernethy. She brought him her inheritance of Ballinbreich castle in Fife. Andrew and Mary de Leslie had four or five sons, the youngest of whom was Walter. After Andrew's death in 1324, Mary married Sir David Lindsay of Crawford, ancestor of the earls of Crawford. Their son Alexander of Glenesk, Walter's beloved half-brother, was to be another crusader favourite of the king.

So what do we know of this Walter who was to marry the Lady Euphemia? First and foremost he was a warrior.

On 20th August 1356 when Euphemia would have been about ten years old, Walter, his brother Norman and others were granted a safe-conduct through England to join the Baltic Crusade in Prussia. According to his descendant, the sixteenth-century historian Bishop John Leslie, Walter served in the Imperial army under the Emperors Louis and Charles IV with great distinction against the Saracens, and was so esteemed for his bravery and for his humanity towards the vanquished that he was styled 'the generous knight'.

He returned briefly to Scotland but a couple of years later he was abroad again, this time fighting for the French against the English Edward III. As a reward for his services he was later granted an annuity of 200 gold francs 'for his good and faithful services against our ancient enemies of England especially at the battle of Pontvalain'.

He was back in Scotland some time before 1363 when Euphemia, now about sixteen or seventeen, may first have met him. On 14th October of that year David granted him a pension of £40 sterling to be paid annually out of the customs of Dundee. This happened at about the same time as David's meeting with King Peter of Cyprus and may have been a reward for Walter's joining the new crusade. Certainly a month later Walter, brother Norman and eight horsemen had another pass to go through England and thence overseas.

In 1364 they were in Florence trying to raise support for King Peter's crusade. There they acted as witnesses to an agreement between that city and the English White Company, a band of mercenaries fighting and plundering for whoever would employ them. Thereafter the White Company agreed to fight for Florence against Pisa, instead of *vice versa*, but its members did not enlist in the crusade, which had obviously been the Leslies' intention. Both brothers were at the storming of Alexandria and the Scot who was stoned to death at the customs-house gate is thought to have been Sir Norman.

King Peter's crusade was quickly over, having achieved little more than bloodshed and plunder. Sir Walter returned to claim his prize, the hand of Euphemia of Ross. They were married sometime before 13th September 1366. Perhaps David's wedding gift to the couple was 'the new forest in the shire of Dumfries to be held of the king in free barony'. The charter was issued from Perth in September 1365.

The following year David granted Walter a charter of the barony and castle of Philorth in Aberdeenshire. Thereafter many gifts of land flowed his way. The thanage of Aberchirder and the lands of Blaresnache, Buchan in exchange for the service of one knight and three suits at three head courts to be held within the shire of Banff was dated Perth 1369. A further charter to Aberchirder and Kincardine followed a few months later. These lands, in fact, had previously belonged to Euphemia's father.

But of course the marriage was not purely a reward for Sir Walter's crusading activities. It was a political move engineered by the king to balance the Steward's marriage to the third Euphemia. It gave David an important foothold in Ross.

Earl William, Euphemia's father, was deeply angry. The king had taken away his Buchan lands and his right to arrange the future of his own daughter. He and his brother Hugh of Rarichies threw off their allegiance to the crown and refused to pay their annual dues towards David's ransom. This was perhaps the excuse the king needed. In a charter dated 23rd October 1370 he compelled William to renounce his earldom and most of his lands. He then regranted him most of his property and his title and permitted him to leave them to any legitimate male heirs he might have, but he could not leave them to his half-brother Hugh or Hugh's heirs, the future Rosses of Balnagown. David changed the entail so that on William's death Ross must go to Euphemia and Sir Walter Leslie, her spouse, and their heirs; whom failing to William's youngest daughter Joanna or Janet Ross and her heirs.

Not an auspicious start to any marriage. Euphemia must have been aware of William's anger, and torn between her loyalties to her father, her husband and her king. No doubt she agonised over the situation in the privacy of the confessional and was told firmly that her duty now was to her husband.

And what was Sir Walter like as a husband? Not surprisingly, for he must have been some ten years older than his bride, he had at least one mistress. A papal dispensation was obtained from Pope Urban V in December 1367 because of his illicit intercourse with a woman related within the fourth degree of kindred to Euphemia. Perhaps she was that other Euphemia de Sancto Claro (Sinclair) to whom in the same year Walter, signing himself lord of Ross, granted a charter of lands in Buchan and those of Bra, Drum and Bron

(Brahan) in Inverness-shire 'to be held of him and his heirs by her and her heirs, for payment of two pennies yearly at the feast of St John the Baptist, if demanded'.

Euphemia would have been conditioned to overlook such a misdemeanour. She might well have been proud of her husband's career which now formed the basis of an exciting crusading epic poem (unfortunately lost) entitled *The Tail of Syr Valtir the Bald Leslye*. She would have admired his coat-of-arms which displayed a fiercesome bearded and turbaned Saracen's head above the Leslie shield of three buckles on a bend.

Walter may have been like Chaucer's pilgrim, a 'veray parfit gentil knight' to women. Or he may have been like the courteous knight's son, with his curly hair and fine clothes, 'embrouded . . . as it were a meede,/ All full of freshe flowres, white and rede'. Perhaps like the Squire he whistled and sang, danced and jousted, wrote poetry and made such hot love to her that 'he slept namore than doth a nightingale.' Let us hope so, but the clues are not encouraging.

In spite of the depredations of war, the expensive annual ransom payment to England and the on-going ravages of plague, David managed to make Scotland richer than it had ever been. He built up an effective civil service which controlled the exchequer and kept the nobles in order. In so doing, Walter Leslie was one of his key men. Richard Oram, a modern medievalist, in conversation has gone so far as to call him a thug. One episode in particular adds substance to that condemnation. After David's unexpected death in 1369, Euphemia's father issued the following *Querimonia* (complaint) to his brother-in-law, Robert II as follows.

> Your predecessor, King David of good memory, gave to Sir Walter de Leslie, knight, all my lands, and also those of my brother Hugh, within Buchan, without our leave, and without legal process.
>
> As soon as I heard of that lawless investiture, I wrote to the Lord Bishop of Brechin, then Chancellor of Scotland, and also to Robert, Steward of Scotland [now king, and others] in order that they might act as my attorneys for suing from my lord the king, my lands and my brother's under causation, and also a letter to my sister Euphemia, countess of Moray [now queen] on the same subject; and I employed my clerk, Sir John of Gamery, Canon of Caithness, to present those letters in due form.

As he was on his journey, he was met by John of Aberkerdor, calling himself the squire of Sir Walter de Leslie. This person arrested my clerk; robbed him of all his letters; cruelly beat his squire, because he refused to bind his master to his horse's tail; carried him among woods and pathless places, nor would he set him free till he undertook to pay eight marks of sterling, and gave Sir Robert the rector of Forglen, and William Bisset of Ochterless, for surety, and swore on the holy gospels, in presence of Sir Cristinus, vicar of Forgue, not to deliver any of my letters, but to carry the box containing them sealed with his seal, to Sir Walter de Leslie, his lord, and enter himself his prisoner. When this was done, my clerk toiled forward to his lord, the Bishop of Aberdeen and to Sir William of Keith who freed him from the payment of the money, and thence came to me in Ross and told me this history.

Perhaps the chaplain was lucky to get away with his life. He was able to return to the earl to relate what had happened. William's complaint continued that he himself had immediately ridden south to Aberdeen where David was in residence, but the king had refused to see him until he renounced certain territorial rights in Forfar. When he had made that concession, David asked him to dinner, after which he had tried to start some discussion on his affairs but instead the king had given him a 'long list of questions to answer containing many authorities from the civil law'.

William explained that he had no desire for litigation with the king, that was not the purpose of his visit, and so he had returned to Dingwall without seeking permission to leave Aberdeen. The story continues:

But the Lady Margaret Logie [then queen], with her council, hearing that I had thus returned without agreeing with Sir Walter nor with her, gave precept and command that my body should be arrested and imprisoned, and all my lands seized and recognosced in the king's hands. The king would by no means suffer my body to be arrested, but permitted all my lands to be seized in his hands.

When the king next visited Inverness William tried to speak to him again but without success. 'Nor could I learn any cause except that the friendship of my lord the king I might not have, until I were agreed with Sir Walter.' He had applied to the court of justice in Inverness.

> And there I and Hugh my brother, deprived of all our land and without lordship, and perceiving that our lord the king was moved against us, and Sir Walter very powerful with him and with the queen, we ratifed the gift of our lands of Buchan made by the king to Sir Walter, because of the great dangers imminent.

The earl's final complaint was that,

> never was my daughter espoused to the foresaid Sir Walter with my will, but quite against my will: nor did I make to them any grant or gift of lands or agreement of any kind of succession at any time up to the day of the death of my lord King David, your predecessor, except through fear of the king's anger.

Robert paid no attention to the complaint, or perhaps he laid it aside to deal with in due course. As we have seen, for political reasons he had no wish to quarrel with the Leslies. It seemed then that Walter not only had David's ear but also a network of spies prepared to go to any lengths to do their master's bidding. A thug perhaps in his service to the king, but that did not necessarily make him a bad husband.

During those first five years of their marriage Euphemia probably remained at court, for her husband was continually in the king's company or on the king's business. He was witness to several charters signed by the king in Edinburgh. He had a pass to England on state affairs in January 1369. He was one of the guarantors of a truce with England signed in July 1369.

Then on 9th February 1372, a year after David's death, the earl, Euphemia's father, died at Delny. Euphemia according to the provision of the 1370 charter became his heir and – perfect timing for 'the generous knight' who would most certainly have been out of a job under Robert II – Sir Walter de Leslie took up his new responsibilities as earl of Ross in his wife's right and travelled north.

LADY OF ROSS

Euphemia and Walter had two children, Alexander and Margaret, both of whom would have been infants or possibly not yet born by the time they took up official residence in Dingwall castle. Alexander was neither a Ross nor a Leslie name but the infant may well have been called after his uncle and possibly godfather, Sir Alexander Lindsay of Glenesk, half-brother and crusading comrade of Walter and another powerful favourite of David II. In several charters Walter refers to his Lindsay relatives as *carissimi fratres* (beloved brothers). Alexander Lindsay's daughter was betrothed to Queen Euphemia's young son David, earl of Strathearn and Caithness. So the connections were close on both sides of the family.

They called their daughter Margaret, again not a Ross nor a Leslie name. She might have been called after Sir Norman Leslie's widow. Walter may have made himself responsible for his widowed sister-in-law after her husband's death on crusade. Certainly a charter exists issued by her and witnessed by him for the disposal of certain lands which had belonged to her great-grandfather, Sir Alexander de Lamberton. Possibly she stood as godmother to the infant Margaret.

Euphemia's mother, the dowager countess – she was still alive and living at Delny – may have been one of the first persons to welcome the couple back to the north and possibly with her would have been Euphemia's younger sister Janet (or Joanna). She had married Sir Alexander Fraser of Cowie and Durris and had inherited or received as part of her dower certain lands in Ross. In 1375 Walter and Euphemia issued a charter arranging for the exchange of all Janet's inheritance in Ross and Galloway for the barony of Philorth in Aberdeenshire. This was probably a friendly and geographically convenient gesture towards Janet and her husband who were to become the progenitors of the Frasers of Philorth and ancestors of the Barons Saltoun.

Philorth castle had originally (as we have seen) been the property of the Comyn earls of Buchan, inherited by the last earl's heiress who had married Sir John de Ross, who, having died childless, left it to his nephew, the earl of Ross. It is thought that the oblong tower was constructed perhaps by Sir Walter or more likely by his brother-in-law Sir Alexander Fraser. His and Janet's son sold off the

13. Dunbar Castle defended by 'Black Agnes' against the English in 1338.

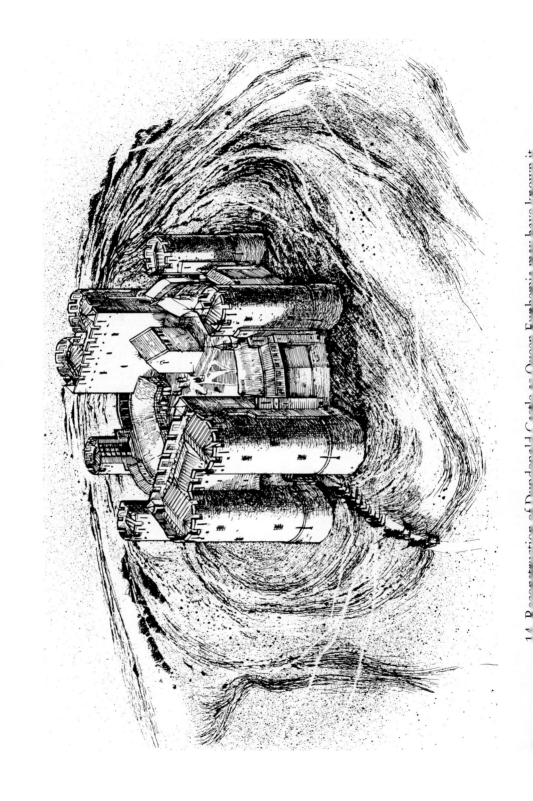

14. Reconstruction of Dundonald Castle as Queen Euphemia may have known it

15a. Dundonald Castle today.

15b. Robert II and Queen
Euphemia from the Seton
Armorial.

16. Edinburgh Castle improved by David I in 1367 and Robert II in 1377

17. All that remains of Dingwall Castle.

18. Ruthven Barracks, Kingussie, built for the Hanoverians after the Jacobite Rising of 1715. The motte was once a seat of the Wolf of Badenoch.

19. The Wolf of Badenoch's splendid tomb in Dunkeld Cathedral. He died *c.* 1405.

20. Fortrose Cathedral showing the chantry chapel and alleged tomb of the fourth Euphemia.

21. Doune Castle built by the Duke of Albany,
grandfather of the fifth Euphemia.

22. Dirleton Castle near North Berwick, home of the fifth Euphemia's stepfather, Sir Walter Halyburton.

23. The Cistercian Nunnery at North Berwick which the fifth Euphemia may have entered *c.* 1415.

24. North Berwick Harbour where pilgrims embarked for St Andrews.

25 Nuns singing in Chapel

lands of Cowie and Durris and Philorth was established as the principal home of the Frasers. In the late sixteenth century it was renamed Cairnbulg, as it is called today.

It is interesting to note that never in the many writs issued by Walter and Euphemia do the couple call themselves earl and countess, but rather *dominus* and *domina*, lord and lady of Ross. Euphemia's seal bore the legend 'Sigillum Eufamie Lescely dne de ros' while his was 'Lesley domini de Ros'. Only on one occasion in 1384 after her second marriage did she actually sign herself as countess of Ross.

During those early years at Dingwall, although they both issued many charters together, Walter was continually away on jousting or hunting parties in other parts of Scotland. He also travelled to England for which he continued to obtain free-conduct passes to visit his crusading cronies. Euphemia no doubt remained at home.

He was staying with the Frasers at Philorth, perhaps on a hunting party, in August 1381 where he granted a charter of Ross lands in the barony of Kingedward and certain annual rents from land in Banff to a certain Andrew Mercer. The witnesses designated were once again his 'dearest brothers' 'Dominis Alexandro et William Lindsay'.

This seems to have been the last charter that Sir Walter issued. He who had been called by Dr Boardman 'the most famous crusading Scot of the fourteenth century' was killed in 1382 in Perth, allegedly in a hunting accident. Ten days after his death on 9th March 1382 the above charter was confirmed by Euphemia at Dingwall. Among the many witnesses were the bishops of Ross and Moray, both of whom were as we shall see strong influences in the Lady Euphemia's life.

A LASTING MEMORIAL

One charter which the couple issued together from Dingwall castle granted 'to the Virgin Mary and Saint Boneface, patron of the church of Ross, the whole town of Drwme [Drummarkie?] for ever for the sustenance of one chaplain doing divine worship in the chapel of St Boneface adjacent to the town of Rosemarkie . . .'

The purpose of the chaplain was to say masses for the salvation of Euphemia and Walter's souls and those of all their ancestors, their heirs and successors, for ever. The appointment of the chaplain was to be left to the dean and chapter of Ross who, with the bishop, were among the several witnesses who signed the charter at Dingwall castle on 20th February 1380. Thus Euphemia and Walter were responsible for building, or starting to build, the south chapel and aisle, all that remains today, apart from the chapter-house, of the cathedral at Fortrose, once the busy centre of the see of Ross.

Compared with others, the diocese of Ross was never particularly wealthy. When David I created it between 1128 and 1131 under the first recorded bishop, a Gael called Macbeth, the cathedral church was a small stone building in Rosemarkie. This had once been a thriving Pictish monastic settlement, originally founded by St Boniface/Curadan in the eighth century. From the foundation of the diocese until 1235 the chapter of Ross had consisted only of a dean, treasurer and four canons, said to have been too poor to reside in the burgh.

As we have seen, it is thought that Farquhar of Ross would have liked to establish a grand new cathedral in Tain, but Bishop Robert had other ideas. When twenty years later Pope Gregory IX enabled him to found and endow new canonries, the Fortrose site, barely a mile from the old church was chosen for the new building. It is thought that the choir, chancel and chapter-house for the clergy and at least part of the nave for the laity were completed between 1280 and 1290, but when the Wars of Independence intervened, every able-bodied man was called up to fight and the building left unfinished.

It is interesting to note that out of the thirteen great medieval cathedrals in Scotland some were served by monastic or regular canons, while others like Fortrose, then called the Chanonry, were administered by secular (non-monastic) priests. These canons of Ross each had a parish within the diocese and enjoyed an income known as a prebend. They lived independently with their own servants in wooden houses built in a rectangle around the cathedral green. At the same time they were responsible for the services in their own little parish churches scattered throughout the diocese. Thus while they were living in the Chanonry they had to pay parsons to take the services in the parishes, and while visiting their parishes they had to provide vicars-choral to take their part in singing the cathedral offices.

By the early fourteenth century the main cathedral building was probably complete, a long rectangle about 70m (200ft) by 9m (36ft). At the north-western corner was a bell-tower which may have been an original feature, but unlikely to have been high, owing to the thickness of its walls. To the north of the choir was the two-storeyed chapter-house. The lower floor was used as the sacristy, with the arched recesses providing seats for the canons in chapter meetings. The upper floor probably housed the treasury, and perhaps a library.

The bishop was sometimes nominated by the king, but always appointed by the pope. He was the spiritual head of his diocese with the power to ordain others. The cathedral chapter consisted of the dean as chairman and the canons, among whom were appointed a precentor, succentor, chanter and sub-chanter. These were in charge of the canons' chief duty which was to sing the divine offices as perfectly as possible. Choristers were taught and trained in a nearby song-school. Indeed the set-up was not unlike the way the great English cathedrals are organised today.

In Euphemia's time the cathedral kirk of the Chanonry dedicated to St Peter and St Boniface was beautiful, built of glowing red sandstone set in a green yard, but incomplete. A chapter-house, a choir and a nave without aisles, however handsome, did not match up to magnificent Elgin in the neighbouring diocese of Moray. Certainly Beauly priory had no aisles either, but at least it had transeptal chapels. No doubt Bishop Alexander de Kylwos was quick to make these points to Euphemia. He knew Elgin well, having been its dean before his elevation to the see of Ross.

No doubt, too, Euphemia and Walter, when he was at home, visited the cathedral for the major festivals and were splendidly entertained by Bishop Alexander who in his turn was a frequent visitor to Dingwall castle. In accordance with the custom of the age, the couple were generous in their gifts to the many parishes and their parsons, but a cathedral with no chapel and no aisles, was that not an affront to the Almighty?

Perhaps in the first instance only a chantry chapel was planned with an altar and a burial place for the family. But when Walter was killed, the bishop may have appealed again to Euphemia, and plans for the south aisle were prepared as his memorial. His paternal arms – not Euphemia's – of three buckles on a bend are said by N. M. Wilby to be 'clearly visible on one of the roof bosses of the south aisle'. Walter however was not buried there. The building was nowhere near complete at the time of his death. He is more likely to have been buried in Fearn abbey, the traditional resting place of the previous earls of Ross.

Euphemia's chapel is more ornate than the aisle and you can still see the *piscina* set into the south wall for the priest to wash his hands and the sacred vessels. Its windows, what is left of them, have elaborate tracery and can be compared to those inserted in the choir aisles of Elgin cathedral after the fire of 1390. What is alleged to be Euphemia's tomb may still be seen within the most easterly of the arcade arches in the chapel. This canopied altar-tomb is the only one of several other memorials which can be said to be contemporary with the building. Richard Fawcess has called it 'a most effective piece of monumental design with a heavy gable surmounted by a cross finial rising above the arch which embraces the tomb.' Sadly, only a small portion of the stone effigy survives.

Thus Euphemia is credited with all that remains today of a once glorious building, a tribute not only to the skills of local architects and masons, not only to the influence of the church and its hierarchy but also to the humbling strength of belief in the Gospel of Christ by rich and poor alike, a belief that had not been matched before and certainly not since those distant times.

There she still lies today in her beautiful ruined chapel which has survived the depradations of the Reformation, the later ravages of Clan Mackenzie and the contempt of the burgh who once used the cathedral green as a midden. Safe today in the careful hands of Historic Scotland, her tomb is now the object of respectful sightseers who know nothing of her life and little of her times.

But that was for the future. After Walter's death she was to need all the prayers that one priest could raise.

THE WOLF OF BADENOCH

So many unpleasant things have been written about the man who was to become Euphemia's second husband that it is hard to separate the truth from the legend. Dr Stephen Boardman has called Alexander 'the most fascinating and maligned figure in the Stewart settlement of the north'. One fact is clear, however. Whatever Euphemia may have felt when she agreed to marry him, she came to hate him.

Bower wrote of the sons of Robert II that 'some were peace-making and benign, some were arrogant and malign'. In his estimation, Alexander fell into the second category. John, the eldest (later Robert III) was a gentle depressive, Walter the second son was dead, Robert was powerful, academic and devious, and Alexander the typical younger brother, competitive, rebellious, argumentative and quick-tempered, a man who since childhood had had to struggle to be noticed, and who had therefore grown big in every sense of the word (if his coffin is any indication) but particularly in his appetites and ambition.

He was the wrong age when his mother died and when his father remarried Euphemia Ross Randolph and had more sons he may have felt unwanted. There may have been childhood jealousies that were rekindled as he watched not only his older brothers receive prestigious titles but also his younger half-brother David step into the earldom of Strathearn before he came of age. Where was his title? Dr Boardman believes he might have resented this.

All Alexander had was control over the lordship of Badenoch and in 1368 he and his father had been imprisoned on Lochleven castle by David I for not keeping better order in that wild locality. In Robert II's first parliament as king in 1371 Alexander formally received Badenoch with Ruthven and Lochindorb castles from his father. This gift had no doubt been made with Queen Euphemia's blessing, for it is thought to have been part of her inheritance as widow of John Randolph. There was a proviso, however, that should Alexander die without an heir, his half-brother David should inherit the lordship that had belonged to his mother. At the same time David, still a boy but already an earl, received the castle and barony of Urquhart on Loch Ness with a similar proviso to Alexander who leased it from him, thus greatly increasing his influence in the north.

Although during the 'seventies many smaller land grants in the north came to Alexander from his father, no doubt he had hoped that Robert II would extend his patronage to the earldom of Moray which still remained in the king's hands. Indeed, for a full year Alexander had collected the rents from the earldom for his father the king, but instead Robert II gave it to placate his daughter Marjorie's husband, John Dunbar.

Then William of Ross died and Walter Leslie became the next earl of Ross. As King David's man, Walter was no friend of the Stewards and here was Alexander, owner of much property in the north, crouched on his doorstep, an insidious threat to him throughout the 'seventies. Indeed, Alexander had been assigned the task of upholding the widow's rights of the dowager countess of Ross, Mary of the Isles, Walter's mother-in-law. Bearing in mind, too, that Walter was often away from home, Alexander's influence in Ross slowly but surely increased.

He may have feasted at Dingwall with Euphemia, whom he might well have known from Dundonald days and hunted with Walter. Dr Boardman suggests that the two men, in an attempt at friendship, may have planned a pilgrimage together in August 1374, though there is no evidence that it ever took place. Slowly but inevitably Alexander became his father's chief representative and law enforcement officer for a territory which stretched from north Perthshire to the Pentland Firth, a huge area which included all his own scattered property gains. A superhuman task but still he had no title.

Then Walter died in February 1382. Alexander was quick to see his opportunity. In March Euphemia was signing charters, as we have seen, witnessed by Bishop Alexander of Ross and Bishop Alexander Bur of Moray, and others who were all friends of Walter and enemies or Alexander. Only a month later in April, Alexander was in Dingwall witnessing Euphemia's grant of land to Hugh Munro. The other witnesses were all Alexander's men.

He must have made himself attractive to the widow in her mid-thirties whose previous marriage may not have been particularly successful. He must have used all his Stewart charm to woo her. Just under forty, he was born about 1343, he was still in the prime of life, a physical giant of a man with a personality to match. No one forced her to marry him. Indeed, her family and friends including the Leslie-Lindsay connections and the bishops of Ross and Moray were decidedly against the match, as must have been her children Alexander and Margaret who cannot have been older than twelve or thirteen at the most. Perhaps they were being fostered at the time and not at home to give an opinion.

On the other hand King Robert was delighted. On 22nd July 1382 he rode north to Inverness to arrange the complicated marriage and property transactions himself and no doubt attend the celebrations. Firstly Euphemia conceded the barony of Kingedward to the king.

(This had been part of the old barony of Buchan inherited by her father from his uncle John de Ross who had married the Buchan heiress and died without children.) Within two days, Robert made Alexander earl of Buchan. Then she agreed that most of her other lands, including the lordships of Skye and Lewis, were now to be held jointly by her and Alexander and inherited by any children they might have together. Failing these, they would go to her son, Alexander Leslie. As for the earldom that, too, would be his but only in life-rent. According to the original charter of David II it was due to go to Euphemia's son by Walter.

So now Alexander had the two earldoms of Buchan and Ross, including the lordship of Badenoch. A couple of years later Robert made him justiciar and king's lieutenant north of the Forth, a post previously held by Alexander Lindsay of Glenesk, thus adding further fuel to that family's resentment. According to Dr Boardman, Euphemia's new husband was now 'unquestionably the most powerful figure in northern Scotland'.

The new earl of Ross's methods of keeping the peace depended not on chivalrous knights in armour but rather on his army of Highland mercenaries, professional native soldiers who were known as caterans. The name is derived from the Gaelic *ceatharn* and means literally 'broken man'. These mercenary warriors moved from one area to another according to who paid the bill and their remit was to collect the dues and rents from bishops and parsons, gentry and peasants, church lands and farm lands alike. It was the way they did it that caused resentment.

Boyce wrote that Alexander was a man 'whose wickedness had earned him universal hatred', the reason being that his caterans devastated fields, stole cattle and killed labourers. Although the bishops of Aberdeen and Moray complained bitterly, Robert took no notice of them. Alexander justified his actions by claiming that he was acting in the king's name and as Boece wrote 'no one cared to punish his insolence lest in so doing he might seem to offend the king'.

While Walter had been earl of Ross his spirit, and all too often his physical presence, had been in the south attending tournaments and pilgrimages and hunting parties. He was no Highlander by birth or inclination. Alexander on the other hand identified with the Highlands and became more and more involved in the politics of the Gael. While he was styled Wolf of Badenoch by Lowland contemporaries, in Gaeldom he was always Alasdair Mor, Mac an Righ, 'great Alexander, the king's son', and seen as a hero.

It may have been his involvement with and commitment to Gaeldom that appealed to Euphemia whose early childhood had been strongly influenced by her Gaelic mother and probably a Gaelic nurse. Indeed if Mary of the Isles was still alive, she may well have encouraged her daughter to wed the man who had upheld her widow's rights.

A DISASTROUS MARRIAGE

Just how soon the marriage started to go wrong it is impossible to say. Seven years later, with no evidence of children to bond the partnership, Euphemia was driven to complain to the two bishops, Alexander Bur of Moray and Alexander de Kylwos of Ross. The result of their ecclesiastical court held on 2nd November 1389 is the nearest we can come to finding out what had gone wrong.

First they listened to:

> what each party wished to offer against each other; and having considered the mode of procedure, pronounce, discern and declare by this writ, that Lady Euphemia, Countess of Ross, must be restored to Lord Alexander, Seneschal, Earl of Buchan, and Lord of Ross, as her husband and spouse, together with her possessions.

It seemed then that Alexander was no longer living with her in Dingwall but in Delny when he was not in one of his Badenoch castles or feasting with chieftains while keeping the king's peace in the west.

The judgement continued:

> And we have restored to her so far as the law can, to be treated honourably with matrimonial affection at bed and board, in food and raiment, and all others, according to what becomes her station, and that Mariota, daughter of Athyn [Mairead Nighean Eachainn] must be sent away; and we do send her away, as by law we are able; and that she shall not hereafter dismiss her [Euphemia].

This may have been the true reason for the break-up of the marriage. Alexander was, as we have seen, unmarried in his late thirties, an unusual situation, it would seem, for one requiring a legitimate heir. The reason was he had a long-term mistress too lowly-born to marry but whom he must deeply have loved and cared for, as well he might. She had given him five sons, 'all chips off the old block', according to the earl of Cromartie.

It seems he had settled Mariota and her children in Delny castle to the outrage of Euphemia and the scandal of Easter Ross. You don't bring your mistress and her large and rowdy family to live in one of your wife's residences, barely a dozen miles away, even if you are twice over an earl and the king's son. Possibly Euphemia had tried to deal with the situation herself and was rudely turned away from the door of her own castle. More likely, however, Alexander was withholding from her the revenues of the earldom. She had no money.

In addition, the judgement continues:

> since the Lady Euphemia alleges fear of death . . . from his men, family and others, [*homines suos nativos et alios*] the said earl shall find and deliver to us by way of surety, and security of great and honourable persons, and that under penalty of two hundred pounds, that he shall treat the said lady becomingly, as above said.

The rows between them perhaps gives an indication of Alexander's dangerous temper. Seriously frightened and no doubt encouraged by her numerous Ross relatives, Euphemia was driven to make a humiliating public complaint.

There was also a political dimension. In 1389 Alexander's elder brother, Robert, earl of Fife, was effectively ruling the country for his ageing father. Robert and Alexander had quarrelled over the latter's handling of his property gains, including Urquhart castle on Loch Ness, and Robert was determined to curb the power of his younger brother in the north. Also his grand-daughter Isabel was betrothed to Alexander Leslie and he was concerned for that young man's inheritance. He may well have advised Euphemia to make the complaints not so much for her sake but on behalf of her son and heir.

On the surface at least, Alexander complied with the bishops'

ruling. He 'personally constituted, promised, and faithfully undertook to perform and fulfil the premises all and sundry enjoined upon
him by us, under the penalty aforesaid; and to this end gave us as
surety the said lord earl of Sutherland, Alexander de Moravia, Lord
of Culbyn, and Thomas de Chisholm, then present, and consenting
to pay to us the foresaid penalty, when and how often he, which
God forbid, would come to do anything against the premises or any
of them.'

The witnesses were 'the great man, Robert, earl of Sutherland,
and the religious man, Adam, abbot of Kinloss, Masters William de
Spynie and William de Dingwall, deans of the cathedrals of Aberdeen
and Ross etc and many other witnesses especially called to the
premises'.

One can so easily imagine the Wolf outwardly all charm, rueful
smiles and deprecating gestures, inwardly a seething cauldron. His
capitulation could not last. Nor did it.

THE SACKING OF ELGIN CATHEDRAL

Robert II died the following year in April 1390 and his ailing eldest
son, baptised John, but calling himself Robert III at fifty-three became
his successor. This was a relief to Alexander who hoped for his
support against his other brother, the powerful earl of Fife. But when
the guardianship of the kingdom by Fife was renewed in May and the
new king still uncrowned, Alexander grew more and more impatient.

At last the opportunity came to stamp his authority on the north.
During the absence of his particular opponents, the earl of Moray
and David Lindsay of Glenesk at a tournament held at the court of
the English king, Richard II, he gathered a gang of 'wyld, wikkit,
heland men' and descended upon Moray. His main target was Bishop
Alexander Bur, with whom he had had many disputes over church
lands in Badenoch. He was also deeply angry with the bishop for
taking Euphemia's part in her recent complaint, a humiliation not
to be endured. The last straw was when Thomas Dunbar, the earl
of Moray's eldest son, undertook to protect the bishop, his life,
possessions and men against malefactors, caterans and everyone else
(except the king) in return for an annual fee. Obviously the bishop
was hinting at Alexander.

With a new king not yet crowned, the earl of Moray and his knights out of the country, Alexander saw his chance for revenge. In late May he attacked Forres, devastating the town, the choir of the church and the archdeacon's house. Three weeks later he descended upon Elgin and burnt the town, the churches and the cathedral. The roofs of the nave, choir and chapter-house were destroyed. To this day you can still see scorch marks on the restored masonry. The west front, central crossing and great tower were all damaged and had eventually to be rebuilt at huge expense. Immediately Bishop Alexander Bur, using the full authority of his ecclesiastical position, had him excommunicated.

Excommunication was the ultimate punishment in those days. 'That person which by open denunciatiom of the Church is rightly cut off from the unity of the Church and excommunicated, ought to be taken of the whole multitude of the faithful as an heathen and publican, until he be openly reconciled by penance and received into the Church by a judge that hath authority thereto.' Excommunication not only meant exclusion from the sacraments, but also isolation 'such as was inflicted on a leper, the cutting off of all intercourse with the faithful'. In other words, no feasting with his friends, no hunting parties, no association with his family. Alexander would have cared deeply for, apart from the disgrace and the inconvenience, he now had no chance of going to heaven. The whole affair reached such crisis proportions in Scotland that Robert II remained unburied and Robert III uncrowned until it could be resolved.

The bishop was not content with spiritual retribution. He also wanted physical reparation, so a bargain was struck. A couple of months later, according to the *Registrum Episcopatus Moraviensis*, 'Lord Alexander Steward, on the special commission of the lord Bishop Alexander Bur, and in the presence of the lord king, the earl of Fife . . . and many others, in Perth before the doors of the church of the Friars Preacher, and afterwards before the high altar, was absolved by Lord Walter Trail, bishop of St Andrews, from the sentence of excommunication on condition that he at once made satisfaction to the church of Moray and sent to the Pope for absolution, otherwise the former sentence of excommunication would apply again.'

This all happened a few days before Robert II's burial at Scone on 13th August and the new king's coronation the following day.

Thus Alexander, having confessed on his knees in the traditional sackcloth and been duly absolved, would have been able to attend his father's funeral and his brother's coronation, both barred to an excommunicant. A let-off? Perhaps, but the start of a new reign was seen as a time for forgiveness and new beginnings.

But there was to be no forgiveness from Euphemia. She petitioned Pope Clement VII for a separation. His judgement on 9th June 1392 stated that 'her marriage has been the cause of wars, plundering, arson, murders, and many other damages and scandals and it is likely that more will happen if they remain united.' Six months later she was granted a divorce *a mensa et thoro*. The marriage was at an end. Alexander lost the earldom of Ross and all the accompanying territories.

He seems to have withdrawn from Moray, though he retained his earldom of Buchan. No doubt he attended the pope in Avignon as instructed to do. Ten years later he made a small come-back as baillie of the earldom of Atholl owned by his younger half-brother Walter Steward. In 1404 he bought various lands in Inverness-shire from Hugh Fraser of Lovat in exchange for £75 and a promise of the earl's 'help and counsel'. Obviously, his old reputation as a 'protector' was not forgotten. He was also granted custody of the royal castle in Inverness in place of the earl of Moray who had probably been its custodian since 1390.

Many of his latter years were spent in controlling his natural sons, particularly the eldest Alexander whose reputation was no better than his father's. He had seized and married the countess of Douglas, Mar and Garioch in her own castle of Kildrummy. More of him anon.

Alastair Mor or the Wolf, earl of Buchan and lord of Badenoch, died in July 1405 in his seventies. He was buried in Dunblane cathedral in a splendid table tomb on which his huge and handsome armoured effigy reclines. Walter Bower, as we have seen, thought him 'insolent and malign'. The council general in 1388 dismissed him as 'useless to the community'. The Gaels saw him as a hero.

And Euphemia? She was undoubtedly attracted to his flamboyant personality and his identification with a Gaeldom disregarded by her first husband. Her petition to the bishops asked that he be restored to her bed and board, not that he be dismissed. That only came after he had committed the ultimate blasphemy of destroying the altar in Elgin. But she was probably well rid of him.

THE AFTERMATH

The following improbably story which has come down to us through the clan historians describes a strange relationship between Euphemia and Alasdair Ionraic (Upright) Mackenzie, fifth or sixth baron of Kintail. In Euphemia's day the Mackenzies, whose ancestral roots are thought to have been shared with those of the Rosses, were a Celtic clan in the ascendant. The first baron had saved the life of Alexander II during a stag hunt in the Royal Forest of Mar and had been granted the *caberfeidh* or stag's head for his coat of arms. He had fought so bravely for Alexander III at the Battle of Largs that he was rewarded with a charter of Kintail and the castle of Eilean Donan in 1266.

Alasdair Ionraic was exceptionally handsome. The story records that Euphemia fell in love with him and suggested that they marry. He refused, making the excuse that he was already betrothed to someone else. However, had she not been only the life-rentrix of the earldom he might well have accepted her proposal. Euphemia was not pleased. Allegedly she had him seized and imprisoned in Dingwall castle dungeon. She then tortured his servant to get hold of his signet ring and sent it by one of her servants to the governor of Eilean Donan castle with a message that he was to come to Dingwall as his master had married the countess.

The governor, recognising the ring, duly set off to find his master in gaol. Fortunately, he did not enter the castle but hung around the burgh until he discovered the truth. Having managed to find out where Alexander was warded, the two communicated 'by means of an allegory in Gaelic'. Alexander told him that the only way to secure his release was by the tit-for-tat capture of Euphemia's cousin, Walter Ross of Balnagown.

The governor raised a troop of Mackenzies and other friendly clansmen and duly captured the laird of Balnagown, after which the Rosses and their supporters attacked them in a bloody conflict which became known as the Battle of the Bealach nam Brog (Pass of the Shoes). The reason for the name was because the Mackenzies had tied their brogues to their chests to protect themselves from enemy arrows. The slaughter was appalling and unforgettable on both sides. The Mackenzie governor won but he released Balnagown and rode home.

Meanwhile, so the story alleges, Euphemia's men had captured Eilean Donan castle where she had appointed her own governor. As the Mackenzies rode home they overtook thirty Rosses sent by Euphemia with provisions for the castle. The Mackenzies captured them, made them remove their plaids, dressed up in them and took the stores – and their weapons – into the castle. Once safely inside they seized Euphemia's governor and held him prisoner until young Alasdair Ionraic was released.

This extraordinary story which entered into the oral tradition of the Highlands, particularly the oral tradition of clan Mackenzie, was a tapestry of half-truths. Alasdair Ionraic was certainly connected with the battle but as he was not born until 1401 – he died aged ninety in 1491 – he cannot have known Euphemia. In 1416 he became chief of clan Mackenzie and after the forfeiture of the earldom of Ross was in charge of south Ross-shire and established at Brahan castle a few miles from Dingwall. The battle, a desperate clan skirmish, actually took place in 1452.

Another extraordinary version of the story which appeared in the Ardintoul MS history of the Mackenzies again involved Euphemia. This tells us that she had been imprisoned by the king for inciting her son Alexander Leslie to rebellion which was the cause of the battle. As Alexander died in 1402 this too is a fabrication.

Why were such unpleasant tales built around the character of Euphemia? Perhaps because she was rich and powerful and therefore fair game to the story-tellers. Also she divorced her husband, an almost unthinkable act in her generation. In so many ways she captured the imagination of the Gael. Those who recognised the Wolf as their hero and his Gaelic mistress as some sort of wronged heroine may have genuinely believed the countess to have been not only a harridan, not just a figure of derision but also an object of hate.

More likely however, the reason why she was to feature so strongly in the oral tradition of the Mackenzies is that there was continual feuding between that clan and the Rosses. The clan seanachies were often inaccurate on facts but correctly reflected the partisan feelings, beliefs and fears of their listeners. Euphemia featured as an elderly woman whose silly passion for their handsome young chief was responsible for the death of so many mothers' sons. This seems to have been how she was remembered in Gaeldom.

Poor sad Euphemia.

THE FINAL MYTH

Nearly every existing account of the earls of Ross tells us that Euphemia, as if in reparation for her follies, retired to the nunnery of Elcho – the very place where her father had murdered Ranald of the Isles – took the veil and became prioress of that community. Not so. But it is easy to see how the mistake arose for there was a prioress of Elcho called Euphemia Leslie.

Little is known about the history of this convent, a Cistercian foundation, thought to have been founded by David Lindsay and his mother, Lady Marjorie, in the early thirteenth century. Before it was burned by the English in 1547 it supported at least twelve nuns, but by 1560 the numbers had dwindled to seven. These women were driven out by the Reformers and their house entirely destroyed. The last prioress was a Euphemia Leslie who died in September 1570.

Our Euphemia's alleged profession is based on yet another mistake. The seal of the prioress was thought to have been that of the countess, whereas the two are very different. The fallacy was exposed in *Scottish Armorial Seals* by W. Rae Macdonald. There would not have been time for her to become a nun, let alone prioress, in the two years of life remaining to her. In addition, she was still signing herself as lady of Ross in August 1394 when she granted a charter to her 'brother' Sir George Leslie of Rothes. Again in the same year she granted a charter, witnessed by her son, of the lands of Wester Foulis to her cousin Hugh Munro.

It is thought that she died on 20th February 1395, a date often ascribed to the death of the Wolf but, as he survived until 1405, it may have been hers. She was buried in that beautiful canopied tomb in the new chapel and south aisle that she had built in Fortrose cathedral and was duly succeeded in the earldom by her son Alexander Leslie.

Perhaps it was as well that she did not live to see what happened to her unhappy grand-daughter and namesake, the final Euphemia of Ross.

SOURCES

p 177 The recent excavations (1990s) of Finlaggan in the centre of Islay are described and illustrated in *Medieval Scotland* by Peter Yeoman.

p 179 Walter Bower was abbot of Inchcolm. His *Scotochronicon*, written in the fifteenth century, was largely based on John of Fordun's *Chronica Gentis Scotorum*.

pp 181–182 F. Marian McNeill's four volumes of Scottish folklore and festivals under the general title of *The Silver Bough* records a great wealth of customs. Only a flavour can be given here.

pp 182–186 Alan Macquarrie's *Scotland and the Crusades, 1095–1560* gives a full and accessible account of crusaders from Scotland.

pp 183, 184 The verses come from 'Two Irish Poems from the Mediterranean in the Thirteenth Century', G. Murphy, *Eigse*, VII (1955).

p 184 Hector Boece (c.1465–1536) was a Latin scholar and historian from Dundee who was appointed principal of the newly founded university of Aberdeen. He published his *Chronicles of Scotland* in 1527. It was he who depicted Gruoch, a direct descendant of Kenneth III, as the ambition-driven, blood-thirsty Lady Macbeth. Holinshed copied Boece and Shakespeare followed Holinshed.

pp 187, 188 *The Historical Records of the Family of Leslie* by H. K. Leslie of Balquain contains a good description of Sir Walter and gives a detailed account of the sources of the charters.

p 188 The charter granted to Euphemia de Sancto Claro is recorded in *The Shires of Aberdeen and Banff*, Vol. II, from the original to be found in the Innes Charter-chest at Floors.

A coloured illustration of Sir Walter's coat of arms from the *Armorial de Gelre* (1369–88) may be seen on Plate 11 of *PSAS*, Vol. XXV.

pp 189–191 The *Querimonia* is recorded in the *Historical Records of the Family of Leslie* and in *Ane Account of the Families of Innes*, 1864.

p 192 The Charter issued by Margaret Leslie is recorded in *Registrum Magni Sigilii*, no. 151.

p 193 Sir Walter's death is recorded in the *Calendar of Fearn*.

pp 193–194 Euphemia and Walter's charter granting the chantry chapel at Fortrose cathedral is recorded in the *Calendar of Writs of Munro of Foulis 1299–1823*, Scottish Records Society.

pp 195–196 The history and descriptions of the cathedral come from *The Chanonry of Ross* by C. G. Macdowall, *Fortrose Cathedral* by N. M. Wilby and *Beauly Priory and Fortrose Cathedral* by R. Fawcett.

p 199 Hector Boece's criticism is made in his *Murthlacensium et Aberdonensium Episcoparum Vitae.*

p 200 *The Book of Pluscarden* described the Wolf as 'great Alexander, the king's son'.

pp 200–204 The findings of the ecclesiastical court are fully recorded in *Registrum Episcopatus Moraviensis* as are the sacking of Elgin cathedral and the sentence of excommunication.

p 203 The description of excommunication is taken from *The Thirty-nine Articles* by B. J. Kidd.

p 204 Pope Clement's judgements are recorded in *The Calendar of Papal Letters to Scotland, 1378–1394,* Reg. Aven. 269, 391v and 272, 569: 269, 391v.

pp 205–207 The myths surrounding Euphemia are recorded in the earl of Cromartie's *A Highland History* and corrected in A. Haddow's *History and Structure of the Ceol Mor.*

p 207 Euphemia Leslie is recorded as prioress of Elcho in 1570 by I. B. Cowan and D. E. Easson in *Medieval Religious Houses in Scotland.*

INTERLUDE

Our fifth Euphemia was the only child of Alexander Leslie, earl of Ross, a grand-daughter of Countess Euphemia on her father's side and, on her mother's side, a grand-daughter of the most powerful man in Scotland, Robert, earl of Fife, soon to be duke of Albany. During her short life he dominated Scotland.

As we have seen, John Steward, earl of Carrick and eldest son of Robert II, was crowned Robert III on 14th August 1390. Annabella, his queen, was crowned the following day. According to Agnes Mure Mackenzie, Robert III at the age of fifty-three has been described as 'gentle, courteous, dignified and kindhearted with a noble presence and a long snowy beard'. He had the best of intentions to give Scotland peace and prosperity and he was genuinely religious. The nation knew and liked him. However, he lacked the ruthlessness needed to control his nobles, his health was poor and he had been lamed by a horse at the age of seventeen and was unable thereafter to ride, an insuperable handicap for a king in those days.

Walter Bower records that the king, well aware of his deficiencies, cried out to his wife in a fit of deep depression: 'I would prefer to be buried deep in a midden, providing my soul be safe in the day of the Lord. Wherefore bury me, I pray, in a midden, and write for my epitaph – "Here lies the worst of kings and saddest of men."'

Annabella was the niece of David II's second wife, Margaret Drummond Logie, and the marriage largely arranged by that king who had recognised Robert as his successor. Annabella was a capable tenacious woman who adored her eldest son, another David. She was determined that he should succeed his father rather than her ambitious brother-in-law, the earl of Fife who had virtually ruled the kingdom during the latter years of Robert II's reign and still wielded enormous power in the country.

Robert III and Annabella had been married for twenty-three years before succeeding to the throne. They already had two sons and four daughters, Robert the eldest boy who died in infancy and David born in 1378. A third son, James, did not appear until after his father had been king for four years. Of the four girls, three married into the powerful house of Douglas, while the youngest, Egidia, died as a child.

Thus the boy David, so long awaited and so important to the succession, was fourteen when his father became king. He was treasured and spoiled, charming and headstrong. As he grew older the court split into three factions, one led by Annabella and David, another by the earl of Fife and the third by the Douglases who controlled the borders. In a vain attempt to reconcile them, Robert III, in imitation of the European custom, initiated the title of duke. In 1398 he created his son duke of Rothesay and his brother, Robert earl of Fife, duke of Albany. *Albainn* was and still is the Gaelic name for Scotland and carried an aura of royalty which probably gratified the new duke.

Those were still the days of tournaments and lavish displays of chivalry. Bower records that in 1398 it was Annabella rather than the king who arranged a great tournament in Edinburgh where Prince David was publicly initiated as a knight. Dr Boardman thinks that her intention was probably to 'focus the loyalty of his knightly companions, and their families, on the young prince'.

Relations with England were better than they had been for many years with rivalries resolved at the tournaments rather than on the battlefield. Wyntoun records that when the most famous jouster in England, a certain Lord Wells, issued a challenge to any Scots knight, it was taken up by Sir David Lindsay, son of Alexander of Glenesk. They met on London Bridge. Glenesk refused to be thrown. When the crowds shouted that he was a cheat tied to his saddle, he galloped up to the royal box, jumped to the ground, then in full armour leapt back on to his horse and returned to the fray. When both men were dismounted, Glenesk hooked his dagger into Wells' armour and lifted him bodily into the air, let him fall with a crash, then politely assisted him to his feet and presented him to the English queen.

Annabella, writing in French from Dunfermline to Richard II of

England just after the birth of her son James in 1394, had great hopes of 'a marriage-treaty to be made between some nearly allied to you by blood and some children of the king my lord and of us'. Her plans came to nothing.

Robert was, therefore, having more trouble with his nobles at home than with the 'auld enemie' and he had not the brute strength or confidence in himself needed to handle them. He was also having trouble in the north. The gap between the English-speaking Lowlanders and the Gaelic Highlanders under the powerful Macdonalds of the Isles continued to widen.

By 1399 the Council General was not happy with his 'misgovernance of the realm and the defaut of the keipying of the common law'. It decreed that government should be transferred into the Council's hands and that the duke of Rothesay 'be the kingis lieutenande generally athroch al the Kinrike afor the terme of thre yher'. The Council consisted of members of all the factions of power. The king's brother, Albany, of course, was one of them and Alexander Leslie, earl of Ross, who was married to Albany's daughter, was another.

The king's son, David, now aged twenty-one took the same oath as a king at his coronation and his father retreated alone to Dundonald and the Steward estates in the south-west, while Annabella remained at court to advise and support her son. Robert III still had seven years left until his death at Rothesay castle on Palm Sunday 1406. At his own request he was not buried with his father and the other kings at Scone but in nearby Paisley abbey. He did not believe himself fit for such an honour.

Meanwhile David was betrothed for a second time. His first fiancée had died untimely. His new bride-to-be, Elizabeth, was a daughter of the earl of March who had paid him a large sum of gold for the privilege. However when Archibald, nicknamed the Grim, earl of Douglas offered an even bigger sum to marry his daughter Marjory, the fickle David jilted Elizabeth who in shame fled to a convent.

Her father in fury crossed the border to England and roused the Percies of Northumberland who were only too glad to invade the borders. When they were driven back by the new earl of Douglas, Archibald the Grim having died, King Henry IV of England himself in retaliation led a huge army north to Newcastle. There he issued an aggrieved and pious summons to King Robert and to his nobles to do homage to the king of England. Henry's letter, dated 6th/7th August 1400, reminded the Scots of the English crown's ancient claims to superiority and of the previous Scots kings who had paid homage to the English sovereign.

Henry gave Robert a fortnight to comply. He then marched with fifteen to twenty thousand men across the border north to Edinburgh. Although he burned the city, Henry is said to have spared the countryside out of respect for Queen Annabella and he also spared the monks of Holyrood because they had once sheltered his father. Although Edinburgh was destroyed, the castle was held securely by David while Albany raised an army. The two forces met at Calder Muir but no battle ensued. Albany, cunning as always, waited and watched while the English warriors froze and starved in atrocious weather. When the great Owain Glyndwr of Wales led a major revolt against the English, Henry was forced to leave Scotland and hastily arranged a six-week truce in order to retreat.

The following year (1401) Annabella, who had been David's guide and support as well as his mother, died. She was greatly mourned. Andrew of Wyntoun described her as:

Faire, honorabil and plesand
Cunnand, curtas in her efferis,
Lovand and large [generous] to strangeris.

Left to stand on his own feet, the headstrong young prince made a fatal error. It concerned a certain member of the Council General, Sir John Ramornie of Fife, a favourite of Albany and his son Murdoch, but also friendly with David. Here was a dangerous man, a scholar and diplomat but entirely without principle. What exactly happened is obscure but seemingly he suggested to David that he could easily get rid of his uncle Albany by having him murdered. David was shocked and said so, whereupon Ramornie sped without delay to Albany and told him that it was David's idea to dispose of him.

David should have gone straight to his father the king but Albany got there first. He now had the excuse he needed to dispose of his nephew and, he claimed, he had the king's permission to arrest him. Sometime towards the end of 1401 Albany, with his half-brother Walter Steward (second son of Robert II and his queen Euphemia),

Ramornie himself and some others all disenchanted by David waylaid him and his escort on the road to St Andrews. He was seized and imprisoned, first in St Andrews castle and then taken to Albany's own castle at Falkland in Fife. Bower, an admirer of Albany, suggested that the reason for the arrest was that David could be 'put into custody for a time until, after punishment by the rod of discipline, he should know himself better'.

Unfortunately, between 25th and 27th March 1402 he died, officially of dysentery, and was swiftly buried at the nearby monastery of Lindores. However it was rumoured that he had been starved to death and the Council was forced to investigate. Loth to start a civil war, their verdict was 'not proven'.

With David out of the way, Albany had the power he craved. All that stood between him and kingship was his ailing elder brother Robert III and a young boy of seven, the king's son, James. He assumed the title *Gubernator Dei gratia*. He spoke of 'his subjects' and had his own great seal on which he is shown seated on a canopied throne wearing a coronet and sword in place of the crown and sceptre.

His was not an enviable task. Between bad weather, bad harvests, another outbreak of plague and the continued lawlessness of the nobility, the country was in bad shape. Also there was trouble again with England. He decided to further secure his own governorship and to ingratiate himself with Henry IV by handing over the boy, Prince James, now living with his tutor Bishop Wardlaw in St Andrews, as a hostage to the English.

Robert was roused at last. He may not have been an effective king but he was still a fond father. He decided to send the lad secretly on a merchant ship to France on the pretext of improving his education. But in the spring of 1406 his ship was captured by an English privateer. In spite of the truce, Henry imprisoned the lad and his entourage in the Tower of London. When Robert protested, Henry told him firmly that the lad could learn French as easily in London as in France. Walter Bower records that poor Robert's 'spirit forthwith left him, the strength waned from his body, his countenance grew pale, and for grief thereafter he took no food'. He was dead within a few days of hearing the news.

Although his followers were freed, James remained a comfortable prisoner for twenty years. Robert died in 1406 and Albany remained not only ruler but also heir to his nephew who was growing up fast in England. He died in his eighties in 1420 to be succeeded in the guardianship by his unpopular son Murdoch.

But now the Scots were determined to have their proper king back. James promised to pay the English 60,000 merks – carefully not called ransom – for his board and lodging over the past twenty years. He also promised not to support France in her wars with England. He and his beloved English bride Joan returned to Scotland to rule with a ruthless efficiency learned in the English court. Sadly his life was to end, in conspiracy and murder.

Meanwhile Alexander Leslie, earl of Ross had died untimely in the same year as Prince David. He left one child who cannot have been older than the young Prince James and whose fate, like that of both princes, lay in the hands of the duke of Albany. She was little Euphemia Leslie, heiress to the earldom of Ross.

SOURCES

Some of the colourful incidents recorded here come from *The Rise of the Stewarts* by Agnes Muir Mackenzie, a graduate of Aberdeen university, who wrote novels and published a six-volume *History of Scotland* between 1934 and 1941. In all her works, whether fact or fiction, she showed herself to be a fiercely pro-Highland Scottish patriot. Although her works are not highly regarded today, she included those small details that bring the history of a difficult period alive.

p 213 The decrees of the Council General are recorded in *The Acts of the Parliaments of Scotland*, Vol. I, edited by T. Thomson and C. Innes.

PART FIVE

———— ◆ ————

THE FIFTH EUPHEMIA
Bride of Christ

Euphemia's father Alexander Leslie, came into his earldom on the death of his mother c.1394. His cannot have been an easy life. If he had been born within the first five years of the marriage of his parents in 1366, he would have been between twelve and sixteen when his father died and his mother remarried the Wolf of Badenoch. With the rest of the Leslie family and his Ross relatives he hated his new Steward step-father, the more so as the marriage deteriorated and he witnessed his mother's increasing humiliation.

Who it was who arranged his betrothal to Isobel Steward, the eldest of nine daughters of the earl of Fife – later duke of Albany – we cannot know. It may have been his father Walter before his untimely death in 1382 who at the same time arranged a marriage for his daughter Margaret with Donald Macdonald heir to the lordship of the Isles. Thus he made provision for his children to unite with two of the most important families in the kingdom.

But it may have been the earl of Fife himself who, with our fourth Euphemia, arranged the betrothal long after Walter's death. As we have seen he visited Inverness and no doubt Dingwall castle in the autumn of 1389. The marriage may have been arranged then. Almost certainly Fife encouraged Euphemia to complain to the bishops of Moray and Ross of his brother's outrageous behaviour to her. Probably he persuaded her also to have the courage to apply to the pope for a divorce. As young Alexander Leslie's prospective father-in-law it was very much in his interests to have the Wolf out of Ross.

As the fourth Euphemia's relationship with one brother deteriorated, so her dependence on the other grew. Indeed she was staying with Fife in his castle at Stirling in the autumn of 1392 when she petitioned the pope. While there she also issued a charter of some lands in Galloway which was approved by her son, the young Alexander, using Fife's seal as guardian of Scotland.

Perhaps the marriage took place then and Alexander took his bride to Delny, as his mother was living in Dingwall castle, and issuing charters with his consent as her heir. We know that in 1398 as earl of Ross he was staying in Perth where he resigned his father's barony in Fife to a relative, George Leslie of Rothes. He was again at Scone a couple of years later granting more lands to the same George Leslie in exchange for 200 merks 'to relieve his lands and earldom of Ross out of the hands of the king, the superior thereof and for his good council and service'.

What exactly happened to Alexander we don't know but he died in his thirties at Dingwall on 8th May 1402, leaving as his heir one unfortunate little girl. She cannot have been more than six or seven years old. Her tragedy, according to the Clan Donald account, was to be born 'crouch-backit'. For any child to be born with a congenital spine disorder is a tragedy; for one born to inherit the vast territories of the earldom of Ross in the fourteenth century it was a disaster.

A SICKLY CHILD

One can only imagine the grief and guilt of Alexander and Isobel as they sought desperately for healing or indeed a miracle cure for their daughter. How often must Isobel have agonised and wondered over her sins, for in those days illness was seen as a punishment from God. Indeed, as she grew older Euphemia herself may have taken on the blame for her own fate and suffered mental torment.

Perhaps her parents were advised to send for some local healer who had been either a breech birth, born with a caul or a seventh child, and therefore credited with the power to cure disease with silvered water, healing stones or intertwined coloured threads. Perhaps they summoned a local bone-setter who would have known instantly that there was nothing he could do. Maybe he suggested the poor child be made to lie for hours flat on the floor while a barefoot attendant massaged her back with his or her feet.

Perhaps secretly they consulted an astrologer. Astrology was uncompromisingly against the teaching of the church which saw any sort of divination as pagan and therefore of the devil. However Mary Beith tells us that Gaelic physicians were well aware of Islamic medicine which included pharmacology, dermatology, alchemy and astrology. A popular pharmacopoeia compiled in Salerno about 1150 was translated in 1415 into Gaelic and in it diagnoses were made by study of the urine and astrology. It was believed that each of the houses of the zodiac and the planets affected the health of those born under them. Unfortunately, we don't have the birth date of our fifth Euphemia.

There would have been those quick to point out that she had been 'overlooked' by some ill-wisher and she would have been given incantations to ward off the evil eye.

> Against eye of man red and harsh-spoken,
> Against eye of woman swift and loud-spoken,
> Against eye of serpent red and venomous,
>   Salve O kindly Colum Cille
>   Salve O holy Patrick of marvels
>   Salve O quiet Brigit of the Boyne
>   Salve O great Mary of the ringlets . . .
>   (from *Carmina Gradelica*)

Perhaps they took her to some sacred shrine. The bronze bell of St Adomnan, kept at Kincraig near Aviemore, for example, was believed to have healing powers. Or perhaps she made regular trips to a sacred well. There were plenty of them to choose from in Ross. Two survive on the Black Isle to this day, one dedicated to St Boniface/Curadan and the other to St Bennet (Benedict) where people still hang up clouts or rags in exchange for a wish. No doubt Masses were doubled at her grandmother's chantry chapel in the cathedral kirk of the Chanonry. Indeed the whole of her childhood may have been spent in one long desperate search for a cure.

It is more than probable that her father would have invited one of the Beatons, hereditary Highland physicians, to Dingwall castle. The earliest known of these Gaelic-speaking doctors practising in Scotland was Patrick MacBeth, who was chief physician and surgeon to Robert I. His son Gilbert looked after David II and there are documents recording his safe-conduct passes to visit the king of Scots in England. In every reign thereafter until Charles I there were

Beatons, sometimes more than one, in attendance at court. Hector Boece in his *History of Scotland*, written in 1527, stated that the Beatons were 'richt excellent' in the practice of medicine.

A lovely story reflecting one Beaton's skill at diagnosis is told of how a certain king of Scots, probably Robert II, summoned a Highland Beaton to his bedside. The other court physicians, determined to make a fool of him, replaced the king's specimen with urine from a cow. Holding the glass phial up to the light, Beaton declared without a twinkle that the king must be in calf.

The Wolf in conjunction with his father (Robert II) confirmed a grant of land in Sutherland to Fearchar Lichiche or *Ffaercado medico nostro* (Farquhar our doctor), and again on 31st December 1386 Robert II granted to 'our esteemed and faithful leech Fearchar' some islands off the north-west coast for services rendered. So there were Beatons in Sutherland who became physicians to clan Mackay, but there were also Beatons much nearer home who became hereditary physicians to clan Munro and claim to have held land in the area as far back as the thirteenth century.

Whether any of them were doctors at the time of Euphemia is not known but there were certainly several branches of the family working alongside other hereditary medical families in the western Highlands and Islands. The most famous were the Beatons of Balinby in Islay, who took care of the lords of the Isles. Perhaps her aunt Margaret married to Donald of the Isles sent over her own personal physician to Dingwall.

Mary Beith in *Healing Threads* tell us that twenty-nine Gaelic medical manuscripts survive to this day though only a fraction of the texts have so far been translated. 'The manuscripts are not only obviously working manuals with jottings in the margins and signs of contemporary wear and tear, but also collections of earlier, mainly classical and Arabic, writings which arguably reflect the individual preferences of the compilers.'

These Gaelic doctors believed in sound common sense. Exercise and prayer first thing in the morning after 'a good clean spit and rub dust and sweat from the skin'. The hair should be combed, hands and face washed and the teeth cleaned. Diet advice warned against eating raw food such as oysters and birds' eggs half-cooked. Peas, beans and other pulses should be cooked with a pinch of cummin to prevent wind. Vegetable dishes were to be eaten after blood-letting, for example kale, sage, mallow and, in season, bugloss, violets, spinach, lettuce and the tops of fennel.

With regard to drink, wine should not be taken in the same mouthful as food, but whisky in moderation was the universal panacea. 'It will heal wounds, and it will brighten brass, and if it be given to epileptics in their drink it will help them.' It would also relieve those suffering cancer, gripes, colic caused by cold, phlegm, tooth-ache, quinsy, sore throats, melancholia, sciatica, dropsy, deafness, leprosy, catarrh and headache. It could even make 'good wine out of stale wine and strong wine out of weak wine and a very good wine out of a good wine'. Above all it could 'preserve youth for everybody'.

But there was little they could do for Euphemia. Blood-letting, so common up to the nineteenth century throughout Britain, was treated with caution by those long-ago Highland physicians. It was considered weakening and not more than four a year were recommended for the young with less as the patient grew older. So no doubt Euphemia grew used to these as regular events, just as she may have acquired a taste for whisky. At the same time she must have come to realise that for her, without the interception of God himself, there could be no betterment. And, as she may have seen God as angry with her, there was little hope.

ALBANY'S WARD

On the death of her father in 1402, she became officially countess of Ross in her own right but as she was under age, her grandfather, the earl of Fife, now the duke of Albany, appointed himself as her guardian and took her and her mother under his wing.

What was Albany really like? According to Bower, 'He was one of the most patient of men, gentle and kind, affable and communicative, ordinarily sociable, somewhat extravagant, open-handed to strangers, singular above all his compeers. In stature he was tall, and comely in form, with white hair and an amiable countenance . . . his speech was always gracious and wholesome, whether in the highest courts of the realm or any other.' Andrew of Wyntoun declared that if all the princes of the world were gathered together, Albany would stand out as the one worthiest of renown.

Above all he was clever. He realised that unfair taxation on the

ordinary people was counter-productive so by keeping this to a minimum he 'acquired the innumerable blessings of the common folk'.
He was also politically astute with an experience of government that
at the end of his eighty years had spanned most of his life.

But his Steward charm and clever mind hid an overwhelming
ambition to be king. Understandably. He had virtually ruled for his
father, his brother and his nephew James I, whose heir he now was.
He had been responsible – at least indirectly – for the death of his
nephew David, and he made no effort to ransom James, or so James
himself believed. There was a determination in Albany to get his
own way at all costs, whether it was by charm or charter, generosity
in land transactions or the drawing up of devious entails that continually benefited himself, his family or his supporters. He was, in the
words of the historian Ronald Nicholson, 'a master of chicanery'.
Euphemia was soon to experience both the charm and the ruthlessness of her maternal grandfather.

Which of his castles he took her to is not recorded. It could have
been Stirling, that formidable royal stronghold perched on a rock
which Robert II had granted to him and his male heirs in 1373. It
could have been Falkland which he had acquired as earl of Fife and
where his nephew David had died untimely. Indeed, she may have
moved from one to the other as was the custom of the day.

Most likely however it was Doune in Perthshire, an impressive
new tower-house castle which he began to build in the 1370s after
his marriage in 1361 to Margaret Graham, countess of Menteith,
through whom he also acquired that earldom. Doune was strategically important as the two great routes from Edinburgh to Inverlochy
and from Glasgow to Perth and Inverness met and intersected here.
Whoever controlled these roads might also control the Highlands.
Therefore this was his preferred seat from where he virtually ruled
the kingdom from 1388 to 1420. Most impressive is its great
cathedral-like hall measuring 170sq m (1,830sq ft) and rising to 11m
(36ft) to the apex of the roof. Without the customary fireplace,
Albany's guests were kept warm with great iron braziers, while his
family lived in the spacious four-storey tower-house beyond.

There would have been room for little Euphemia and her mother
here and plenty of opportunity for his family to pressure her into
renouncing her inheritance. Although handicapped, young and in
need of protection, there can be no doubt that she was also a prisoner

of her grandfather who from a precept of 11th July 1405 was signing himself lord of the ward of Ross.

According to the *History of the Macdonalds* Albany and his family 'persuaded her by flattery and threats to resign her rights to the earldom of Ross to John, Albany's second son, earl of Buchan, as it was given out and *that* much against her will'. Euphemia was being persuaded to enter a convent. As a nun, Euphemia would be legally dead to the world and not able to keep or dispose of her earldom. Euphemia may have been weak, handicapped and young, but she must also have been stubborn. She resisted, at least for the time being.

About three years after her father's death, her mother remarried in February 1408 Sir Walter de Halyburton, probably as his second wife. He was a border nobleman whose stronghold was Dirleton castle near North Berwick in East Lothian. Sir Walter had taken part in many a border skirmish against the English in an attempt to recapture Scottish lands and castles and was present at the Scots defeat of the Percies at Otterburn in August 1388. His castle at Dirleton had been built by Sir John de Vaux, steward to Marie de Coucy after her marriage to Alexander II in 1239, and its multi-turreted design is thought to have been based on Chateau Gaillard on the river Seine. It stood on a small craggy knoll at the eastern end of a long low ridge of rising ground adjoining the road to North Berwick where a Cistercian convent and refuge accommodated pilgrims on their way to the shrine of St Andrew in Fife.

De Vaux's descendant Sir Walter Halyburton inherited it in a ruinous condition and as part of his renovation included a splendid tower-house residence for his family. Today all that is left is the basement with a chapel above a particularly grim prison and pit, and storage vaults beneath the great hall and cathedral-like kitchens.

Probably Euphemia went to Dirleton with her mother. Perhaps she and her nurse occupied the attic at the top of the spiral staircase, well out of sight of the other occupants. It is tempting to imagine her wistfully looking over the crenellated walls of the square tower, watching the pilgrims passing by, and wondering bitterly what would become of her and who if anyone would ever want to marry her. Perhaps she was visited from time to time by her mother's attractive brother John Steward, who had been created earl of Buchan in 1307. With soft words and pretty speeches he would have given her plenty of good reasons why she should resign her rights in Ross to him. But still she resisted.

In spite of the pressure from her grandfather and uncle, and no doubt her mother, Euphemia did not have the right to give away her earldom to Buchan or anyone else. According to the entail, should she die without children – and to enter a nunnery was to be legally dead – her heir was her father's sister and Margaret was, as we have seen, married to the most powerful man in the west, Donald Macdonald of the Isles.

Rumours and counter-rumours about Euphemia's fate reached Donald and Margaret. Donald sent messengers to the guardian demanding clarification but, according to the *History of the Macdonalds*, 'could get no hearing from Albany but lofty menacing answers. Neither could he get sight of the rights' informing him that Euphemia had signed away her earldom. Donald's sense of injustice was strong, his Celtic blood was fired. Besides, he had no love for Albany. *The Calendar of Patent Rolls 1403–8* records that he had already had 'colloquy with his liege lord the king of Scotland [James]', and in 1408 English envoys from Henry IV had visited Donald at Finlaggan to negotiate, perhaps even to overthrow Albany and restore James to the throne. James may even have approved of Donald's plans to gain the earldom of Ross in his wife's name by force. Indeed, Boece tells us that within the Highlands Donald was seen as the true heir to Ross.

The territory in question was huge, comprising not only Skye, Ross and Cromarty but part of old Argyll west to Loch Broom with the coastlands of Kintail, Lochalsh, Loch Carron, Applecross and Gairloch. South it reached to Urquhart on Loch Ness and east into Inverness with superiority over land in Nairn and Aberdeenshire. Donald was determined to have it 'or else be graithed in his graif' (steeped in his own urine).

He challenged Albany that 'he would either lose all or gain the earldom of Ross'. Albany called his bluff. Donald, no doubt with the use of the fiery cross carried from hilltop to settlement, called out his men and some ten thousand flocked to his castle at Ardtornish on Morvern on the Sound of Mull. Out of the number he picked some six and a half thousand men and sent the rest home. There were Macleans and Mackinnons, Macleods, clan Chattan of Lochaber, men from Mull and Morvern and as many Macdonald kinsmen and vassals as he could muster. Dressed in their eagle plumes and quilted saffron tunics, carrying long axes and two-handed broadswords, the chiefs led out their red-shanked warriors to battle.

As John Major described them, 'the Wild Scots go out to battle with the whole body clad in a linen garment sewed together in patchwork, well daubed with wax or with pitch, and with an overcoat of deer skin.' They were rearin' to fight.

They sailed to Stroma, an island off the northern coast of Scotland, and marched south to Dingwall drawing in others on the way. Their only resistance came from the Mackays who were routed. Dingwall castle was occupied and Inverness taken, its famous oak bridge burned because the burghers would not join the clans. Camerons and Macintoshes, however, pledged their support and Donald's army was said to number some ten thousand men. Although he now held Ross that was not enough. Albany must be taught a lesson. Besides the Ross earldom had lands in Banff and Aberdeenshire and his men wanted more loot. He planned to march through Moray and sack Aberdeen.

Leading the defence was the earl of Mar. He was none other than Sir Alexander Steward, illegitimate son of the Wolf and his mistress Mariota. He had acquired his earldom by besieging the widowed countess in Kildrummy castle and marrying her by force. He was also Donald's first cousin. His father and Donald's mother had both been children of Robert II. This made no difference. No doubt Donald also remembered the Wolf's treatment of his mother-in-law and there was a score to settle there.

At dawn on 24th July 1411 the two armies met near Inverurie close to the village of Harlaw some fifteen miles from Aberdeen. Donald's bard Lachland Mor MacVurich chanted a battle song – three hundred lines of genealogy and proud words – to incite the Gaels. Mar's army, possibly not more than two thousand men clad in armour with lance, mace and battle-axe, consisted of nearly all the local barons and knights, Ogilvies, Lindsays, Carnegies, Frasiers, Arbuthnots, Burnets, with Errol, the lord marischal, and Sir James Scrymgeour, constable of Dundee and standard-bearer of Scotland.

For several hours the battle raged. Donald lost about a thousand men and about half of Mar's army was slain. Nearly every leading family in Aberdeenshire lost a laird or his son. The lord marischal was captured and died later of a broken heart. Donald's casualties included the Maclean chief, a great number of Camerons, John MacLeod and the heir to Ulva.

An old anonymous ballad recalls the tragedy:

> The Hielan' men wi' their lang swords,
> They laid on us fu' sair;
> And they drive back our merrymen
> Three acres breadth or mair . . .
>
> And sic a weary burying,
> The like ye never saw,
> And that was the Sunday after that
> On the muirs down by Harlaw
>
> And gin Hielan' lasses speer at you
> For them that gaed awa',
> Ye may tell them plain and plain enought,
> They're sleeping at Harlaw.

That night Donald withdrew without going on to sack Aberdeen. No one quite knows why.

And who won? Lowland historians claimed that Donald was defeated, even killed. But according to Highland tradition Donald was the victor. The sides were too equally matched for the one to claim outright victory over the other. What Harlaw did, however, was to emphasise and entrench the antagonism that already existed between the Gaelic-speaking clans and the English-speaking Scots.

Donald retreated back to the Isles and Albany roused himself to recover Dingwall castle in the autumn of 1411 where he installed a garrison. The following summer he raised three armies, ostensibly to crush Donald. There is an uncorroborated tale that the two men met at Lochgilphead where Donald handed over hostages and promised to keep the peace.

Thereafter Donald led a life of religious seclusion and died about

1422 at his castle at Ardtornish and was buried on Iona. He and Margaret had a number of children, many of whom died in infancy, but he was survived by three sons and a daughter. One son became a monk, another a bishop and his daughter married a Sutherland of Dunbeath. His heir Alexander – of whom more anon – succeeded him.

Whatever the outcome of 'reid Harlaw', that tragic conflict between Highlander and Lowlander, between Gael and Scot, between east and west, Donald failed to win for his wife little Euphemia's earldom of Ross.

BETROTHAL

It has been said by some historians that Euphemia, through no fault of her own, was responsible for the disaster of Harlaw and perhaps it could be seen that way. Had she been fit and strong and marriageable Albany, her grandfather, and her uncle Donald of the Isles would not have tried to take her inheritance.

But still she held on, at least until 1415 when it was proposed that she should be betrothed to Thomas Dunbar, son and heir to the earl of Moray and one of Albany's supporters. Thomas was a grandson of Robert II through his daughter Marjorie who had married John Dunbar, created earl of Moray by his father-in-law. His father, Thomas the second Dunbar earl of Moray, had married in 1392 and his son Thomas must have been about the same age as Euphemia. Pope Benedict XIII was petitioned for a dispensation on the grounds that they were related in the third and fourth degrees of consanguinity, and a commission issued on 3rd June 1415 granted the necessary permission for the marriage.

However on 12th June, probably before the papal writ arrived in Scotland, she finally resigned the earldom to her grandfather. Possibly Albany persuaded her to do so in anticipation of her marriage in order that it could be regranted to her, her husband and their heirs. On 15th June Albany certainly granted her back the earldom and certain lands, but failing her it was to go to his own son, John, the earl of Buchan, whom failing to his third son Robert and his heirs, whom failing to the king. On the same day she resigned the lands of Kingedward in Buchan to the earl of Buchan and his heirs. She is not styled as countess in either of these writs, but simply Euphemia Leslie.

What happened is not recorded. One can only assume that young Dunbar, having visited her at Dirleton and seen her for the first time, realised that because of her handicap and delicate health she would not be able to give him children. To put it crudely, the earldom was not inducement enough to marry a hunch-back. Possibly Albany dangled the betrothal as a carrot to induce her to sign away her heritage, knowing full well that the marriage would never take place. Whatever the truth of the tragedy, she had no heart to continue the struggle. Thomas also never married though he may have had an illegitimate daughter who was betrothed to a Fraser of Lovat. He was succeeded by a cousin.

Euphemia allegedly entered the nunnery at North Berwick and thus became dead to the world. The earldom was assumed by her uncle John Steward who by 1417 and until his death in battle at the head of a troop of Scots in France at the Battle of Verneuil in 1424 bore the double title of earls of Buchan and Ross.

Donald of the Isles too was signing himself 'lord of the Isles and of the earldom of Ross'. The earldom was finally conferred upon Donald's son Alexander in 1437, but that is another story.

DAME EUPHEMIA

When Euphemia, who must have been about seventeen, finally agreed to enter a convent, North Berwick nunnery was the obvious choice. Apart from being one of the wealthier houses, it was close to her mother's home at Dirleton. She would have been able to take her own nurse and probably another servant with her. Although nuns were expected to work the wealthier sisters employed their own servants. She could look forward to the companionship of other aristocratic women. Perhaps for the first time in her life, away from the heavy pressures of her mother's family, she began to know some happiness as Dame Euphemia, bride of Christ.

North Berwick had been established by Duncan, first earl of Fife in about 1150. He is mentioned in a charter of his successor as having made a donation of land to the nuns whose objective was to care for the poor and accommodate passing pilgrims. It was one of nine Cistercian houses for women in Scotland the most northerly of which was Elcho near Perth. Six of them had been founded in the twelfth century.

The Cistercian priories were by far the largest group of monasteries for women. The Benedictines had had a house at Lincluden in Kircudbrightshire already closed while there were Augustinian canonesses at Iona and Perth, Dominicans at Sciennes in Edinburgh and Franciscans at Aberdour and Dundee. Cistercian houses were usually dedicated to St Mary and intended for a minimum of thirteen nuns, though that number may not always have been reached. They were probably founded as Benedictine but later claimed to be Cistercian 'to obtain the privileges of that order'. They followed the Rule of St Benedict which, according to Father Paul Bonici of Fort Augustus abbey, a Benedictine monk himself, was (and still is) 'gentle and wise'. It aimed at moderate rather than severe austerity and community life rather than complete solitude and silence.

To this day the most impressive ruins in the town are those of Euphemia's convent. You may still find them, not inappropriately, in the grounds of an old people's home in Old Abbey Road. Colin MacWilliam tells us that the walls were built of rubble dressed with yellowish-white stone. The west part raised on a series of four barrel-vaulted rooms was once the hall. The south wall had small oblong windows wider than high. The west gable had a fireplace and the east gable a large door. The square tower projecting from the north wall may have been added after the Reformation by a certain Alexander Hume in 1587. If the previous year 'the place quhair the Albany Kirk and Closter of Northberwick' was described as a ruin, it must have been a huge site. 'The extent of the monastic buildings can be gauged from the segmental-arched gateway on the east side of the garden and the continuation of the north wall for 17m east of the kitchen before it turns south.'

There may have been as many as twenty nuns at North Berwick during Euphemia's time where it seems that they wore the black habit rather than the traditional white undyed wool of the Cistercians but no explanation for this has survived. Their lives must have been very busy catering for the needs of passing pilgrims.

Most Scots attempted to go on pilgrimage during the Middle Ages. They could be counted as penances, and certificates of indulgence were granted to reduce time spent in the dreaded purgatory. For those who could not afford to go to the Holy land, Rome or Sanatiago de Compostela in Spain there was always Our Lady of Paisley, the chapel of the Holy Cross in Montrose, St Catherine's well in Liberton and the relics of St Duthac in Tain amongst others. Most popular of all was the shrine of St Andrews and it was for these pilgrims going by ferry to Fife that the North Berwick nuns catered. The North Berwick nunnery was particularly prosperous with lands yielding revenue both in Lothian and in Fife. The pilgrims themselves would have brought in money by buying special badges. A stone mould for making these tokens, one of which showed St Andrew on his cross, was found in a nearby graveyard.

If Chaucer's Madame Eglentyne, created about 1387 in *The Canterbury Tales*, is a true example of a nun in Euphemia's age – and Eileen Power in her superb evaluation of that lady in *Medieval People* certainly thinks she was – than Euphemia's life, depending upon the temper of her prioress, would be regulated but not unpleasant. Although many nuns in the fifteenth century had genuine vocations, there were increasingly more who regarded it, or indeed were forced to regard it, as a profession. It would seem that Euphemia's decision was not based so much on religious zeal but because there was no other option open to her. Among her new companions may have been some genuinely called to a life of poverty, chastity and obedience but also younger daughters too plain or too poor to find husbands and widows turned from their homes by newly-married sons. All would, however, have seen themselves as nobly born and as Scotland was a very small place in those days all would have known each other, if not personally, at least by family and repute. Many, indeed, would have been related.

One can picture Euphemia's arrival at the convent escorted by her stepfather, perhaps her mother too, and the excited interest of the other nuns as they watched her arrival. The countess of Ross, handicapped or not, was an important acquisition and her new sisters were ready to make her welcome. Her dowry amounting to several thousands of pounds in today's money would have been paid out of Ross revenues by Albany's steward, who would also have provided her with a bed, some furniture and of course a habit, black rather than the traditional white.

As a novice she would have been taught the rule of St Benedict, perhaps how to read and certainly how to sing the services. If she was fit, she would have been shown how to embroider the beautiful vestments worn by the priests in chapel or, as Eileen Power describes, 'make little silken purses for her friends and finely sewn bands for them to bind round their arms after a bleeding'.

There would be no time for boredom. The nuns sang nine services called 'the Hours' during the course of the day and night beginning with Nocturns at about 2 a.m., followed by Matins and Prime in the chapel by candlelight. One can imagine the agony of that early rise in winter, back to bed for an hour or so then up at 6 a.m. for Mass with Terce, Sext, None and Vespers spread throughout the rest of the day. Compline was sung at seven in winter and eight in summer, after which they went, or were supposed to go to bed.

They ate three meals during the day. Breakfast after Prime consisted of bread and beer. A good dinner was served at midday, with a small supper after Vespers in the early evening.

The afternoons were for recreative work, perhaps ministering to a sick pilgrim, perhaps offering spiritual advice or answering questions about the journey to St Andrews. Maybe there was time to take her little dog for a walk in the gardens. Madame Eglentyne 'of smale houndes had she, that she fedde/ with roasted flesh, or milk and wastel-breed'. So why not Dame Euphemia?

Eileen Power tells us that reports of the bishops' visitations to nunneries are full of their objections to pets as bad for discipline. Dogs were favourites, though monkeys, rabbits and birds not unknown, but cats less popular than today. In those days pets accompanied their owners into church and ladies would fondle them on their laps – a warm muff in winter – while men kept their hounds at their feet or held their hawks on their wrists. Starved of affection, little Euphemia may well have had a pet to sleep on her bed and smuggle into chapel during the offices.

The nuns, like their male counterparts, would have kept a guest house as well as a refuge for pilgrims and, although they were forbidden, according to Eileen Power, 'all manner of minstrelsy, interludes, dancing or revelling', they could hardly have denied their worldly married visitors these luxuries. Nor had they any wish to refuse these wealthy visitors, for like the pilgrims they paid for their keep and the nuns relied on the extra income.

Saints days and Christmas were times for special food and modest partying. Perhaps on the feast of the Holy Innocents, the nuns with much whispering and giggling among themselves dressed Euphemia – their newest novice – as prioress for the day and made her feel important for the first time in her life.

Nor could they avoid seeing the latest fashions among their noble guests. As Eileen Power writes 'for six weary centuries the bishops waged a holy war against fashion in the cloister, and waged it in vain.' Remember Madame Eglentyne?

> Ful fetis was hir cloke, as I was war,
> Of smal coral aboute hir arm she bar
> A pair of bedes, gauded al with grene,
> And ther-on heng a broche of gold ful shene,
> On which there was first write a crowned A,
> And after, *Amor vincit omnia*!

Dame Euphemia, too, may have had her gold hairpins, jewelled rings, beads and brooches, her furs, girdles and scarlet stockings, while her habit, far from being simply fashioned and coarse to the touch, may have been made of the costliest wool and lined with silk. Some compensation perhaps for her small misshapen body. As for her veil, it was supposed to hide her brow but as the fashion in those days was for a high forehead – Madame Eglentyne's was 'almost a spanne broad I trowe' – then Dame Euphemia too may have worn hers higher and learned to pinch her wimple in the most fashionable way.

Her movements too may not have been totally restricted. She may have gone home for family celebrations such as christenings, weddings and funerals. It is unlikely that she went further afield or on pilgrimage like Chaucer's prioress, not necessarily because she was a nun but on account of her health.

It is probable, too, that the nuns at North Berwick as elsewhere may have bent the rules a little when it came to what Eileen Power calls the three D's, dances, dresses and dogs. They may have been late on occasion for the offices, quarrelled among themselves, told tales of their prioress to the bishop, gossiped after Compline instead of going straight to bed and gabbled through the services. All these peccadilloes were very human faults and their prevalence depended upon the authority of the prioress.

So Dame Euphemia may not have been as zealous in her religious duties as the Rule required, but she still believed in the practice of charity and almsgiving, the reality of heaven and hell, the importance of dying confessed and the supreme efficacy of the Mass. There is no record of her death. One account suggests that she may have been poisoned but of this there is no proof, nor was there any need. As a nun and dead to the world, she was no longer a threat to anyone. Other accounts say she died young, but who knows.

So let us take our leave of Dame Euphemia, respected within and without her cloister as nuns were in those days, surrounded perhaps by a litter of little dogs, in the company of a confidente or two, busy as her health permitted and content for the first time in her short sad life.

SOURCES

Most of the scant information that exists about Euphemia comes from the clan histories, including Hugh Macdonald of Sleat's *History of the Macdonalds* (1914) and *The Book of Clanranald*, translated by A. Cameron from *Reliquiae Celticae* (1892). These accounts are readily combined and the period further researched in *The Lords of the Isles* by Ronald Williams.

p 223 This excerpt extolling the virtues of whisky, recorded by Mary Beith in *Healing Threads*, comes from a manuscript held in the National Library of Scotland (Advocates' Library MS 72.1.2). It was assembled in the first half of the seventeenth century by several of the Mull Beatons and is here translated from the Gaelic by Ronald Black.

pp 226–229 The descriptions of the Battle of Harlaw are included in *Grampian Battlefields*, P. Marren, 1990.

p 229 The commission granting permission for Euphemia to marry is quoted in the *Calendar of Papal Letters to Scotland*, Vol. XIII (Reg. Aven. 347, 356v).

Albany's charter granting Euphemia back her own lands is in General Register House, Edinburgh, no. 243 and Euphemia's charter resigning the lands of Kingedward etc. to the earl of Buchan is in *Father Hay's Collection*, Advocates' Library MS 34.1.10.i.

p 230 *Medieval Religious Houses in Scotland* by I. B. Cowan and D. E. Easson gives a good account of the number, origins and variety of the monastic orders and their houses.

Tom Gray while photographing the North Berwick site comments on the place today. 'The gardens around the nunnery are delightful. There is one secluded area of lawn with a high solid hedge around it, and only one tiny carved stone saying "Here lie the nuns of the Cistercian Order". Very moody in an area of fine homes of the well-to-do.'

p 235 The suggestion that Euphemia may have been poisoned is recorded in the *Historical Records of the Family of Leslie*.

AFTERWORD

HOME TO APPLECROSS

When Albany died in 1420, his son Murdoch inherited the dukedom, became heir presumptive to the throne and was chosen to be guardian of Scotland as James I was still a prisoner in London. He did not however inherit either his father's popularity or his guile. The country seethed with lawlessness and the Scots were determined to have their proper king back.

In exchange for 60,000 merks (£40,000) and twenty-seven hostages (one of whom was our fifth Euphemia's intended husband, now earl of Moray), the young king, with his beloved bride Queen Joan riding beside him, arrived in Melrose in 1424, free at last after eighteen years.

Walter Bower records that it was his ambition to rule well. 'Let God grant me life and aid, and there shall not be a place in all my kingdom where the key shall not keep the castle, the bracken-bush the cow, though I lead the life of a dog in securing it.' James' time in England had been wisely spent. At thirty he was well-educated, strong, athletic, clever and determined to govern well. He was also a poet and musician, author of *The Kingis Quair*, an allegorical poem of courtly love in the Chaucer style, full of subtlety and symbolism.

He was fortunate to fall in love with the woman he married, Lady Joan Beaufort, who was Henry IV's niece. Some of the most charming verses in *The Kingis Quair* describe their first meeting in a garden.

> And when she walked had a little throw [space]
> Under the sweete greene boughis bent,
> Her fair fresh face as white as any snow,
> She turned has, and forth her wayis went;

And then began mine axis [fever] and torment
To see her part, and follow I na might;
Methought the day was turned into night.

James was also a scientist with a particular interest in the mechanics of warfare. He had a logical mind and a passion for making laws. In spite of his sensitivity and undoubted charm he understood the need to be ruthless, and his enemies found him implacable. He made it clear that he would tolerate no factions among his nobles, either Gael or Scot, and for those who disobeyed his laws, poacher, cattle reiver or warmonger, there were fines, imprisonment or execution.

Two years into his reign he had Murdoch Albany and his two sons arrested, tried and executed, thus extinguishing the power of the Albany Stewards for ever. The barons were shocked to the core and stunned into submission, while the people were pleased to have a king who administered justice equally to rich and poor. For thirteen years, until he was assassinated, his powerful personality dominated Scotland.

Meanwhile Donald of the Isles, too, had died and had been succeeded by his son (Euphemia's first cousin) Alexander. He had been a member of the jury convicting Murdoch Albany in 1426 and hoped to be confirmed in the earldom of Ross. James seems to have recognised his mother Margaret as the countess of Ross in her own right, but Alexander, though he signed himself master (*magister*) of Ross, was not granted the title or the revenues. James also kept the revenues of the earldoms of March, Fife, Mar, Buchan and Lennox, at least for the time being. His main objective was to curb the unruliness of the nobility.

The following year he turned his attention to the north. In view of the continual cattle-raiding and feuding between the clans he called a parliament in Inverness consisting of fifty of the most important chiefs. Although Alexander had been warned not to attend, he and his mother both travelled to Inverness together and with the other chiefs they were summoned individually to the castle. Immediately they were arrested. Some were executed and Alexander was kept in prison for two months. He was outraged and his whole clan with him. As soon as he was released he raised an army of allegedly ten thousand men who attacked and burned Inverness.

Equally determined to crush the rebellion, James himself at the head of an army drove Alexander out of Inverness and south to Lochaber. Gathering Mackenzies (always loyal to the king) on the way, with clan Chattan and some of clan Cameron, James routed Alexander somewhere near Lochaber. Alexander was advised by his chieftains to go into hiding in Ireland or the Hebrides, but instead decided to make a great show of submission to the king at Holyrood Palace on Easter Day 1429.

Always attractive to women, he owed his future to Queen Joan, who pleaded to the king for his life. Instead of having him immediately executed, James imprisoned him at the grim fortress of Tantallon castle near North Berwick to await his decision. As for his mother Margaret, she was charged with inciting her son to lawlessness and she too was imprisoned on the island of Inchcolm in the Firth of Forth.

It looked as if Alexander was done for, especially as a number of clans once loyal to him decided that it was in their best interests to support the king's man, the recently appointed earl of Mar, warden of Inverness castle and justiciar of the north. However Alexander managed to send a message to his kinsmen who appointed the eighteen-year-old Donald Balloch as clan war-leader. His galleys carrying six hundred warriors sailed through the Sound of Mull, up Loch Linnhe, to land near Inverlochy where Mar's men were encamped just north of the present town of Fort William.

Mar was routed with a loss of nearly a thousand men, while Donald who had lost merely twenty-seven ravaged Lochaber, particularly the lands of those clans who had deserted to Mar. James again marched north, demanding that Donald Balloch be delivered to him alive or dead. Eventually a head was produced and James appeased. In fact Donald had escaped to Ireland where he married the O'Neill of Connaught's daughter.

Alexander was released from Tantallon as part of the general amnesty celebrating the birth of the king's heir. He was restored to his ancestral rights in the Isles but not to the earldom of Ross. That had to wait until after James I's assassination in Perth on 21st February 1437.

As Mar was dead, the guardians of the six-year-old James II appointed Alexander in his place as justiciar of the north, and therefore keeper of Inverness castle and warden of the town he had once destroyed. He was also granted Ross, thus the lordship and the earldom were united for the first time under one man.

Alexander died in Dingwall on 8th May 1449 and was buried, not in Iona like the other lords of the Isles, but in the cathedral kirk of the Chanonry in Fortrose. Nor was he buried in his grandmother's chantry chapel but in the nave which was destroyed after the Reformation in 1560.

The combined earldom and lordship was by far the largest territory in Scotland, apart from the kingdom itself. It was inherited by Alexander's eldest son John who within fifty years was to lose both for ever to the crown in whose hands it still remains. John, once the eleventh earl of Ross and fourth lord of the Isles, died penniless in a small lodging house in Dundee in 1503. At his own request he was buried in Paisley abbey by the tomb of his ancestor Robert II.

But Alexander had other sons. His first wife Elizabeth Seton, a daughter of the lord of Huntly and Gordon, was mother to his heir. After many years of marriage he fell in love with the beautiful Christina MacIaide and installed her in his bed to the fury of his wife who petitioned first the bishop of the Isles and then the pope.

After Elizabeth's death he allegedly married a daughter of Macphee of Lochaber by whom he had a son called Celestine who inherited the lands of Lochalsh. After her death Ronald Williams in *The Lords of the Isles* believes he married a third time, a great-grand-daughter of the notorious Finnon, known as the Green Abbot of Iona.

However the earl of Cromartie in his *Highland History* believes that he was married only twice and that his second wife was the daughter of the last Mactaggart of Applecross and heiress of Lochalsh, a descendant of Earl Farquhar's second son Malcolm who was also known as the Green Abbot. Her eldest son Celestine inherited Lochalsh, while her second son Hugh became progenitor of the lords of Sleat in Skye. For the last word perhaps we should look to Donald Macdonald of Castleton's *History of Clan Donald*. He states that Alexander married for a third time, a daughter of Gilpatrick Roy, son of Ruari, descendant of the Green Abbot of Applecross, by whom he had Hugh, founder of the family of Sleat.

So if it is true that the Applecross heiress whose name is lost to us today married the penultimate earl of Ross, then the wheel had come full circle in that green and hallowed place where it began its long revolution some two hundred and fifty years before.

Afterword

THE FIVE EUPHEMIAS

How much do we really know of those five women whose lives spanned parts of the central and later Middle Ages?

Because such records as are left to us were kept by churchmen whose attitude to women was at best ambivalent, we know far too little about Scottish medieval women in general. Only a few like Black Agnes of Dunbar dusting the battlements of her fortress in the face of the besieging English spring to life from the aged parchments of the day. Yet from the little we do know about the five Euphemias, a pattern emerges. Each individual is a small reflection of her times, each woman in her personal life adds to the portrait of her generation, each Euphemia is an essential thread in the tapestry of Scottish medieval history.

Thus we have watched little Eighrig leave Applecross, the ancient Celto-Nordic cradle of her childhood, to cross those mountains, as metaphorical as they were real, to become Euphemia I in a different world. That journey from east to west was so much greater than the sum of mere miles, for it was to lead to her adoption by marriage into the French-speaking feudalism of the Anglo-Norman knights. We can only imagine how she – and countless other women of her age – coped with the change of culture.

One fact is certain. Euphemia and her Celtic sisters must have taught their children to respect and remember their own inheritance. Feudalism, for all its strength, did not dominate the Celt. It adopted the best in Gaelic tradition, just as the Celts took from the Normans what they needed to survive. That delicate blend of cultures, Irish, Pictish, Norse, Anglian and Norman from which the modern Scot has emerged is due to Euphemia and her generation of mothers and wives, foster-mothers and nurses who nourished their children with pride in their original race.

And there was leisure to do it well, for Euphemia I lived in an age of blessed peace that saw a flourishing of the arts and architecture, and the flowering of all that was best in chivalry and religion. Hers was the age of the establishment of magnificent cathedrals, monasteries and churches, of great castles, towns and markets, the golden century of the two Alexanders. A hierarchical society certainly, both in lay life and in the church, where it was infinitely more comfortable to be a knight than a *neyf*, a bishop than a *scoloc*, a merchant than a *stallager* – but so it has always been.

As for women, they were either virgins or widows, wives and mothers, the property of their fathers, husbands or sons. This would not have caused Euphemia I a moment's concern. She was steeped in the doctrine of Christian duty which included the fifth commandment, 'Honour they father and mother that thy days may be long in the land which the Lord thy God giveth thee.' Her sorrows were those shared by all women throughout all ages, sickness, cruelty and death, while her joys were equally universal, birth, love and good health.

Local battles happened from time to time and friends were killed at home or on crusade but there was no external foe. England was a neighbour not an enemy. Indeed most of her acquaintance among the Scottish knights had English relatives and English lands. Both Alexanders had married English princesses. To outward appearances then Euphemia I lived a secure and prosperous life reflecting the golden age she inhabited. Of her inner feelings we have no record.

Euphemia II was not so fortunate. She lived through one of the most difficult periods of Scottish history. Conflict with England for the first time became a struggle which was to drag on one way or another right up until the sixteenth century and to leave its scars into the twentieth and beyond. She was alive during one of that conflict's most virulent phases, the determination of Edward I to control Scotland. Brought up as a true child of her generation to believe in the supreme importance of family and land-ownership, she saw it as her own personal crusade to preserve the territory of Ross at all costs, particularly during the imprisonment of her husband in the Tower of London.

To her credit she succeeded. Whether she actually used her womanly wiles to appease the English king is a matter of speculation. If so, she merely reflected the actions of her peers. For seven years she, in common with the rest of the nobility, swung from Balliol to Edward and from Edward to Bruce and back again in order to survive. During her lifetime she and her fellow countrymen and women came slowly to understand the meaning of nationhood, the importance of independence and the nature of freedom.

Euphemia III became the first Stewart queen, whose line was to include Mary, Queen of Scots and Queen Anne who was the last monarch of an independent Scotland at the time of the Act of Union in 1707. Indeed, she can claim among her descendants the royal family of today.

In her personal life Queen Euphemia symbolised not only the rivalries between the House of Bruce and the House of Stewart but also their resolution. Married first to one guardian of the kingdom who was friend and loyal supporter of David Bruce and then to his rival guardian, Robert Steward whose queen she became, her loyalties must have at times been tested to the limit. How she felt we can only guess but through her perhaps we can begin to understand how the nation itself was torn between those who supported the uncle and those the nephew. In the light of future events those who, like Euphemia, stayed with the Steward made the right decision.

Euphemia IV reflects the role of aristocratic women in the Middle Ages with startling clarity. All marriages were arranged but hers was done with more calculation than most. Usually a father's motive in bestowing his daughter's hand and dowry was as much for her benefit and happiness as his own gain. Often, too, he would seek the king's approval for an important match. But Euphemia's marriage was arranged for her by David II who did not seek her father's consent. She was given, together with her inheritance, as a gift by the king to his current favourite. A purely political act. Her happiness was never considered. Or so it would seem.

As for her second husband, the Wolf of Badenoch, he married her entirely for her lands and title, not at all an unusual motive. Nor was his flagrant and unchivalrous disrespect for his wife that uncommon then as throughout history. However her courage in seeking a divorce was in those days extremely unusual. A husband's cruelty was not normally a reason for the dissolution of a marriage and, as we have seen, every effort was made, as in the case of Euphemia and the Wolf, to mend the situation.

One interesting fact emerges from Euphemia IV's matrimonial quarrel with the Wolf. Although women had little say in the choice of partner, when it came to serious disagreement within the marriage, or the downright cruelty of one partner to the other, the clerical judges were scrupulously fair. As Henrietta Leyser writes, 'every effort seems to have been made to pay equal attention to both men's and women's stories.'

Usually the disastrous marriage ended in annulment. Divorce was rare and the fact that Euphemia was granted one probably reflects the power of her Albany supporters more than her own. As for remarriage after divorce, that was absolutely forbidden by the church. This is one reason why the tale of her relationship with Mackenzie of Kintail must be fantasy. Euphemia IV cared as much as any other medieval Christian for a place in heaven. Had she not been responsible for building the chantry chapel at Fortrose cathedral for the sole purpose of saving her and her family's souls?

Euphemia V, the little 'crouch-backit' heiress, tells us as much about her generation as any of her forerunners. As handicapped, she was considered unmarriageable and as there was no place for unmarried women in secular society she was forced to enter a nunnery, there to become conveniently dead to the world. And yet in practical terms the nun was at least as useful to society as her married sisters. R. Gilchrist in *Gender and Material Culture: the Archaeology of Religious Women* tells us that 'medieval female religious experience was different from that of men, not less successful.' Many convents had the only schools available for girls, raised orphans and provided refreshment and hospitality for discarded widows, ailing aristocrats and weary pilgrims, as well as feeding the ubiquitous poor that begged at the convent gates. Others, such as the nunnery of Wherwell in Hampshire which was famed for its healing abbess, another Euphemia, specialised in medical care.

It was only in convents such as North Berwick where women lost their worldly status that they found a welcome measure of freedom and equality. Here they could express their various talents, whether of leadership, scholarship or piety. Within the wider community they were loved and respected. Some, indeed, whose holiness elevated them to spiritual pedestals were in continual demand for their prayers, and their advice continually sought. So perhaps Euphemia V's confinement in a nunnery was in fact her release into a happier existence, her worldly death a renewal of life in which for the first and only time she found a measure of happiness and security.

And so we bid them farewell, the wife, the adventuress, the queen, the divorcée and the nun, five aristocratic women whose individual personalities will always remain hidden but whose lives reflect those of countless others whose genes and experience have helped to make us what we are today.

APPENDIX I

Abbreviations used in the tables

b.	born
d.	died
d. sp	died *sine prole* (without issue)
dtr	daughter
e.	earl
ex.	executed
k.	killed
m.	married

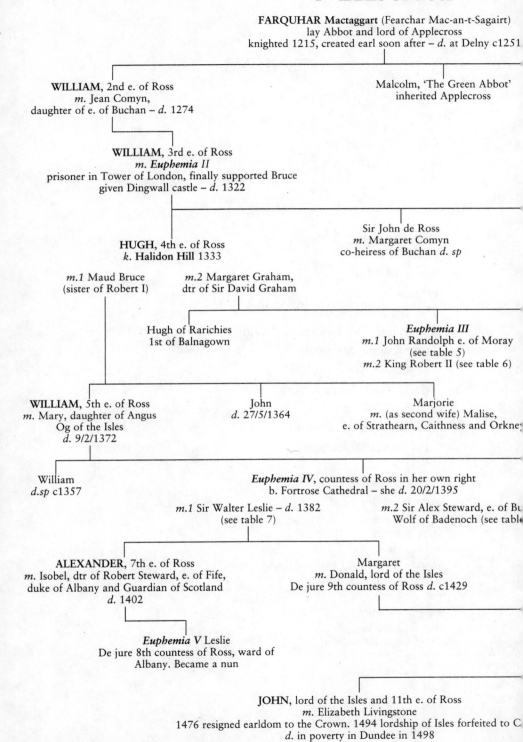

1 – EARLS OF ROSS

FARQUHAR Mactaggart (Fearchar Mac-an-t-Sagairt)
lay Abbot and lord of Applecross
knighted 1215, created earl soon after – *d.* at Delny c1251

WILLIAM, 2nd e. of Ross
m. Jean Comyn,
daughter of e. of Buchan – *d.* 1274

Malcolm, 'The Green Abbot'
inherited Applecross

WILLIAM, 3rd e. of Ross
m. Euphemia II
prisoner in Tower of London, finally supported Bruce
given Dingwall castle – *d.* 1322

Sir John de Ross
m. Margaret Comyn
co-heiress of Buchan *d. sp*

HUGH, 4th e. of Ross
k. **Halidon Hill** 1333

m.1 Maud Bruce
(sister of Robert I)

m.2 Margaret Graham,
dtr of Sir David Graham

Hugh of Rarichies
1st of Balnagown

Euphemia III
m.1 John Randolph e. of Moray
(see table 5)
m.2 King Robert II (see table 6)

WILLIAM, 5th e. of Ross
m. Mary, daughter of Angus
Og of the Isles
d. 9/2/1372

John
d. 27/5/1364

Marjorie
m. (as second wife) Malise,
e. of Strathearn, Caithness and Orkney

William
d.sp c1357

Euphemia IV, countess of Ross in her own right
b. Fortrose Cathedral – she *d.* 20/2/1395

m.1 Sir Walter Leslie – *d.* 1382
(see table 7)

m.2 Sir Alex Steward, e. of Bu
Wolf of Badenoch (see table

ALEXANDER, 7th e. of Ross
m. Isobel, dtr of Robert Steward, e. of Fife,
duke of Albany and Guardian of Scotland
d. 1402

Margaret
m. Donald, lord of the Isles
De jure 9th countess of Ross *d.* c1429

Euphemia V Leslie
De jure 8th countess of Ross, ward of
Albany. Became a nun

JOHN, lord of the Isles and 11th e. of Ross
m. Elizabeth Livingstone
1476 resigned earldom to the Crown. 1494 lordship of Isles forfeited to C
d. in poverty in Dundee in 1498

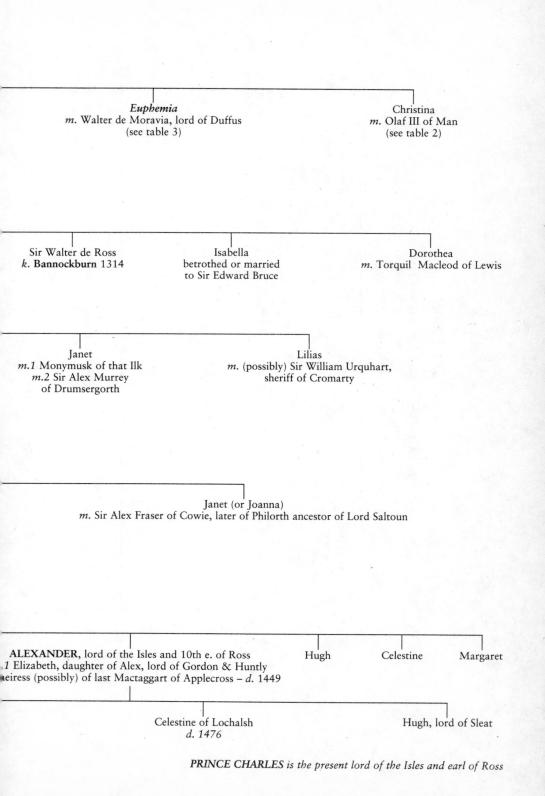

Euphemia
m. Walter de Moravia, lord of Duffus
(see table 3)

Christina
m. Olaf III of Man
(see table 2)

Sir Walter de Ross
k. **Bannockburn** 1314

Isabella
betrothed or married
to Sir Edward Bruce

Dorothea
m. Torquil Macleod of Lewis

Janet
m.1 Monymusk of that Ilk
m.2 Sir Alex Murrey
of Drumsergorth

Lilias
m. (possibly) Sir William Urquhart,
sheriff of Cromarty

Janet (or Joanna)
m. Sir Alex Fraser of Cowie, later of Philorth ancestor of Lord Saltoun

ALEXANDER, lord of the Isles and 10th e. of Ross
1 Elizabeth, daughter of Alex, lord of Gordon & Huntly
heiress (possibly) of last Mactaggart of Applecross – *d.* 1449

Hugh   Celestine   Margaret

Celestine of Lochalsh
d. 1476

Hugh, lord of Sleat

PRINCE CHARLES is the present lord of the Isles and earl of Ross

2 – KINGS OF MAN

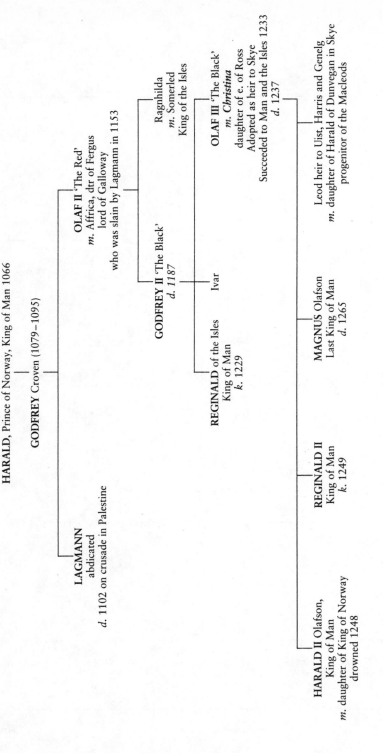

HARALD, Prince of Norway, King of Man 1066

GODFREY Croven (1079–1095)

LAGMANN
abdicated
d. 1102 on crusade in Palestine

OLAF II 'The Red'
m. Affrica, dtr of Fergus
lord of Galloway
who was slain by Lagmann in 1153

Ragnhilda
m. Somerled
King of the Isles

GODFREY II 'The Black'
d. 1187

Ivar

OLAF III 'The Black'
m. *Christina*
daughter of e. of Ross
Adopted as heir to Skye
Succeeded to Man and the Isles 1233
d. 1237

REGINALD of the Isles
King of Man
k. 1229

Leod heir to Uist, Harris and Genelg
m. daughter of Harald of Dunvegan in Skye
progenitor of the Macleods

MAGNUS Olafson
Last King of Man
d. 1265

REGINALD II
King of Man
k. 1249

HARALD II Olafson,
King of Man,
m. daughter of King of Norway
drowned 1248

3 – FRESKIN THE FLEMING

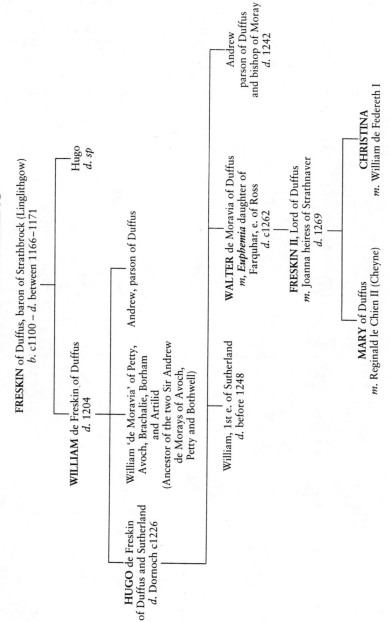

FRESKIN of Duffus, baron of Strathbrock (Linlithgow)
b. c1100 – *d.* between 1166–1171

Hugo
d. sp

WILLIAM de Freskin of Duffus
d. 1204

HUGO de Freskin
of Duffus and Sutherland
d. Dornoch c1226

William 'de Moravia' of Petty,
Avoch, Brachalie, Borham
and Artiid
(Ancestor of the two Sir Andrew
de Morays of Avoch,
Petty and Bothwell)

Andrew, parson of Duffus

William, 1st e. of Sutherland
d. before 1248

WALTER de Moravia of Duffus
m, Euphemia daughter of
Farquhar, e. of Ross
d. c1262

Andrew
parson of Duffus
and bishop of Moray
d. 1242

FRESKIN II, Lord of Duffus
m. Joanna heiress of Strathnaver
d. 1269

MARY of Duffus
m. Reginald le Chien II (Cheyne)

CHRISTINA
m. William de Federeth I

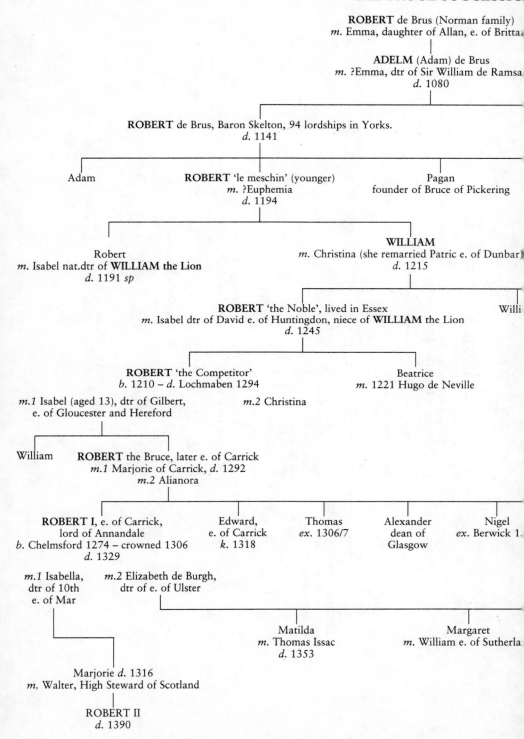

ROBERT de Brus (Norman family)
m. Emma, daughter of Allan, e. of Britta

ADELM (Adam) de Brus
m. ?Emma, dtr of Sir William de Ramsa
d. 1080

ROBERT de Brus, Baron Skelton, 94 lordships in Yorks.
d. 1141

Adam

ROBERT 'le meschin' (younger)
m. ?Euphemia
d. 1194

Pagan
founder of Bruce of Pickering

Robert
m. Isabel nat.dtr of **WILLIAM the Lion**
d. 1191 *sp*

WILLIAM
m. Christina (she remarried Patric e. of Dunbar)
d. 1215

ROBERT 'the Noble', lived in Essex
m. Isabel dtr of David e. of Huntingdon, niece of **WILLIAM** the Lion
d. 1245

Willi

ROBERT 'the Competitor'
b. 1210 – *d.* Lochmaben 1294
m.1 Isabel (aged 13), dtr of Gilbert,
e. of Gloucester and Hereford
m.2 Christina

Beatrice
m. 1221 Hugo de Neville

William

ROBERT the Bruce, later e. of Carrick
m.1 Marjorie of Carrick, *d.* 1292
m.2 Alianora

ROBERT I, e. of Carrick,
lord of Annandale
b. Chelmsford 1274 – crowned 1306
d. 1329

Edward,
e. of Carrick
k. 1318

Thomas
ex. 1306/7

Alexander
dean of
Glasgow

Nigel
ex. Berwick 1

m.1 Isabella,
dtr of 10th
e. of Mar

m.2 Elizabeth de Burgh,
dtr of e. of Ulster

Matilda
m. Thomas Issac
d. 1353

Margaret
m. William e. of Sutherla

Marjorie *d.* 1316
m. Walter, High Steward of Scotland

ROBERT II
d. 1390

am, prior of Gisborn
d. 1155

Agatha

John

Isabel	Mary	Christina	Maud	Margaret
b. 1275	m.1 Sir Neil Campbell,	m.1 e. of Mar	(Matilda)	m. Sir William
Sir Thomas Randolph	anc. of Argylls	m.2 Christopher	m. 1308 to	de Carlyle
Eric, King of Norway	m.2 Sir Alex Fraser	de Seton	e. of Ross	
	d. 1323	m.3 Andrew		
		de Moravia		

DAVID II
m.1 Joan of England
ı.2 Margaret Logie Drummond
d. sp 1371

John
d. sp

Robert I's Illegitimate Family
1. Sir Robert Bruce, *k.* **Dupplin** 1333
2. Nigel of Carrick, *d.* 1346
3. Margaret, *m.* Robert Glen

4. Elizabeth, *m.* Sir Walter Oliphant of Aberdalgie
5. Christina of Carrick

5 – THE RANDOLPH FAMILY AND DUNBAR CONNECTION

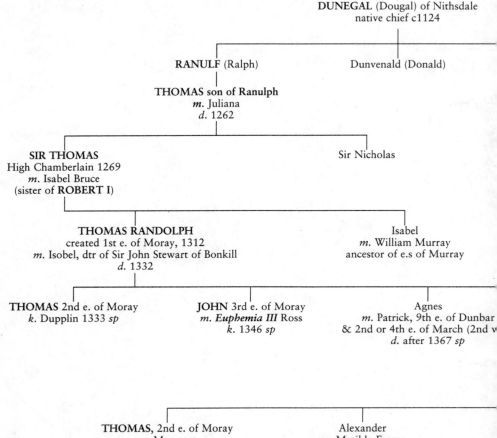

DUNEGAL (Dougal) of Nithsdale
native chief c1124

RANULF (Ralph)   Dunvenald (Donald)

THOMAS son of Ranulph
m. Juliana
d. 1262

SIR THOMAS   Sir Nicholas
High Chamberlain 1269
m. Isabel Bruce
(sister of **ROBERT I**)

THOMAS RANDOLPH   Isabel
created 1st e. of Moray, 1312   *m.* William Murray
m. Isobel, dtr of Sir John Stewart of Bonkill   ancestor of e.s of Murray
d. 1332

THOMAS 2nd e. of Moray   JOHN 3rd e. of Moray   Agnes
k. Dupplin 1333 *sp*   *m. Euphemia III* Ross   *m.* Patrick, 9th e. of Dunbar
                          k. 1346 *sp*   & 2nd or 4th e. of March (2nd v
                                                   d. after 1367 *sp*

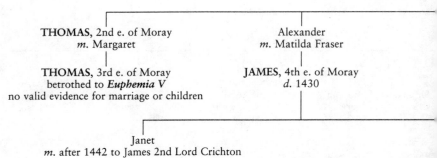

THOMAS, 2nd e. of Moray   Alexander
m. Margaret   *m.* Matilda Fraser

THOMAS, 3rd e. of Moray   JAMES, 4th e. of Moray
betrothed to *Euphemia V*   *d.* 1430
no valid evidence for marriage or children

Janet
m. after 1442 to James 2nd Lord Crichton

Gillepatric

Isabel
m. Sir Patric Dunbar

OHN DUNBAR, created e. of Moray
Marjorie Steward, daughter of **ROBERT II**
d. 1392

James

Euphemia
m. Alexander Cumming
(ancestor of family of Altyre)

Elizabeth (also called Mary and Agnes)
Archibald Douglas who was created e. of Moray

6 – THE STEWARD SUCCESSION

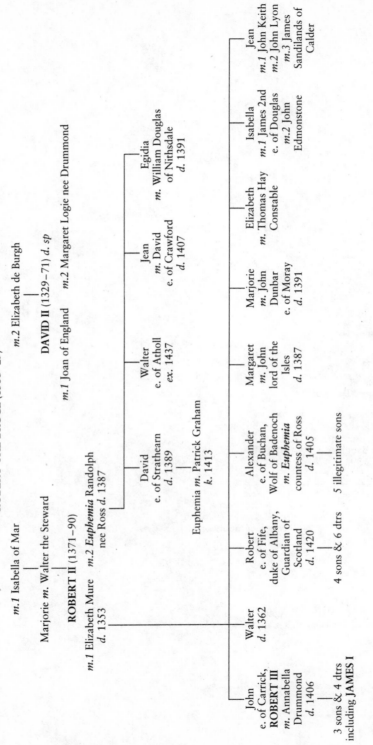

ROBERT THE BRUCE (1306–29)

m.2 Elizabeth de Burgh

DAVID II (1329–71) *d. sp*

m.1 Joan of England *m.2* Margaret Logie nee Drummond

m.1 Isabella of Mar

Marjorie *m.* Walter the Steward

ROBERT II (1371–90)

m.1 Elizabeth Mure *m.2* **Euphemia** Randolph
d. 1353   nee Ross *d. 1387*

Euphemia *m.* Patrick Graham
k. 1413

Walter *d. 1362*

Robert
e. of Fife,
duke of Albany,
Guardian of
Scotland
d. 1420

4 sons & 6 dtrs

John
e. of Carrick,
ROBERT III
m. Annabella
Drummond
d. 1406

3 sons & 4 dtrs
including **JAMES I**

David
e. of Strathearn
d. 1389

Walter
e. of Atholl
ex. 1437

Alexander
e. of Buchan,
Wolf of Badenoch
m. **Euphemia**
countess of Ross
d. 1405

5 illegitimate sons

Jean
m. David
e. of Crawford
d. 1407

Egidia
m. William Douglas
of Nithsdale
d. 1391

Margaret
m. John
lord of the
Isles
d. 1387

Marjorie
m. John
Dunbar
e. of Moray
d. 1391

Elizabeth
m. Thomas Hay
Constable

Isabella
m.1 James 2nd
e. of Douglas
m.2 John
Edmonstone

Jean
m.1 John Keith
m.2 John Lyon
m.3 James
Sandilands of
Calder

Robert II's Illegitimate Family:
1. Sir John Stewart Heritable Sheriff of Bute
2. Thomas Stewart Archdeacon of St Andrews, Dean of Dunkeld
3. Alexander Stewart, Canon of Glasgow
4. Sir John Stewart of Dundonald, Lord of Burley
5. Alexander of Inverlunas
6. James Stewart of Kinfauns
7. Sir John Stewart of Cardney
8. Walter Stewart

7 – THE LESLIE FAMILY

BARTOLF (Hungarian?)

MALCOLM de Leslyn in Aberdeenshire
d. c1200

NORMAN de Leslie, constable of Inverurie
d. 1243

ANDREW de Leslie
(alive in 1253)

NORMAN de Leslie of Fetkil (now Leslie in Fife)

ANDREW lord of Leslie
Signatory of Declaration of Arbroath in 1320
m. Mary, co-heiress of Sir Alex Abernethy of Ballinbreich Castle
d. 1324

Son
(name
unknown)

Sir Norman de Leslie,
ward of Ballinbreich
m. Margaret
grand-daughter of
Sir Alexander Lamberton
k. Alexandria c1366

Sir GEORGE Leslie of Rothes
inherited Ballinbreich
progenitor of earls of Rothes
d. 1395/6

Sir Andrew Leslie of Leslie
inherited Ballinbreich
d. before 1366

Walter Leslie of Fetkil
m. Euphemia
countess of Ross
and became e. of Ross
(see table 1)

8 – THE LINDSAY CONNECTION

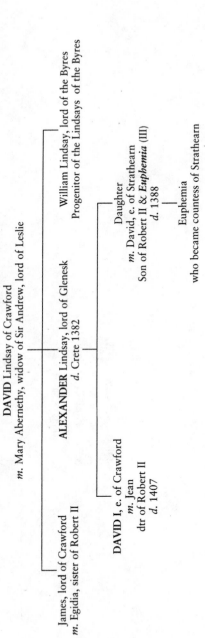

DAVID Lindsay of Crawford
m. Mary Abernethy, widow of Sir Andrew, lord of Leslie

James, lord of Crawford
m. Egidia, sister of Robert II

ALEXANDER Lindsay, lord of Glenesk
d. Crete 1382

William Lindsay, lord of the Byres
Progenitor of the Lindsays of the Byres

DAVID I, e. of Crawford
m. Jean
dtr of Robert II
d. 1407

Daughter
m. David, e. of Strathearn
Son of Robert II & *Euphemia* (III)
d. 1388

Euphemia
who became countess of Strathearn

9 – ALBANY'S FAMILY

ROBERT earl of Fife, duke of Albany

m.1 Margaret Graham, countess of Menteith   *m.2* Muriela, dtr of Sir William de Keith, Marischal of Scotland

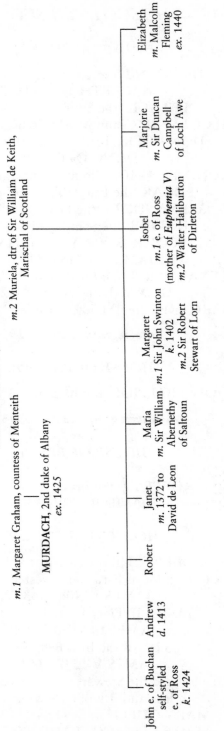

MURDACH, 2nd duke of Albany
ex. 1425

John e. of Buchan
self-styled
e. of Ross
k. 1424

Andrew
d. 1413

Robert

Janet
m. 1372 to
David de Leon

Maria
m. Sir William
Abernethy
of Saltoun

Margaret
m.1 Sir John Swinton
k. 1402
m.2 Sir Robert
Stewart of Lorn

Isobel
m.1 e. of Ross
(mother of *Euphemia V*)
m.2 Walter Haliburton
of Dirleton

Marjorie
m. Sir Duncan
Campbell
of Loch Awe

Elizabeth
m. Malcolm
Fleming
ex. 1440

10 – THE SCOTTISH SUCCESSION

HOUSE OF DUNKELD

DUNCAN I 'the Gracious' 1034–1040
MACBETH 1040–1057
LULACH 'the Simple' 1057–1058
MALCOLM III 'Ceann Mor' (big head) 1058–1093
DONALD III 'Ban' (white) 1093–1097
DUNCAN II 1094
EDMUND 1094–1097 (joint ruler with DONALD III)
EDGAR 'the Peaceable' 1097–1107
ALEXANDER I 'the Fierce' 1107–1124
DAVID I 'the Saintly' 1124–1153
MALCOLM IV 'the Maiden' 1153–1165
WILLIAM I 'the Lion' 1165–1214
ALEXANDER II 'the Little Red Fox' 1214–1249
ALEXANDER III 1249–1286
MARGARET 'the Maid of Norway' 1286–1290

Interregnum 1290–1292

HOUSE OF BALLIOL

JOHN BALLIOL 'toom tabard' 1290–1292

Interregnum 1296–1306

HOUSE OF BRUCE

ROBERT I 'the Bruce' 1306–1329
DAVID II 1329–1371

HOUSE OF STEWART

ROBERT II 'the Steward' 1371–1390
ROBERT III 'John of Faranyeir' (yesteryear) 1390–1406
JAMES I 1406–1437
JAMES II 'Fiery Face' 1437–1460
JAMES III 1460–1488
JAMES IV 'of the Iron Belt' 1488–1513
JAMES V 1513–1542
who said the Stewart dynasty 'came wi'
a lass and it will pass wi' a lass'
MARY QUEEN of SCOTS 1542–1567
JAMES VI of SCOTLAND 1567–1625
and I of ENGLAND 1603–1625

11 – THE ENGLISH CLAIM

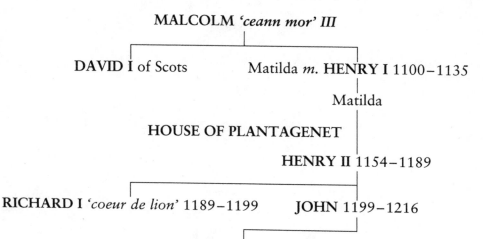

MALCOLM *'ceann mor' III*

DAVID I of Scots   Matilda *m.* HENRY I 1100–1135

Matilda

HOUSE OF PLANTAGENET

HENRY II 1154–1189

RICHARD I *'coeur de lion'* 1189–1199   JOHN 1199–1216

HENRY III 1216–1272

EDWARD I 'Hammer of the Scots' 1272–1307
EDWARD II 1307–1327
EDWARD III 1327–1377
RICHARD II (grdson of above) 1377–1399
HENRY IV (cousin of above) 1399–1413
HENRY V 1413–1422
HENRY VI 1422–1461
EDWARD IV (cousin of above) 1461–1483
EDWARD V (murdered in Tower) 1483
RICHARD III (uncle of EDWARD V) 1483–1485

HOUSE OF TUDOR

HENRY VII 1485–1509
HENRY VIII 1509–1547
EDWARD VI 1547–1553
LADY JANE GREY 1553
MARY I dtr of HENRY VIII 1553–1558
ELIZABETH I dtr of HENRY VIII 1558–1603

UNION OF THE CROWNS: HOUSE OF STEWART

JAMES VI of Scotland and I of England
(son of Mary Queen of Scots)

APPENDIX II

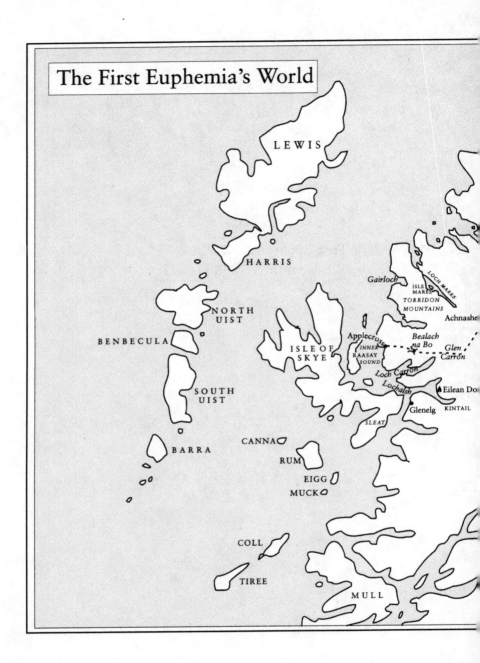

The First Euphemia's World

LEWIS

HARRIS

Gairloch

LOCH MAREE

ISLE
MAREE

TORRIDON
MOUNTAINS

Achnashe

NORTH
UIST

BENBECULA

ISLE OF
SKYE

Applecross

Bealach
na Bo

Glen
Carron

INNER
RAASAY
SOUND

Loch Carron

SOUTH
UIST

Lochalsh

Eilean Do

Glenelg

KINTAIL

SLEAT

BARRA

CANNA

RUM

EIGG

MUCK

COLL

TIREE

MULL

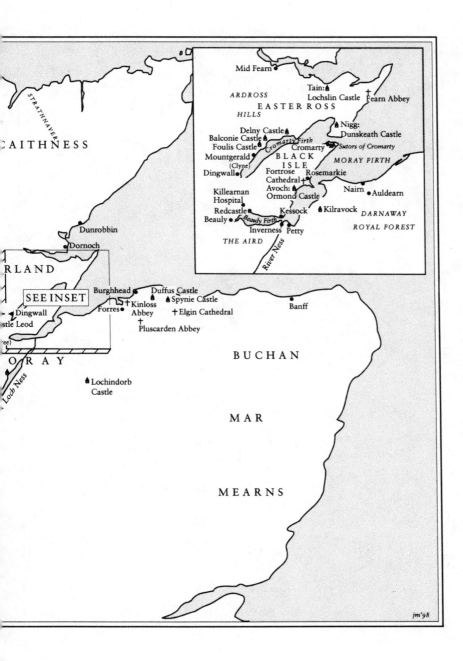

STRATHNAVER

CAITHNESS

Dunrobbin

Dornoch

RLAND

SEE INSET

Dingwall
stle Leod

ree)

ORAY

Lochindorb
Castle

Mid Fearn

Tain:
Lochslin Castle   Fearn Abbey
ARDROSS
EASTER ROSS
HILLS
Delny Castle   Nigg:
Balconie Castle   Dunskeath Castle
Foulis Castle   Cromarty
Mountgerald   Cromarty   Sutors of Cromarty
(Clyne)   BLACK
Dingwall   ISLE   MORAY FIRTH
Fortrose   Rosemarkie
Cathedral
Killearnan   Avoch:
Hospital   Ormond Castle   Nairn   Auldearn
Redcastle   Kessock
Beauly   Kilravock   DARNAWAY
Beauly Firth
Inverness Petty   ROYAL FOREST
THE AIRD
River Ness

Loch Ness

Burghhead   Duffus Castle
Kinloss   Spynie Castle
Forres   Abbey   Banff
        Elgin Cathedral
Pluscarden Abbey

BUCHAN

MAR

MEARNS

jm'98

[263]

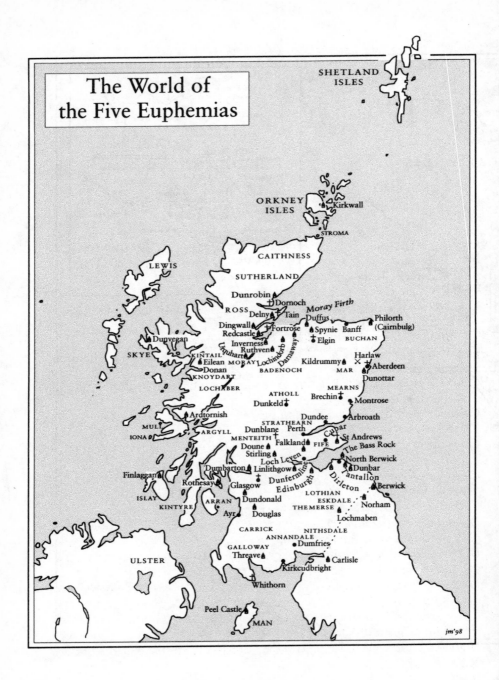

The World of
the Five Euphemias

SHETLAND
ISLES

ORKNEY
ISLES
Kirkwall
STROMA

CAITHNESS

SUTHERLAND

LEWIS

Dunrobin
Dornoch
ROSS
Delny
Tain
Moray Firth
Dingwall
Duffus
Philorth
Spynie
Banff
(Cairnbulg)
Redcastle
Fortrose
Elgin
BUCHAN
Inverness
Dupvegan
Ruthven
SKYE
Urquhart
Harlaw
KINTAIL
Lochindorb
Kildrummy
Aberdeen
Eilean
MORAY
Darnaway
Donan
BADENOCH
MAR
Dunottar
KNOYDART
MEARNS
LOCHABER
ATHOLL
Brechin
Montrose
Dunkeld
Ardtornish
Dundee
Arbroath
STRATHEARN
MULL
Dunblane
Perth
Cupar
St Andrews
IONA
ARGYLL
MENTEITH
Falkland
FIFE
The Bass Rock
Doune
 Stirling
North Berwick
Dumbarton
Loch Leven
Dunbar
Finlaggan
Linlithgow
Tantallon
Rothesay
Dunfermline
Dirleton
Glasgow
Edinburgh
Berwick
ISLAY
LOTHIAN
Dundonald
ESKDALE
Norham
KINTYRE
ARRAN
THEMERSE
Ayr
Douglas
Lochmaben
CARRICK
NITHSDALE
ANNANDALE
GALLOWAY
Dumfries
Threave
ULSTER
Carlisle
Kirkcudbright
Whithorn

Peel Castle
MAN

jm'98

BIBLIOGRAPHY

RECORD SOURCES

Ane Account of the Family of Innes, Spalding Club, Aberdeen, 1864

Anglo-Scottish Relations 1174–1328: Some Selected Documents, ed. E. L. G. Stones, Oxford, 1965

The Acts of the Parliaments of Scotland, eds. T. Thomson and C. Innes, (12 vols) Edinburgh, 1814–75

The Book of Buchan, The Buchan Club, Peterhead, 1910

The Book of the Thanes of Cawdor, ed. C. Innes, Spalding Club, Aberdeen, 1859

Calendar of Documents Relating to Scotland, ed. J. Bain, 5 vols, Edinburgh, 1881–8

Calender of Fearn: Text and Additions, 1471–1667, ed. R. J. Adam, Scottish History Society, 1991

Calendar of Papal Letters to Scotland of Clement VII of Avignon, 1374–1394, ed. C. Burns Vol xii, Scottish History Society, 1976

Calendar of Papal Letters to Scotland of Benedict XIII of Avignon, 1394–1419, Vol xiii, ed. F. McGurk, Scottish History Society, 1976

Calendar of Patent Rolls, 1399–1441, 8 vols., London, 1903–7

Documents Illustrative of the History of Scotland, 1286–1306, ed. J. Stevenson, 2 vols, Edinburgh, 1870

Documents and Records Illustrating the History of Scotland, ed. F. Palgrave, London, 1837

Foedera, Conventiones, Litterae et Cuiuscunque Generis Acta Publica, ed. T. Rymer, 20 vols, London, 1704–35

A Genealogical Deduction of the Family of Rose of Kilravock, ed. C. Innes, Spalding Club, Aberdeen, 1898

Highland Papers, ed. J. R. N. Macphail 1914–41, Scottish History Society, 4 vols, Edinburgh, 1914–34

Illustrations of the Topography and Antiquities of the Shires of Aberdeen and Banff, eds., J. Robertson and G. Grut, 4 vols, Spalding Club, 1847–69

An Index, drawn up about the year 1629, of many Records of Charters, ed. W. Robertson, Edinburgh, 1798
Origines Parochiales Scotiae, Spalding Club, Aberdeen, 1850–55
Proceedings of the Society of Antiquaries of Scotland, Edinburgh 1851–
The Records of Elgin, New Spalding Club, 2 vols, Aberdeen, 1903–8
Regesta Regum Scorotum: David II, ed. B. Webster, Edinburgh, 1982
Registrum Episcopatus Moraviensis, ed. C. Innes, Bannatyne Club, Edinburgh, 1837
Registrum Magni Sigilii Regum Scotorum, eds., J. M. Thomson and J. B. Paul, 11 vols, Edinburgh, 1882–1914
The Voice of the Middle Ages in Personal Letters 1100–1500, ed. C. Moriarty, Oxford, 1989

HISTORICAL SOURCES
J. Barbour, *The Bruce*, ed. and trans. A. A. M. Duncan, Canongate Classics, Edinburgh, 1997
H. Boece, *The Chronicles of Scotland*, trans. into Scots by John Bellenden 1531, Scottish Text Society, Edinburgh, 1938–41
W. Bower, *Scotichronicon*, ed. D. E. R. Watt Aberdeen, 1987
Early Travellers in Scotland, ed. H. Hume Brown, Edinburgh, 1891
J. de Fordun, *Chronica Gentis Scotorum*, ed. W. F. Skene, Edinburgh, 1871–2
J. Froissart, *Chronicles*, trans. T. Johnes, 2 vols, London, 1868
Bishop J. Leslie, *Rebus Gestis Scotorum*, Rome, 1578
M. Martin, *A Description of the Western Islands of Scotland*, London, 1716. Facsimile ed. Edinburgh, 1981
J. Major, *Historia Majoris Britanniae 1521*
M. Paris, *Chronica Majora*, ed. and trans. R. Vaughan, 1984
Liber Pluscardensis, ed. F. J. H. Skene, 2 vols, Edinburgh, 1877–80
A. of Wyntoun, *The Orygynale Cronykil of Scotland*, ed. D. Laing, 3 vols, Edinburgh, 1872–9

LITERARY AND FOLKLORE SOURCES
Blind Harry, *The Actes and Deidis of the Illustre and Vallyeant Campioun Schir William Wallace*, c.1508, trans. and adapted by W. Hamilton of Gilbertfield, Glasgow 1722. This edition Edinburgh, 1998
J. F. Campbell, *Popular Tales of the West Highlands*, 4 vols, London, 1890–3
J. G. Campbell, *Witchcraft and Second Sight in the Highlands and Islands of Scotland*, Glasgow, 1902
A. Carmichael, *Carmina Gadelica*, Edinburgh, 1900, Floris edition, 1992

Bibliography

G. Chaucer, *The Canterbury Tales*, begun c.1386. Penguin Classic edition, 1969

T. D. Lauder, *The Wolf of Badenoch: A Historical Romance of the Fourteenth Century*, 3 vols, Edinburgh, 1827

E. Lhuyd, *A Collection of Highland Rites and Customes*, 1699, ed. J. L. Campbell for the Folklore Society, 1975

J. M. Macinlay, *Folklore of Scottish Lochs and Springs*, Glasgow, 1893

J. Marian McNeill, *The Silver Bough*, 4 vols, Glasgow, 1956–68

R. C. Maclagan, *Evil Eye in the Western Highlands*, London, 1902. Reprinted Wakefield, 1972

Poems and Ballads of Scottish History, ed. D. M. Robb, Glasgow, 1926

A. Ross, *The Folklore of the Scottish Highlands*, London, 1976

Sir W. Scott, *Tales of a Grandfather*, Edinburgh, 1827–9

Transactions of the Gaelic Society of Inverness, vols 6, 7, 8, 18, 23, 24, 25, 28, 30, 32, 48, 51, Inverness

SECONDARY SOURCES

F. Adam, *The Clans, Septs and Regiments of the Scottish Highlands*, London and Edinburgh, 1908

J. Anderson, *The Family of Frizel or Fraser*, Edinburgh, 1825

M. Ash, *This Noble Harbour, A History of the Cromarty Firth*, Invergordon and Edinburgh, 1991

R. Bain, *History of the Ancient Province of Ross*, Dingwall, 1899

G. W. S. Barrow, *The Anglo-Norman Era in Scottish History*, Oxford, 1980

G. W. S. Barrow, *Kingship and Unity, Scotland 1000–1306*, New History of Scotland Series, revised ed., Edinburgh, 1989

G. W. S. Barrow, *Robert Bruce and the Community of the Realm of Scotland*, 3rd ed., Edinburgh, 1988

P. Basing, *Trades and Crafts in Medieval Manuscripts*, London, 1990

M. Beith, *Healing Threads*, Edinburgh, 1995

S. Boardman, *The Early Stewart Kings*, Edinburgh, 1996

M. H. Brown, *James I*, Edinburgh, 1994

The Cambridge Illustrated History of the Middle Ages 1250–1520, ed. R. Fossier, 1986

I. B. Cowan and D. E. Easson, *Medieval Religious Houses Scotland*, London, 1976

J. N. Claster, *The Medieval Experience 300–1400*, New York, 1982

M. Clough, *The Field of Thistles, Scotland's Past and Scotland's People*, Edinburgh, 1983

The Hamlyn History of Medicine, ed. A. Crane, London, 1996

The earl of Cromartie, *A Highland History*, Berkhamsted, 1979

Abbot M. Dilworth, *Scottish Monasteries in the Late Middle Ages*, Edinburgh, 1995

G. Donaldson and R. S. Morpeth, *Who's Who in Scottish History*, Oxford, 1973

G. Duby, *Love and Marriage in the Middle Ages*, trans. J. Dunnett, Cambridge and Oxford, 1994

J. T. Dunbar, *The Costume of Scotland*, London, 1984

P. B. Ellis, *Celtic Women*, London, 1995

R. Fawcett, *Scottish Abbeys and Priories*, Historic Scotland, 1994

R. Fawcett, *Scottish Medieval Churches*, HMSO, Edinburgh, 1985

I. Finlay, *The Lothians*, Glasgow, 1960

J. Fraser, *Polichronicon Seu, Policratica Tempora*, Wardlaw M.S. History of Clan Fraser, 1882

J. M. Gilbert, *Hunting and Hunting Reserves in Medieval Scotland*, Edinburgh, 1979

Women in Medieval English Society, ed. P. J. P. Goldberg, Stroud, 1997

Sir R. Gordon, *History of the Family of Sutherland*, Edinburgh, 1813

L. G. Graeme, *Or and Sable: A Book of the Graemes and Grahams*, Edinburgh, 1903

A. Grant, *Independence and Nationhood, Scotland 1306–1469*, New History of Scotland Series, Edinburgh, 1984

I. F. Grant, *Highland Folk Ways*, London, 1961

I. F. Grant and H. Cheape, *Periods in Highland History*, London, 1987

D. Gregory, *History of the Western Highlands and Isles of Scotland*, 1881, reprinted Edinburgh, 1975

A. J. Gurevich, *Categories of Medieval Culture*, London, 1985

A. Haddow, *The History and Structure of the Ceol Mor*

Plague, Pox and Pestilence, Disease in History, ed. K. F. Kiple, London, 1997

L. and J. Laing, *Medieval Britain, The Age of Chivalry*, London, 1996

K. H. Leslie of Balquhain, *Historical Records of the Family of Leslie*, 3 vols, Edinburgh, 1869

H. Leyser, *Medieval Women, a Social History of Women in England 450–1500*, London, 1995

M. Lynch, *Scotland, a New History*, London, 1991

D. J. Macdonald of Castleton, *Clan Donald*, Edinburgh, 1978

C. G. Macdowall, *The Chanonry of Ross*, Fortrose, 1963

R. R. McIan, *The Clans of the Scottish Highlands*, 1845, Pan edition, 1980

A. M. Mackenzie, *The Rise of the Stewarts*, London, 1935

A. M. Mackenzie, *Scottish Pageant, 55BC–1513AD*, London, 1937

The Middle Ages in the Highlands, ed. L. Maclean of Dochgarroch, Inverness Field Club, Inverness, 1981

Bibliography

C. McNamee, *The Wars of the Bruces*, Edinburgh, 1997

A. Macquarrie, *Scotland and the Crusades*, Edinburgh, 1997

N. Macrae, *The Romance of a Royal Burgh, Dingwall's Story of a Thousand Years*, Dingwall, 1923

C. McWilliam, *Lothian (Except Edinburgh)*, Buildings of Scotland Series, ed. N. Pevsner

P. Marren, *Grampian Battlefields*, Aberdeen, 1990

R. W. and J. Munro, *Tain Through the Centuries*, Tain, 1966

Sir H. Nicholas, *History of the Earldoms of Strathern, Monteith and Airth*, London, 1842

R. Nicholson, *Scotland, the Later Middle Ages*, The Edinburgh History of Scotland, Vol 2, Edinburgh, 1974

The Ross and Cromarty Book, ed. D. Omand, Golspie, 1984

F. Piponnier and P. Mane, *Dress in the Middle Ages*, New Haven and London, 1997

E. Power, *Medieval People*, London, 1924

M. Prestwich, *Edward I*, London, 1988

G. Redpath, *Border History*, 1948, reprinted Edinburgh, 1979

P. Reese, *Wallace, a Biography*, Edinburgh, 1996

F. N. Reid, *The Earls of Ross and Their Descendants*, Edinburgh, 1894

J. L. Robertson, *Lost Kingdoms, Celtic Scotland and the Middle Ages*, Edinburgh, 1997

A. M. Ross, *History of the Clan Ross*, Dingwall, 1932

J. R. Ross, *The Great Clan Ross*, Canada, 1972

S. Ross, *Monarchs of Scotland*, Moffat, 1990

The Frasers of Philorth, ed. Lord Saltoun, 3 vols., Edinburgh, 1879

Moray Province and People, ed. W. D. H. Sellar, Edinburgh, 1993

L. Shaw, *The History of the Province of Moray*, 3 vols, Glasgow, 1882

S. Thompson, *Women Religious, the Founding of English Nunneries after the Norman Conquest*, Oxford, 1991

P. F. Tytler, *The History of Scotland*, 9 vols, Edinburgh, 1828–43

J. Warrack, *Domestic Life in Scotland*, Rhind Lectures, Edinburgh, 1919–20

J. and W. Watson, *Morayshire Described*, Elgin, 1868

J. Wormald, *Lords and Men in Scotland: Bonds of Manrent, 1442–1603*, Edinburgh, 1985

P. Yeoman, *Medieval Scotland*, Historic Scotland, 1995

A. Young, *Robert the Bruce's Rivals: The Comyns, 1212–1314*, Edinburgh, 1997

REFERENCE SOURCES

R. Douglas, *The Peerage of Scotland*, revised and corrected by J. P. Wood, Edinburgh, 1813

E. Dwelly, *The Illustrated Gaelic-English Dictionary*, Glasgow, 1901

J. and J. Keay, *Collins Encyclopaedia of Scotland*, London, 1994

P. McNeill and R. Nicholson, *An Historical Atlas of Scotland c.400–c.1600*, St Andrews, 1975 and 1996

F. H. Nicolaisen, *Scottish Place-Names*, London, 1976

The Scots Peerage, ed. J. B. Paul, 9 vols, Edinburgh, 1904–14

The Statistical Account of Scotland, 1791-1799, vols xv and xvii, ed. Sir J. Sinclair, republished 1981, 1992

W. J. Watson, *Place-Names of Ross and Cromarty*, Inverness, 1904. Republished by Ross and Cromarty Heritage Society, Inverness, 1976

ARTICLES, BOOKLETS AND UNPUBLISHED MANUSCRIPTS

A. E. Anton, 'Handfasting in Scotland', *Scottish Historical Review*, XXXVII (1958)

R. Fawcett, *Beauly Priory and Fortrose Cathedral*, Guide Book, HMSO

Kildrummy Castle and Glenbuchat Castle, Guide Book, ed. C. Tabraham, Historic Scotland, 1995

J. S. Richardson, *Dirleton Castle*, Guide Book, 1950

R. MacDonald, *Bishops and Archbishops of St Andrews*, (manuscript)

I. Moncreiffe of Easter Moncreiffe, *The Royal Palace of Falkland*, Guide Book

A. G. Reid and S. D. M. Lye, *Pitmiddle Village and Elcho Nunnery*, Perthshire Society of Natural History, 1988

D. M. Rose, 'The Sutherlands of Duffus and Skelbo', a series of articles in the *Northern Times*, Helmsdale

A. C. G. Ross, *The Chronicles of Ross*, (manuscript), 1967–9

W. D. H. Sellar, 'The Origins and Ancestry of Somerled', *Scottish Historical Review*, Vol lxv 1966

D. Simpson, *Doune Castle*, Guide Book, 1968

C. J. Tabraham, *Duffus Castle and Church*, Leaflet, HMSO, Scotland

N. M. Wilby, *Fortrose Cathedral, Ross-shire*. Published privately c.1965

INDEX

Index

Index

Index